Islam's Predicament

Islam's Predicament

Perspectives of a Dissident Muslim

Salim Mansur

GYAN

ISBN : 978-81-212-1327-1

Price : ₹ 900

First Published, Mosaic Press in North America

Republished in 2016

Gyan Publishing House
5, Ansari Road
Daryaganj, New Delhi-110002
(India) Phones: 9811692060
E-mail: books@gyanbooks.com

Printed at: G. Print Process, Delhi.

Cataloging in Publication Data—DK
Courtesy: D.K. Agencies (P) Ltd. <docinfo@dkagencies.com>

Mansur, Salim, author.
Islam's predicament : perspectives of a dissident Muslim / Salim Mansur.
pages cm
Reprint. Originally published: U.S.A. : Mosaic Press,c2009.
Includes bibliographical references (pages 253-259).
ISBN 9788121213271

1. Islam and politics. 2. Islam—21st century. I. Title.

BP173.7.M36 2016DDC 297.272 23

for Ines, Samir and Yasmina
with love & gratitude

There is no compulsion in religion.

Quran, 2:256.

To each of you We have given a law and a pattern of life. If Allah had pleased He could surely have made you one people (professing one faith). But He wished to try and test you by that which He gave you. So try to excel in good deeds. To Him will you return in the end, when He will tell you of what you were at variance.

Quran, 5:48

Any who believe in God and the Last Day, And work righteousness, Shall have their reward with their Lord: on them shall be no fear, nor shall they grieve.

Quran, 2:62

Contents

Foreword by George Jonas

When people say, as they do from time to time, "Where are the moderate Muslims?" one is tempted to answer: Why, they're all around us. Hundreds of millions live in Indonesia, Pakistan, India, Afghanistan, and Bangladesh. Millions more live in the Middle East. And, of course, a great many live in the West.

Moderate Muslims service our cars, take our X-rays, and fix our computers. We probably know dozens without knowing we know them. We don't know they're moderate precisely because they are – and since they're moderate we may not even know they're Muslims.

This is as it should be. It would be incongruous for a deliveryman to ring the doorbell and say: "Your loveseat is in the truck, but before I bring it in, I want you to know I'm a moderate Muslim."

We're grateful for Salim Mansur, though. Professor Mansur, teacher and pundit, delivers opinions rather than loveseats. When he rings our doorbell, or rather his newspaper does, we are keen to know where he is coming from, and he doesn't keep us guessing. The House of Islam has mansions ranging from the contemplative to the martial, and Mansur comes from one whose central pillar is peace.

It is hardly news that the edifice of Islam contains mansions of peace, but it is still a comfort to hear it authoritatively from a courageous and clear-thinking writer. When measuring the world for numbers and noise, moderate Muslims lead the census, but immoderate Muslims lead the chorus. They have the decibels. With the overwhelming din of militant Islam drowning out all other sounds, it is necessary to be reminded that peaceful Islam isn't just an illusion, a liberal fantasy, a fairy tale, a Santa Claus for Virginia. No: it is Mansur and others like him. It is reassuring to hear that compassionate Islam with which Western civilization isn't remotely on a collision course is significantly larger than political Islam with which it is, and that militant, medieval Islam clashes not only with modernity and Western civilization but also with millions of peaceful Muslims who worship a just and merciful God.

A professor at the University of Western Ontario, Salim Mansur is a Canadian Muslim, as comfortable in his citizenship as in his faith. Far from being an apostate, as some have characterized him, he is a champion of Islam, ready to defend it even against Islam itself – that is, what he regards as a noxious distortion of Islam, a rapidly metastasizing malignancy variously described as political or fundamentalist Islam or "Islamism."

"The West is confronted by an enemy clearly recognizable at war against its values of individual freedom and reason," is how Mansur puts it. "The enemy is the Islamists." The West's best allies in this war aren't the detractors but the friends and followers of Islam. If Islamism is the malady, Islam is the medicine.

Falsehood isn't cured by concession to falsehood, but by truth. "When we need clear thinking and clear prose to dismantle our false sense of safety," Mansur writes, "we find instead the weakening of our critical faculties essential for discriminating between our friends and our foes." He makes it clear that he is not impressed with U.S. president Barack Obama's apologetic approach as manifested in his June 4, 2009, address to the Muslim world in Cairo. While Mansur finds it commendable that the president cited verses from the Qur'an, "[t]he verse Obama needed to quote – if he were truly honest both in disclosing his knowledge of the Qur'an and in speaking to Muslims – is God's admonishment that He does not change the condition of any people unless they change what is in their hearts."

Calling Mansur a "moderate" Muslim may be a misnomer. It is more accurate to describe him as a militant moderate: a Muslim who recognizes that appeasement, pussyfooting, and politically correct groveling is unlikely to carry the day against the Islamist enemies of

Islam as well as the West. The professor calls on us to understand that we cannot give peace a chance until we have given a chance to clarity and courage.

Which is what he does in this collection.

George Jonas
Toronto,
June, 2009

Preface

The essays in this book, both the longer and the shorter pieces, were written in the period after the events of September 11, 2001. For me 9/11 came to represent the moment when all hesitations, skepticism and inner doubts about Muslim history dissolved, and it became clear that the principal conflict within Islam is between the forces of tyranny and the desire for freedom. Muslim or Islamist terrorism is the ill-begotten offspring of this history of tyranny. The origin of this conflict is coterminous with the beginning of Muslim history, and tyranny being the dominant element in Muslim history since the demise of Muhammad (the Prophet) it has shaped the religious understanding and practice of Islam among Muslims.

In the face of Muslim extremism and terror that went global with 9/11, there remains the urgent need for Muslims to confront and repudiate those who have perverted their faith, or hijacked it, and made of Islam an ideology of bigotry and war (jihad). Mine has been a small effort in that urgently needed larger and wider struggle against radical Muslims, or Islamists, who have wrecked the Muslim world and have spread fear and violence indiscriminately among non-Muslims.

Muslims, Arabs and non-Arabs alike, will not make progress as people and countries unless they subject their history to a critical examination. Their religion, Islam, has been conditioned by their history much more so than the other way around. Subjecting their history to critical examining will open the necessary space for Muslims to progress and reconcile themselves with the requirements of the modern world by separating religion from politics, and by making faith a personal matter between man and God. This is a long, unavoidable and necessary historical process of Muslim reform of their society and of the reformation of Islam. It is this perspective I brought to my writings in the public media after 9/11, and from this perspective I have opposed Muslim extremism and fanaticism that brought ruin to Muslims in the past, and continue to do so in the present. It is the thread that runs through my writings collected here.

The longer pieces were initially prepared for public lectures at academic meetings, conferences and public gatherings. The paper on Sadat's journey to Jerusalem was given at a public event held at the University of Toronto in November 2006 marking the 25th anniversary of his murder in 1981. The lecture was subsequently broadcast by TVO. The essay on Jewish-Muslim relations was given at a meeting organized at the Jewish Centre in London, Ontario in January 2005. The event in a small way was a milestone for the Jewish Centre since I was the first Muslim invited to speak there. The essay on Danish cartoons is based on a keynote address given at the annual meeting of the Society for Academic Freedom and Scholarship (SAFS) in London, Ontario in May 2006. The essays on Muslim on Muslim violence and a Sufi saint's response to Khomeini were papers read at the annual meetings of the American Council for the Study of Islamic Societies (ACSIS) in May 2003 and April 2004 in Victoria, British Columbia and in Washington respectively. The essay on Pakistan was a paper for a conference on the country organized by the Aspen Institute, Berlin in April 2006. The essay on the West's decline and Islam's stormy rise was the theme of the Civitas annual meeting in May 2007 at Halifax, Nova Scotia. The essay on the war within Islam was an invited talk given at a meeting organized on Islam and terrorism at St John Fisher College, Rochester, New York, in November 2005. The two essays on Democracy and Muslim perspectives respectively were published in the Middle East Quarterly, and I am thankful to the journal for permission to include them in this collection. The paper on keeping faith in the age of Islamist terror was an invited talk given at an annual meeting of the senior alumni of the University of Western Ontario in February 2002. The shorter pieces are essays and columns written for the public media.

I have taken liberty to edit and do some re-writing of the longer pieces so that they may read as essays and not as they were originally presented as lectures. I have not done editing of the shorter pieces except for making uniform the spellings of proper nouns. And since these pieces were written independently of each other to be read accordingly, there are repetitions which have not been removed through editing.

The writings collected here were all done under pressure of the circumstances which occasioned them, and in an environment of threats and intimidations from Muslim extremists and fanatics that have been directed at individuals who have taken a public stand against them, their politics, their ideology and their abuse of Islam. I have had my own share of these threats. Yet during this entire period, and one that by no means have come to an end, I have been fortunate to have friends whose support and kindness are of enduring comfort. The most important person in my life remains my wife and partner, and ever since 9/11 without her support and her courage I could not have functioned. My friends want to remain private, and I must not break their trust. But to each one of them I owe a debt of life-long gratitude. Finally, I could not have arranged this selection and done the editing and proof-reading without the help of Adrienne Dain. I owe her an immense thank you.

Salim Mansur
July, 2009

1

The War within Islam

In an authoritative essay published in *The Wall Street Journal* Abdurrahman Wahid, the former first president of newly democratic Indonesia from 1999 to 2001 described what constitutes "right Islam" contrary to "wrong Islam."[1] He warned people of good will to recognize "a terrible danger threatens humanity." This peril, Wahid wrote, emanates from an "extreme and perverse ideology in the minds of fanatics," specifically "Wahhabi/Salafist ideology – a minority fundamentalist religious cult fueled by petrodollars."

The importance of this essay, and the warning in it, comes with the prestige of the author. Abdurrahman Wahid is an Islamic scholar and heads Nahdatul Ulama (NU), the largest Muslim organization in the largest Muslim country, Indonesia, with a population of some 240 million. NU membership is estimated at 40 million, and the Islam its leadership preaches and practices while being mainstream traditional Sunni Islam strives to be open, tolerant, inclusive, moderate, respectful of local traditions, embracing of Sufi learning and spirituality, and not inimical to the modern world of science and democracy. The progress of the Muslim world greatly depends on how the leadership of NU, and similar organizations of Muslims across the Arab-Muslim world, prevail over the ideology of *jihad* (holy war) preached by radical Islamists.

In the struggle for the hearts and minds of Muslims Wahid lists the formidable organizational strengths of the worldwide fundamentalist Muslim/radical Islamist movement, and then offers a counter-strategy.

Among strengths of this movement are: "a claim to and aura of religious authenticity and Arab prestige;" "an appeal to Islamic identity, pride and history;" and "networks of Islamic schools that propagate extremism" financed by oil-rich Wahhabi sponsors with "scholarships for locals to study in Saudi Arabia and return with degrees and indoctrination, to serve as future leaders." The counter-strategy Wahid presents is primarily one to harness the essential desire for goodness in the hearts of Muslims shared in common by all individuals irrespective of their faith traditions.

The unavoidable struggle for Muslims, the vast majority who are not doctrinally and politically in league with the proponents of "Wahhabi/Salafist ideology," is one of expunging bigotry and violence from their faith-tradition. It requires of them acknowledging how violence and bigotry right from the outset of Muslim history as a community of believers undermined the simplicity of Islam's teaching of bearing witness to the truth of One God. The defeat of Islamists requires discrediting the crude "Wahhabi/Salafist ideology" that insists on *jihad* (holy war) as one of the central pillars of Islam, and in contemporary times is filled with anti-Jewish and anti-West bigotry. Since September 11, 2001 when Islamist terrorists hijacked passenger airplanes and flew them into buildings in New York and Washington, the focus and drive of the anti-Islamist struggle has been on waging a military campaign against the network of terrorists. This external aspect of the struggle has received much attention in the public media. The internal aspect of the struggle, of reconnecting Muslims to the original impulse of Islam and reclaiming its spirituality soiled by the inherently corrupt nature of politics, however, is more important if "right Islam" is to prevail over "wrong Islam."

"Right Islam" will not prevail over "wrong Islam" unless a fresh new reading of the Quran and a revised understanding of Muslim history take precedence over the layered traditional readings and often bigoted interpretations of the text Muslims as an article of faith accept to be the words of God. Wahid is cautious and sensitive. He is a non-Arab when Muslims – a global population exceeding one billion – in reading the Quran and recalling Muslim history of the founding generation generally defer to the views of ethnic Arabs who make up less than twenty percent of Muslims worldwide. This is what Wahid means when he writes about how Wahhabi/Salafist claim to an "aura of religious authenticity and Arab prestige" sets the requirement in advance for a certain limited reading of the Quran shaped by the prevalent cultural reality of a segment of the Muslim world, that of the Arabs, but is not representative of the Muslim world in its entirety nor consistent with views of those Muslims, including Arabs, striving for an understanding of the Quran and Muslim history in harmony with the modern world of science and democracy.

Islam means peace, but Muslim history from its origin in the post-Prophetic period has been marked by violence. This fact is deliberately obscured by those who preach the Salafist ideology of regaining Islam's purity by returning to the practice of the faith of the first generation of Muslims, the companions of the Prophet, revered as being righteous. The irony is that it was this generation with whom the template of historical Islam was crafted and this historical Islam, unrevised and resistant to revision by most Muslims, Arabs and non-Arabs, instructs them in the understanding and practice of their faith tradition. This history provides the Islamists the basis for their ideological promotion of *jihad* as one of the core pillars of Islam.

The Prophet's demise in 632 in Medina ended the heavenly-guided mission of Muhammad in accordance with Muslim belief that lasted for 22 years. During the first 12 years Muhammad preached in Mecca, his native city, the message of Islam as the belief in One God, of returning to the path of Abraham, of repudiating the practice of idol-worship, and of living an ethical life based on moral values instructed by the heavenly voice guiding him. The last ten years of his life Muhammad spent in exile in Medina. His enemies, the Meccan elite and defenders of the pagan ways, pursued him and Muhammad was forced to take arms in defence of his mission. He triumphed over his enemies, conquered Mecca, established Islam over the pagan culture, and more or less unified the tribes of Arabia before his final illness and death.[2]

The bare facts of Muhammad's life and mission against the tremendous odds he had to contend with are inspirational. By the time of his death he was acknowledged by all the tribes of Arabia as their leader, and to him alone the tribes and their chiefs pledged their allegiance in accepting Islam by abandoning the idol-worshipping ways of their ancestors. But Muhammad did not establish authority in any form that could be construed as the basis of an Islamic state, nor did he nominate his successor as the head of such a state. His mission, as stated in the Quran, was to deliver the message and warn the people of the errors of their pagan customs and their worshipping of idols while denying God and His messenger (*rasul Allah*), and that he was not their keeper. Muhammad fulfilled his mission, and with his demise the brief period in history when heavenly-voice was engaged in directing and protecting him among pagan Arabs ceased. After Muhammad Muslim history is no different than the history of any other people, the affairs of fallible men and women motivated by the mix of their virtues and vices where is found great nobility of purpose and achievements as well as hideous wrongs.

The best that might be said of the immediate events following Muhammad's demise in which his companions engaged themselves, and which set in motion the making of the template of Muslim history in the year 11 of the Islamic calendar, is that the activities of Abu Bakr and Umar were hurried and spontaneous reactions to actions contemplated by others around them. The unleashing of struggle for power on the death of Muhammad and the quarrels that plagued the first community of Muslims are the irrefutable evidences that no practical thought was given and steps taken by the Prophet for administering the affairs of the community through some institutional arrangement however rudimentary that could be viewed as the makings of a state, and for an orderly line of succession from among his companions and their responsibility laid out for the community to accept as set forth by him ahead of his demise. This was not any part of his mandate as Muhammad understood his divinely guided mission. On the completion of his mission as a messenger of God, of securely establishing the monotheism of Abraham among the idol-worshipping pagans of Arabia, he passed away just as the Quran reminded Arabs that he was mortal and in this respect no different than any other human being.

When the news of the Prophet's illness and death spread among the inhabitants of Medina, a gathering of the native clan elders of that city was arranged at a place called Banu Sa'idah to nominate and elect one of their own as the leader. Sa'ad ibn Ubadah was a native of Medina and one of the *Ansars* (helpers) who had received the Prophet on escaping from Mecca with others joining him as *Muhajiruns* (refugees), and given them shelter. The support for Sa'ad ibn Ubadah among his people assured him of being appointed as the leader of the Muslim community in Medina, but the challenge thrown at the people gathered at the portico of Banu Sa'idah by Abu Bakr and Umar as the most senior and closest companions of the Prophet changed the situation. It was a *coup de force* by Abu Bakr, Umar and their supporters that led to a rout of the *Ansars*, and in the accompanying violence Sa'ad ibn Ubadah was wounded, and later assassinated. Abu Bakr was declared by Umar as the *khalif* (caliph), meaning the successor or deputy of the Prophet. The basis of Abu Bakr's claim to the leadership of the Muslim community, and the denial of the same claim made on behalf of Sa'ad ibn Ubadah by the *Ansars*, was that of tribal precedence claimed for the new Muslim order in which the Prophet's tribe, the Quraysh of Mecca, carried the most prestige and next to the Quraysh were other tribes of Mecca standing ahead of non-Meccan tribes. This claim had no basis in the Quran, no reference of such nature could be provided for, nor did the Prophet make any claim of such nature, yet all contrary arguments were dismissed with force by Abu Bakr (632-34) and his supporters.[3]

Abu Bakr's leadership was not recognized by all Muslims. Sa'ad ibn Ubadah did not acknowledge Abu Bakr as leader before he was killed. Ali, the Prophet's cousin, son-in-law and the closest in kinship, refused to recognize Abu Bakr for the six months after the events at Banu Sa'idah until the death of Fatima, the Prophet's daughter and his wife. But Abu Bakr was faced with an even greater challenge than the refusal of those in Medina to give their allegiance to him by the swelling ranks of Arabian tribes declaring they were no longer bound by their allegiance to the deceased Prophet. For the next two years Abu Bakr and his supporters were engaged in putting down what came to be viewed as apostasy by the Arab tribes. These wars, known as the *Riddah Wars* (or Wars against Apostasy) were in effect tribal wars driven by competing interests and rivalry of tribes.[4] Abu Bakr prevailed by the superior tact of dividing and conquering his opponents, and in the process imposing the power of Medina and the Meccan tribes whose loyalty he secured over the "apostatizing" tribes. The Quran's command about there being no coercion in religion was cast aside, and Islam in its Arabian environment and among desert Arabs came to be inseparable from the power and sweep of the sword. It was the nature of these wars, brutal and mercilessly fought, that established the rule of force and terror in coercing submission to God, and it was this culture based on the authority of those wielding the sword that shaped the practice of Islam and the religious attitude of the Arabs in the immediate period after Muhammad. Since then the Arabs, and through their influence the non-Arabs, have conceived of Islam more as a collective identity of a people – in modern terms, nationalism – rather than the personal faith of individuals.

The wars that followed the violence unleashed in Banu Sa'idah became the dominant feature of Muslim history in which politics and religion became indistinguishable. There were civil wars, murders and killings among the companions of the Prophet culminating in the bloodshed in Karbala, Iraq, where the grandson of the Prophet, Husayn, and his companions were brutally massacred by the Arab armies of the rulers in Damascus. The unity of the Muslims was irreparably broken and Islam became divided between the majority Sunni adherents of Islam and the minority Shiites. The division was the result of power struggle under the banner of Islam, and the authority of the Quran was sought by competing factions according to the various interpretations they gave to the text.

These internal wars pushed by rival claims to rule among various individuals and companions of the Prophet were prelude to the wars of the Arab-Islamic expansion that came in the reign of Umar (634-44) and after.[5] Conquest of lands brought booty as spoils of war and conquered people to be administered on behalf of a central authority, and from such circumstances the rubric of an Islamic state or *khilafat* (caliphate) was put together. The rulers required their authority be given legitimacy in the name of Islam, and religious scholars provided the requisite interpretations of the Quran along with the traditions (genuine and manufactured) of the Prophet narrated by his companions and collected by scribes to support the claims of the power-holders. The religious scholars, or clerics, in support of the majority Sunni rulers became subservient to the state and ever since have served men in power. Those who did not and remained opposed to the Sunni rulers preserved their autonomy from the state and their right to interpret the Quran and the traditions of the Prophet according to their oppositional needs.

The war within Islam that Abu Bakr and Umar initiated at the moment when the Prophet died, and which has continued to the present times, was and remains about power and legitimacy. It was their political innovation – the caliphate – that became within a generation an Arab-Muslim version of dynastic authority, and which was embellished with the trappings of Islam even as it acquired the pomp and splendor of the Byzantine and the Persian emperors. Under the authority of the caliphate in the first two centuries of Islam a legal system, *shari'ah*, was elaborated by religious scholars that was remarkable for its time and served the requirements of the empire. This elaborately worked out legal system carried the imprimatur of an empire, reflected the prejudice of the age and served the interests of the power-holders. But as Mohamed Charfi, the Tunisian scholar, indicates the *shari'ah* was "based on three fundamental inequalities: the superiority of men over women, of Muslims over non-Muslims, and of free persons over slaves."[6]

The caliphate and the *shari'ah* were human artifacts provided with the gloss of religious sanctions that served the interests of the power-holders. Ali Abderrazak, the Egyptian jurist and religious scholar at al-Azhar University in Cairo, in *Islam and the Foundation of Power* showed at great length that Islam did not set forth the requirements of political authority, and that the caliphate was purely a product of historical circumstances. Abderrazak's book came out some months after Mustafa Kemal, the founding ruler of modern Turkey, abolished in 1924 the thirteen centuries old institution of the caliphate situated in Istanbul since the 15th century. In the midst of the uproar across the Arab-Muslim world against Kemal's decision, the authorities at al-Azhar condemned Abderrazak, dismissed him from his position and banned his book.

Abderrazak's efforts represented the current of modernist thinking in the Arab-Muslim world to salvage or liberate the spiritual truth of Islam from its historical setting, and in the process advance the essential requirement for the progress of Muslims in the modern world by separating religion and politics as European Reformation did for Christianity. While this effort recognizes the Islamic civilization bearing the initial imprints of Arab culture was a great advancement over other civilizations in the pre-modern world during the first half of the second millennium of the Christian era, it failed to keep pace with changing times and fell behind Europe from about the 16th century.

The modernist thinking among Muslims is one of reconciling reason with revelation, and the root of this thinking within Muslim history pre-dates the modern age reaching back to the early history of Muslim free-thinkers (Mutazilites) in the 8th and 9th century.[7] Mutazilites insisted on the free-will of individuals and of reason to comprehend and explain the Quran. They pointed to the evidence of the orderly functioning of nature in discerning the rational will of God as creator, and they conceived God of the Quran as rational Law-Giver and not as a reified arbitrary Despot whose earthly representation was to be found in the conduct of rulers in Muslim history. They were mercilessly hunted as infidels by the caliphs in Baghdad from the mid-9th century onwards and with their repression a brief flirtation with reason as the key to expounding the truths of religion in Islam ended. In the work of later philosophers such as Ibn Rushd (Averroes to Europeans) from the 12th century the rationalist approach of the Mutazilites briefly reappeared. Ibn Rushd, for instance, echoing the method of the first victims of inquisition in Muslim history wrote, "We categorically state that, whenever there is a contradiction between the result of a proof (or of rational explanation) and the apparent meaning of a revealed text, the latter must be subject to interpretation."8 Ibn Rushd meant by interpretation that the text be understood figuratively, not literally, as supported by reasoning or rational knowledge.

Abdurrahman Wahid's essay calling upon Muslims to distinguish between the "right Islam" and the "wrong Islam" in the post-9/11 world is about once again picking up the defeated efforts of the Muslim modernists and their illustrious ancestors going all the way back to the Mutazilites. This effort cannot succeed without an accompanying social revolution in Muslim countries supported by reform-minded power-holders. And for this social revolution to be meaningful it would have to be democratic, respecting of human rights, gender equity and individual freedom that would then open space for free and vigorous debate between the modernists on the one side and the gathering of traditionalists, fundamentalists and Wahhabi/Salafists on the other. It is a debate that modernists will win for Islam since a religion cannot remain entombed within the structure primarily shaped by the Arabs of the first generation of Islam and bearing the stamp of their culture rendered obsolete by history.

The war within Islam that began with the *coup de force* arranged by Abu Bakr and Umar at Bani Sa'idah continues into our time. For a period in history this internal war within Islam was displaced with the outward expansion and conquests by Arabs whose ranks grew as Persians, Afghans, Turks and other ethnicities embraced Islam, and the Islamic civilization flourished in the first half of the second millennium of the Christian era. The rise and advancement of Europe squeezed the Islamic civilization and its imperial power, and eventually Muslim lands passed into the control of the European powers. The retreat of Europe from its overseas empires in the last century brought independence to Muslims organized for the first time in their history within the modern settings of nation-states. The experience of administering nation-states for Muslims is relatively recent and Muslim history offers little guidance. The disconnect existing between Muslim political-legal and religious thought inherited from the past and the contemporary reality of the modern world in the 21st century is immense, and hugely difficult if not unlikely to be bridged. In this situation the long raging war within Islam is no longer limited to Muslims and has gone global as evident by the events of 9/11.

It is in the transformation of the war within Islam into a global confrontation between Wahhabi/Salafists or the radical Islamists and the West that Muslims might ironically find an eventual exit out of their impoverished history at odds with the modern world. The wars for regime change in Afghanistan and Iraq precipitated by 9/11 have opened these societies for the first time in their respective history to engage with the demands of modern politics based on the principles of democratic government and the ideas of freedom. The social revolution as a result of regime change in Afghanistan and Iraq that will come, however slow and difficult it is in making progress, will also help bring about the reform of Islam. Other Muslim societies will be affected by these changes even as the pressures of the modern world bear down upon them, and the war within Islam will be increasingly similar to the wars of Reformation and Counter-Reformation that raged across Europe for several centuries as part of the historical process in the making of the modern world.

The "right Islam" of which Abdurrahman Wahid speaks will prevail over the "wrong Islam" when Muslims in sufficient numbers within their societies also awaken to the understanding that all the events relating to Islam from the moment of the Prophet's death to the present time were and remain historical in nature, secular and profane, and not religious. This understanding when it eventually arrives and is affirmed in practice might take hold of the men holding power in independent nation-states as much out of the necessity imposed by the conditions of the modern world as by the reform wrought in their minds about the meaning and nature of Islam as a religion distinct and separate from politics. The costs in terms of lives and properties destroyed in the eventual defeat of the "wrong Islam" will remain tragically high and unavoidable, and this too is the result of the manner in which Muslim history was set in motion by the companions of the Prophet.

The "right Islam" is not entirely invisible in our world though it goes unreported in the mainstream media and in public discussions. This "right Islam" is also the "other Islam" as described by Stephen Schwartz.[9] It is found in the quiet existence of Sufi Muslims, and in the influence of Sufi Muslims on their surroundings. The core reality of the "right Islam" is the emphasis on right conduct of Muslims as individuals, and in repudiating the bigoted thinking based on the triumphal view of Muslim history claiming Islam as superior to all other faith traditions. This supremacist view, unsupported by the Quran, is derived from the untenable proposition that since the Quran is the final revelation of God to man Islam is the *only* true faith superseding all previous revelations, in particular Judaism and Christianity as the two monotheistic faith traditions most proximate to Islam. Such a view acquired political reality with the rapid military advances of the Arabs into the making of the Arab-Islamic Empire in the years following the Prophet's demise.

The "wrong Islam" of Wahid became the "official" Islam of the Arab-Islamic Empire institutionalized and defended by the power of the sword. It continues to rule the Muslim world as in modern Iran under the authority of the Shiite clerics and in Saudi Arabia under the compact of the Saud family and the Wahhabi/Salafist clerics of the kingdom. There is no mandate, or requirement, for empire in the Quran, nor was empire essential for the spread of Islam. Islam travelled beyond the central core of the Arab-Muslim world – the area of the greater Middle East and North Africa conquered by the Arab armies during the first century of the Islamic calendar – into India, Central Asia, the borderlands of China, and south-east Asia without arms or conquest by the Arab-Muslim armies. But the making of empire had a lasting effect on Islam as religion. Islam became the triumphal faith of the empire's ruling class acquiring superior standing over other faiths within the empire, and providing most Muslims with an undisputed sense of their faith being superior to those of non-Muslims.

Islamic empires disintegrated a long time ago, but the Muslim mindset shaped by the politics of empire persists. Christians and Jews by faith and conduct have exposed the hollowness of Muslim belief that Islam is a superior religion. Instead Islam is as a historical reality one faith-tradition among others, and it is this acceptance of pluralism as a natural order of things and beliefs that distinguishes Sufi Muslims from the vast majority of Muslims who still persists in the path of the "wrong Islam." But such persistence against the evidence of history invariably becomes fanaticism, and this is what the world has been witnessing in the politics of *jihad* preached and practiced by Islamists. Fanaticism can wreak havoc for a period of time, even a long time, but it cannot endlessly endure. The war within Islam reached a crisis point at the beginning of the 21st century culminating with the events of 9/11. Since then it has begun to exhaust itself as most Muslims however reluctantly eventually concede to the reality and demands of the modern world. The eventual collapse of "wrong Islam" through the sheer burden of its internal contradictions, its falsehood, its opposition to reason and democracy, will bring peace for Muslims among themselves and with others as Muhammad from the outset of his heavenly guided mission, which is as an article of faith for Muslims, instructed those who would pay heed.

2

Enlightenment's Dusk? The West's Decline and Islam's Stormy Rise

The events of September 11, 2001 have given greater credence to Samuel Huntington's thesis of the unfolding of the "clash of civilizations" following the end of the Cold War, than the efforts of those to belittle or be dismissive of his analyses and warnings. Even as 9/11 precipitated the "war on terror" and has taken the United States into the heart of the Arab-Muslim world by demolishing al Qaeda supporting Taliban regime in Afghanistan and the removal of the Iraqi tyrant, Saddam Hussein, there are misgivings in the West about its future as it confronts the rise of militant Islam. These misgivings, as reflected in the chapter heading, suggest that the spread of religious fundamentalism places the gains of the Age of Enlightenment at risk as the West is riddled with doubts indicating its decline and, inversely, the world of Islam is on the ascent given the militancy of Muslims. I view, however, the militancy of the Muslim world as a display of its increasing weakness and evidence of its failure to reconcile itself with the modern world.

We need to pay close attention to the role of ideas in shaping history even as the unfolding of events shape ideas in ways unanticipated. I like the phrase Richard Holbrooke used in introducing Paul Berman's book, *Power and Idealists*, "the savage intersection where theories and personalities" collide. "Enlightenment's Dusk? The West's Decline and Islam's Stormy Rise," I take to mean as that moment in our contemporary history when we stumbled into the "savage intersection" where ideas that went into the building of the modern world of science and liberal-democracy are in collision with other ideas hostile to this world as represented by the West. In this collision to which we are witness there will be unforeseen consequences as there were in past collisions, and unanticipated developments will place tomorrow's generation into situations resulting from decisions of the present generation in response to the events of 9/11.

In the millennium year of 2000 Jacques Barzun published his chronicle of ideas in the making of the West over the past five hundred years titled *From Dawn To Decadence: 500 Years of Western Cultural Life*. Barzun's narrative begins with the generations to which Martin Luther belonged. Luther's posting of his 95 theses on the doors of All Saints' church at Wittenberg in October 1517 was a seminal moment in the history of the making of the modern world, sparking Salim Mansur 11 as it did the beginnings of the Protestant Reformation. The Reformation was carried into the period known as the Enlightenment and then followed by what Marshall Hodgson, in writing the *Venture of Islam*, described as the "great western transmutation" that placed Europe ahead of all other existing civilizations. Barzun's choice of the word "decadence" instead of "dusk" is pregnant with allusions that would have been otherwise missing, for "dusk" foretells of the "night" ahead arriving as a closure to any history with a distinct beginning. "Decadence" suggests that closure is not a given, that though age brings infirmity and the passage of time breeds corruption, that ideas and the accompanying human spirit can become revitalized, and that in the Biblical sense an Abraham of much advanced age can still bring off-springs into the world and with them his world's renewal.

The slogan of Enlightenment was given by Kant. "Enlightenment is humanity's departure," Kant declared, "from its self-imposed immaturity. This immaturity is self-imposed when its cause is not lack of intelligence but failure of courage to think without someone else's guidance. Dare to know! That is the slogan of Enlightenment."[10] Not only man alone without intermediaries may reach God directly as Luther proclaimed, but man alone aided only by rational thinking can unlock the mysteries of God's creation as Newton demonstrated.

Enlightenment was the opening wide of human intellect to reach for the stars and beyond. Its premise was the unlimited power of unfettered reason among individuals. Reason and Freedom would be the two faces of the Enlightenment's coin, each supporting and enhancing the other's widening horizon. Both on their own were fragile and precariously situated; but together they would be nearly invincible in the making of the modern world. In the five centuries since this adventure began the ideas of Reason and Freedom have had innumerable collisions with countervailing and hostile ideas. There would be moments of great doubts about the survival of Enlightenment's ideas from enemies who placed the authority of the collective – be it of the church, the general will, class or race – ahead of individuals to be free and to think for themselves in constructing a society where Reason and Freedom remain protected and are unassailable.

Of the West's decline and Islam's stormy rise, I will place "decline" and "rise" within quotation marks. For the past century, at least since Oswald Spengler's pessimistic ruminations in *The Decline of the West* published in 1918, western historians and philosophers in regular intervals have speculated on West's passage to some end state of irreversible weakening. The story of ancient Rome's decline and fall stalks such speculation which, ironically, is also an attribute of the modern West's resilience. Hence, "decline" is more apparent than real, though concerns about the loss of vitality are genuine.

Islam, unlike Christianity, has yet to have its own reformation. Here we need to recognize that "reform" of a faith-tradition accompanying an institutional framework of order is neither an *event* nor an *instant* in time but a *process* deeply frustrating, confounding, ugly, prone to violence, and of end state not entirely predictable. Luther posting his 95 theses stands out in the flow of that long winding *process* of Reformation in Europe as does the royal prerogatives of Henry VIII's break with Rome when refused annulment of his marriage to Queen Catherine and establishing the Anglican Church, and so does the Reign of Terror in France that made a mockery of a revolution in the name of the Rights of Man.

It might also be said that 9/11 for what it now has come to represent – i.e., an episode illustrating the intensity of turmoil inside the world of Islam – is indicative of the unpredictable nature of the reform process at work. The stormy "rise" of Islam is the action-reaction of Muslims as they seek either to embrace or to resist and reject the modern world. Europe's reformation process took place over a period when boundaries separating civilizations and continents were sufficiently impenetrable, and even adjacent cultures could be closed to each other. The squeezing of the world of Islam is taking place in the full glare of globalization, and the world that Canada's Marshall McLuhan imagined as a "global village" is one we inhabit in which boundaries have dissolved and no culture remains unaffected by what occurs in another.

When we speak and write of Islam, as we do for example of Christianity, we mean simultaneously a faith-tradition with its non-negotiable core doctrine and an institutional framework of socio-political order built by human enterprise in the name of that faith-tradition. This distinction is worth bearing in mind since much confusion is generated by conflating the two. In discussing Islam we mean generally more or less what Muslims do in practicing their faith-tradition as they variously understand its meaning provided primarily in the Quran, which is taken by them to be divinely revealed words to Muhammad. But the practice of Islam comes in great variety, as there is much diversity in ethnicity among Muslims. The world of Islam is not monolithic though its domain is vast. Yet Islam as a monotheistic faith-tradition belongs to the family of faith-traditions which includes Judaism and Christianity. We know from experience that no quarrel tends to be more difficult than the quarrels within a family as what is common gets neglected and differences are amplified.

Mohammed Arkoun of Berber-Algerian origin and professor of Islamic studies at Sorbonne, Paris, observed, "Christianity in its Catholic and Protestant forms is the only religion which, in what it has rejected and what it has accepted, has been continuously exposed to the challenges of a modernity which was forced and which developed in Europe and exclusively in Europe until the Second World War."[11] In other words, Arkoun's observation indicates Christianity's experience in the development of the modern world has important lessons for other faithtraditions whose followers are in various degrees yet to make as full a transition from pre-modern to modern world as Christians of

Europe did. This lesson bears upon Muslims with urgency and with demands that Jews do not confront in the like manner, for Jews in Europe both participated in and contributed to the making of the modern world.

Christianity influenced and shaped the moral foundation of the modern world even as it retrenched and conceded space to secular thought in the realm of politics. Rodney Stark in *The Victory of Reason* contends, "Christianity created Western Civilization...Without a theology committed to reason, progress, and moral equality, today the entire world would be about where non-European societies were in, say, 1800: A world with many astrologers and alchemists but no scientists."[12] Stanley L. Jaki, the Hungarian-born scientist and Benedictine priest, similarly but less stridently has pointed out the "science" we are familiar with and which has been central in the making of the modern world is uniquely European, and this "science" owes its "viable birth in a Europe which Christian faith in the Creator had helped to form."[13]

In the long arc of history the world of Islam for several centuries in the medieval period, from the 8th to the 12th, stood ahead of Christian Europe in terms of civilization. This was the period dominated by Muslim thinkers of Arab, Persian, Turkish and Afghan origins within the commonwealth of Islam. But during this period a confrontation among Muslims took place between men of doctrinaire faith and men of rational thought, and the doors of reasoning in matters of faith and law were closed. It brought to an end development in science within the world of Islam situated at the crossroads of civilizations and the role of Muslims as the bridge between the ancient world of Greece and the modern world's awakening in Europe.

The world is constructed and reconstructed by ideas. This notion is inherent in Islam as the Quran insists people observe nature and its working and see in them signs revealing of God. But once authoritarian politics shut the door on speculative reasoning, the creative impulse dwindled at a time when Europe was to take its "great leap" forward. The result was a breach opened between Europe and the world of Islam; it soon became a chasm and the present widening distance between these two worlds – one modern and the other pre-modern – seems insurmountable. Abdus Salam, the first Muslim scientist to win the

Nobel Prize for Physics in 1979 reflected upon this parting of ways. Salam wrote:

> [A]round the year 1660, two of the greatest monuments of modern history were erected, one in the West and one in the East; St. Paul's Cathedral in London and the Taj Mahal in Agra. Between them, the two symbolize, perhaps better than words can describe, the comparative level of architectural technology, the comparative level of craftsmanship and the comparative level of affluence and sophistication the two cultures had attained at that epoch of history.
>
> But about the same time there was also created – and this time only in the West – a third monument, a monument still greater in its eventual import for humanity. This was Newton's *Principia*, published in 1687. Newton's work had no counterpart in the India of the Mughals. I would like to describe the fate of the technology which built the Taj Mahal when it came into contact with the culture and technology symbolized by the *Principia* of Newton.
>
> The first impact came in 1757. Some one hundred years after the building of the Taj Mahal, the superior firepower of Clive's small arms had inflicted a humiliating defeated on the descendants of Shah Jahan. A hundred years later still – in 1857 – the last of the Mughals had been forced to relinquish the Crown of Delhi to Queen Victoria. With him there passed away not only an empire, but also a whole tradition in art, technology, culture and learning.[14]

The emergence of the Muslim world into independence and statehood in the middle years of the 20th century after two hundred years of European control is one motif of Islam's "stormy rise" and Europe or the West's retrenchment, not "decline." But the Muslim world was not alone in this emergence into independence and statehood; India's independence, China's nationalist revolution under the banner of Marxism, and the gradual withdrawal of European powers from Africa is part of this singularly over-arching history. What makes Islam's "stormy rise" noteworthy is the close proximity of the central core of the Muslim world, the Arab-Muslim Middle East, to Europe geographically and historically, and its many threads of relationship with Europe. This intricate web of history places the Middle Eastern societies in a special tension with Europe that is not similarly present in the story of modern India, or China.

There is the memory – however vague, uncertain or imprecise – recalled when a Muslim mind is scratched of a past when the Islamic world was at par with Europe, and even in some respect ahead. This memory works in many different ways to question, obstruct, rattle, and also defeat efforts of that segment of Muslims who want to engage with the modern world, learn from it, adopt its ways and make the social transition from the traditional premodern arrangements to the modern world of science and democracy. This is what we have witnessed in Iraq and Afghanistan where the collision between the modern world and the pre-modern world due to circumstances that brought about 9/11 has been most dramatic. We will witness more of such collisions as the Muslim world, in particular its central core, exhausts itself in pushing back on the modern world. This is because instead of learning from Christianity's long standing experience with modernity and the process of modernization, as Mohammed Arkoun suggests, openness to learning that is embracing of science and democracy is under siege among Muslims.

Let us take a bird's eye view of the past fifty years, or the second half of the 20th century. In 1957 Wilfred Cantwell Smith, Canada's foremost scholar of Islam and comparative religions, published *Islam in Modern History*. Smith had traveled in the Middle East before the Second World War, and lived and taught in Lahore of pre-1947 India. He witnessed India's partition, followed closely the developments in Pakistan, and his book was an effort to put in perspective history's challenge for Muslims as they were beginning to work out their place in the modern world. Smith wrote,

> The massive uncertainties of the nineteenth century have given way to the bewildering complexity of the twentieth. The resurgence of Asia has included the strenuous, gradual emancipation of Asian countries from European political control, an emancipation now almost but not quite complete. A radical modernity in living, western in provenance, has shown a continually expansive, determined, seemingly irresistible penetration of all areas, including the Muslim. In this process it would be difficult to overestimate how fundamentally involved the Islamic societies are; in the cities psychologically and culturally, in all parts economically and administratively.[15]

Smith was a student of Sir Hamilton Gibb, the doyen of Anglo-Islamic scholars of the first half of last century. In 1932 Gibb published *Whither Islam* in which he wrote,

> The most remarkable feature of the Moslem world in these early decades of the twentieth century is not that it is becoming westernized, but that it desires to be westernized. It would be difficult to point to a single Moslem country which entirely rejects the contributions of the West in each and every field of life and thought.[16]

Between the two observations of Gibb and Smith the world was politically wrenched out of its moorings as a result of wars and revolutions. The Muslim world was deeply affected by these events as were other cultures. Independence came, or was won as in Algeria, and the ruling class in the Muslim world made a bid to establish political order and engage with tasks that Smith described. But other forces were also at work abroad and domestically. Cold War logic on either side of its divide lent support to ruling elites across the Muslim world as they placed their survival in power ahead of the need to work out some institutional arrangement allowing for participation of the widest segment of the population in meeting the requirements for democracy and socioeconomic progress. Domestically the ideas of secular nationalism gave way to the politics of religious exclusion, and the insistence of religious authorities that the political order of Muslim societies conform with the legal principles of Islamic law (*shari'ah*) worked out in the early period of Islam between the 9th and the 11th century.

The rulers of the Muslim world in the decades after Smith's landmark book was published went into retreat from their early adherence to the "desire", as Gibb had written, of making their societies "westernized," or "modernized" in the vocabulary of a later time. The retreat was occasioned by military defeats in Muslim encounter with non-Muslim countries, primarily Israel and India. There was also loss of authority of those in power, as of the Shah in Iran, when confronted by populist movements such as the Muslim Brotherhood in Egypt and the Jamaat-i-Islami in Pakistan.

By the end of the last century the guarded optimism of Gibb and Smith had faded. Paul Kennedy, a Harvard historian, in *Preparing for the Twenty-First Century* published in 1994, summarized differently the situation of the Muslim world. Kennedy observed,

> It is one thing to face population pressures, shortage of resources, educational/technological deficiencies, and regional conflicts which would challenge the wisest governments. But it is another when the regimes themselves stand in angry resentment of global forces for change instead of (as in East Asia) selectively responding to such trends. Far from preparing for the twentyfirst century, much of the Arab and Muslim world appears to have difficulty in coming to terms with the nineteenth century, with its composite legacy of secularization, democracy, laissez faire economics, transnational industrial and commercial linkages, social change, and intellectual questioning. If one needed an example of the importance of cultural attitudes in explaining a society's response to change, contemporary Islam provides it.[17]

Those Muslims most acutely tormented by the collision of their inherited world with the modern world are, and not surprisingly as witnessed in similar circumstances with other people in other cultures, members of the social elite educated in the traditional value system of their society and exposed to the currents of modern thinking. It is from this class the opposition has come to the modern world based on *identity* politics. It is the much-privileged children of this class whose alienation, resentment and awareness of the increasing gap between their societies and the West morphed into the politics of terror. Their rage would have been of little consequence but for the upheavals inside the traditional world of Islam resulting from globalization. They succeeded in fusing their anger and grievances against the modern world, born of failure and defeats, with the protests of uprooted peasantry and unemployed workers in sprawling urban slums of failed economies into the making of populist movements within the Muslim world.

Khomeini and Osama bin Laden are the two faces of Muslims irrespective of their differences joined together in the fight against the modern world, as are the faces of Mohammed Atta, the lead pilot of one of the hijacked airplanes on 9/11, and Khalid Sheik Mohammed, the al Qaeda mastermind of global terrorism in the name of Islam. In the opposite end are Muslim faces in the crowd of those rallying in support of democracy and the modern world as in Turkey and Lebanon, Indonesia and Iraq, or coerced into silence as in Iran. Marshall McLuhan would remind us that what occurs in one corner of the global village will affect other corners since the global village is now wired and connected. This was the lesson of 9/11. This is the struggle into which the West has been drawn: its battlefields in the post-9/11 world are in Afghanistan and Iraq, and the West can no more afford to turn its back on this struggle than Muslims can opt out of being engaged in bringing their societies to adapt to the requirements of science and democracy.

For the West the confusion is how to assist Muslim countries make the transition into modernity as much out of historical necessity as its self-interest demands in terms of security. For Muslims the confusion is how to restore the centre to their civilization that collapsed a long time ago, and to reconstruct it in harmony with the modern world. So long as the world was predominantly an agrarian economy, Muslim civilization maintained vitality. Once the Europeans pioneered in the making of the industrial civilization, the Muslim world fell behind. For Muslims the need is to acknowledge they have to learn in new ways how to hear and understand the words of the Quran, if they are going to contribute as a people positively to their advancement in a dramatically altered world as once in the past other Muslims did.

3

Muslims, Democracy, and the American Experience

The subject of Islamic reform is old, even as it has emerged in recent years as one of urgency. Since 9/11, the subject has become even more pressing. It would be more proper, however, to speak about the reform of Muslims. For whatever is Islam and however Islam is received, understood, practiced, and made the template of cultures and civilization, it is at the human level a reflection of the conduct of Muslims.

The reform of Muslims, as was that of Christians, is neither an event nor an instant in time but a process deeply frustrating, ugly, and, at its end, not entirely predictable. This is true of any reform process but even more so of reform driven by the ideals of a religion.

It is the human condition to persist, to push on the boulder of reform like Sisyphus, and to strive despite disappointments and defeats to improve upon the existing situation. The Qur'an sets an imperative tone on the need for reform by insisting that it must come from within people themselves. A well-known Qur'anic verse reads, "Verily God does not change the state of a people till they change themselves."[18]

The subject of reform (*islah*) and renewal (*tajdid*) within Islam is as old as the history of Muslims. There exists a vast number of Muslim writings and reflections on this matter, and much of the effort behind this cumulative labor of the mind has been driven on the assumption that reform may be brought about by a better textual understanding of

Islam. No matter that such an assumption is contrary to Qur'anic instruction and that reform of the mind and the heart must precede a better reading of the sacred text.

The concern for reform from the late nineteenth century to the present has been driven in part by the objective of reconciling Islam and Muslims with the requirements of modernity and democracy, both products of European history and most compellingly manifest in the United States.

The Growing Cry for Reform

The six lectures which Muhammad Iqbal (1877-1938), the poetphilosopher of India-Pakistan, gave in Madras in the late 1920s, subsequently published as *The Reconstruction of Religious Thought in Islam*,[19] remains one of the most thoughtful and provocative attempts by a Muslim to reconcile Islam and the modern world. In the opinion of the late historian Hamilton Gibb (1895-1971), this attempt reflected an approach almost bordering on heresy.[20] But Iqbal's efforts were not the work of a recluse; he was deeply involved as a spokesman for Muslims in the politics of undivided India and an active supporter of Muslims across Asia and Africa in their effort to gain independence from European rule. His efforts were also part of a nineteenth century Muslim intellectual movement questioning the traditional formulation and representation of Islam as Muslims became increasingly aware of the gap between civilization of their world and that of Europe.

Iqbal is important because the effort he expended in rethinking Islam exemplifies the modernist approach of Muslims – to name just a few such as Jamal ad-Din al-Afghani (Iranian, 1838-97), Sayyid Ahmed Khan (Indian, 1817-98), Muhammad Abduh (Egyptian, 1845-1905), and Ali Abd ar-Raziq (Egyptian, 1888-1966) – before Iqbal, and those after him such as Adonis[21] (Syrian, b. 1930), Ghulam Ahmad Pervez[22] (Indian/Pakistani, b. 1903), Nasr Hamid Abu Zayd (Egyptian, b. 1943), Abdolkarim Soroush (Iranian, b. 1945) and Mohammed Arkoun (Algerian, b. 1928). They contended that closing the gap between Europe and the Muslim world requires preeminently an interpretation of Islam taking into account the philosophical and scientific foundation of the modern world. The foundational assumption of the modernist approach is that by demonstrating reason and revelation to be in harmony, then such a reading, understanding, and application of the Quran by Muslims to their lives will also be harmonious with the requirements of the modern world. Hence to speak about *Islam and Modernity*[23] as Fazlur Rahman (1919-88) did, or about *Islam and Democracy*[24] as Fatima Mernissi (b. 1940) does, is to suggest that if the Qur'an is properly read and rightly understood in keeping with the spirit of the age in which Muslims reside, then Islam may be reconciled with modernity and democracy respectively. This is the faith and optimism of the modernist approach; the reality, however, is sobering about a civilization that may well be irreparably broken.

Iqbal anticipated the argument for partitioning India and the making of a Muslim majority state within the subcontinent. He died in 1938, some nine years prior to the formation of Pakistan. At the end of the twentieth century, Pakistan, in light of Iqbal's dream of a Muslim majority state coming to terms with the modern world economically, politically, and socially, has turned out to be a nightmare of failed expectations. But Pakistan is not alone, nor is its political and economic failure unique – the country broke apart in 1971 when East Pakistan became independent as Bangladesh after a bloody civil war. Neither is its continuing internal sectarian violence exceptional within the larger Muslim world. From Algeria to Indonesia, from the Central Asian republics to Sudan, the entire Muslim world has retreated from meeting the challenge of modernity and has turned its back on modernity. Writing in the 1930s, Hamilton Gibb observed that the "most remarkable feature of the Moslem world in these early decades of the twentieth century is not that it is becoming Westernized, but that it desires to be Westernized."[25] Without injury to Gibb's choice of words, readers can assume that "to be Westernized" means "to be modern." In contrast to Gibb's observation Yale historian Paul Kennedy, writing at the end of the twentieth century, wrote, "Far from preparing for the twenty-first century, much of the Arab and Muslim world appears to have difficulty in coming to terms with the nineteenth century, with its composite legacy of secularization, democracy, laissez-faire economics, transnational industrial and commercial linkages, social change, and intellectual questioning."[26]

The difference between the observations of Gibb and Kennedy is the distance between the restlessness of Muslim elites exposed to the

Western world under colonialism and a civilization constrained by its cultural system in the post-colonial age. Kennedy astutely stated, "If one needed an example of the importance of cultural attitudes in explaining a society's response to change, contemporary Islam provides it."[27] The weakness in the modernist approach is the assumption and expectation that a new textual interpretation or modern hermeneutics applied to the reading of the Quran will enable the Muslim world to be reconciled culturally and politically with the relentlessly revolutionary process of change that Marshall Hodgson in *The Venture of Islam* termed the "great Western transmutation."[28]

The problem and challenge for Muslims in coming to terms with the modern world, shaped by the social power of the West, resides in the cultural resistance of their societies taken individually and together as the Muslim world. Textual interpretations are part of a cultural enterprise and for any interpretation, whether modern, traditional, or something other, to become absorbed into majority thinking requires that society is receptive to new ideas. The failure of modernist thinkers in Islam such as Iqbal to find majority support among Muslims suggests that culturally they remain averse, if not entirely hostile, to the values of the contemporary world associated with the West. British sociologist Anthony Giddens described modernity as "modes of social life or organization which emerged in Europe from about the seventeenth century onwards and which subsequently became more or less worldwide in their influence."[29] The problem of the Muslim world in terms of being open to modernity is not with Islam awaiting "reconstruction" in the sense Iqbal used the term but that Muslims in their majority culture are resistant both to the change demanded by the modern democratic age and to the need for self-reformation.

How Did Orthodoxy Become Orthodox?

To focus on Muslims and their culture, and not on Islam, requires acknowledgment that Islam as a lived reality is a human construction in historical time. From the earliest accounts of Islamic historians Ibn Ishaq (d. 761), Al-Waqidi (d. 823), and At-Tabari (d. 923) among others, it is clear that the founding of Islam was neither a peaceful affair nor did the new religion eliminate tribal and familial conflicts. Blood readily flowed. Muslims in the first age of Islam were not simply moved to accept the new faith as taught by Muhammad and by the wonder of the sublime majesty of divine revelation that descended upon him. They had to be subdued forcibly. The Quran itself provides testimony to the obduracy and violent resistance of those among whom Muhammad was born, lived, and preached. Islam prevailed, but the cultural predisposition of the desert Arabs remained sufficiently strong in shaping the message of Islam for posterity.

What became consecrated as orthodox Islam of the Muslim majority from its beginning in the eighth century was initially arbitrary. It was the opinions of those who succeeded in holding the centers of power against dissidents that became the dominant cultural value of the Arab-Muslim society. It was the political views of Mu'awiya and his chosen successors who defeated 'Ali ibn Abi Talib and his sons. It was the Umayyads over the Hashemites. Contests between claims and counterclaims over time and place slowly shaped orthodoxy. In that moment of great plasticity in Islam's infant history, when the Prophet died and all could have been lost in the succession dispute that followed, those who seized power and legitimated it in the Prophet's name set the tone of what came to be defined as orthodoxy. Within a few short decades, that orthodoxy provided legitimacy for those in authority even though they did not possess the virtues exhibited by the Prophet and by his family and close companions. Ever since then, it is that orthodoxy – more a product of the cultural markings of the desert Arabs and tribal manners – that has had an immeasurable influence on what later Muslims made of their religious inheritance.

Should anyone depart from orthodoxy, for example, by adhering to Sufi ethics and mysticism, they would need to reconcile their private or minority views with the public face of orthodoxy or suffer the consequences. In time, this orthodoxy became idealized as the norm of Muslim culture. The merits this cultural system once possessed in premodern history became incongruent with the values – secular, rational, democratic – of the modern age.

To use Western terms, this culture became authoritarian, due both to deference to rulers and the unaccountability of authorities to their subjects. The *sulta* (those in authority) were always right, for the *sulta* held both the Quran and the sword. The orthodox ulema (religious scholars) provided the key judgment for all time within this cultural system: since order is preferable to anarchy, the tyranny of the *sulta* is preferable to the consequences of resistance and rebellion. In South Asia, the word for *sulta* is *sarkar,* meaning that all rights emanate from those in power and all obligations are due to them. This is the culture of deference which in Pakistan resulted in Supreme Court judgments on the basis of the "doctrine of necessity" legitimizing the right of men in uniform to seize power."[30]

The success of the orthodoxy in this cultural system of deference is not entirely a function of coercion; rather, it reflects the values of the people, which in turn reinforce those values as norms and ideals. Indicative of this phenomenon is the manner in which the orthodoxy uses *hadith* (accounts of the Prophet's words and deeds) to constrain the reading of the Qur'an according to the interests of the orthodox. The use of *hadith* – a human product of a certain time and, therefore, of questionable authenticity in contrast to the Quran, the Word of God – to fix the meaning of the Quran has reinforced the conservatism of the *sulta* and the culture of deference.

The symptoms of this cultural system can be seen in the prevalent attitude of Muslims toward women, minorities, and dissidents. The microcosm of this cultural universe is the family and the mosque. Within the family, patriarchal values dominate; women are the property of men, beholden to their opinions and their needs. The violence done to women reflects the reaction of men when women are unwilling to submit to those values. A culture of deference is also one in which the collective consensus takes precedence over individual thinking, where an individual is suspected of being misguided and subversive unless he remains beholden to the collective. Minorities are tolerated so long as they acknowledge the rights and privileges of the majority and recognize their appropriate place in society. Dissidents are punished for not submitting to the *sulta*.

In the mosque, the cultural rhythm of Muslim societies finds routine expression. The place of the *imam* (prayer leader) in the congregation, the authority he wields when he ascends the *minbar* (pulpit) and delivers the Friday *khutba* (sermon) is unmistakable and amplified by the chain of authority leading ultimately to the person of the *sulta*. The *imam* cannot be questioned on what he preaches on the pulpit, and what he preaches is sanctioned by the wisdom residing in the consensus of the orthodoxy. He protects the values by which Muslims live, sanctifying and validating them by referring to the *hadith* and reading the Quran through the perspective of that literature, irrespective of the vast changes in time and place from the context of the age in which the *hadith* was compiled.

It is through the family and the mosque that the Muslim cultural system is reproduced daily and maintained in all its complexity. While this cultural system has been challenged by the modern world, it has also resisted it by maintaining the autonomy of its culture from the economic linkages it has with the West. Moreover, the dominance of fundamentalism in the discourse and practice of Muslims since the 1970s represents the stern resistance of a traditionalconservative cultural system against the forces of modernity.

The face of the Taliban in Afghanistan and Pakistan is a particular variant of this cultural system, as is the Saudi Wahhabi variant, the Iranian Shi'ite variant, and the Malay Indonesian within the larger complex of the Muslim world. The autonomy of the cultural system has assisted each of these variants to maintain its authenticity in the midst of global changes. This autonomy also provides Muslim immigrants in the West, protected by the Western liberal values of pluralism and multiculturalism, with the ability to maintain in their personal lives and within their private domains the norms of the Muslim cultural system. So long as by choice and conviction the Muslim majority adheres to, approves of, and reinforces this cultural system, the Muslim world will recede further from the modern world. The consequences of a fifth of humanity being resistant to the West and the occasional eruption of this resistance into reactionary violence will remain one of the more difficult and troubling challenges for global politics in the twenty-first century.

Is Islamic Culture Compatible with Democracy?

Democracy is a political-cultural system describing the norms of a society rather than just the workings of a government. Such a reference to democracy indicates how great the cultural distance is between the Muslim world and democracy, and how profound reform will be if democracy is to become reality among Muslims beyond periodic elections to give a façade of legitimacy to those in power. Anthony Arblaster, a political philosopher, defined democracy as "the idea of popular power, of a situation in which power, and perhaps authority too, rests with the people."[31] This idea of popular sovereignty resting with the people is an anathema to Islamists.

Democracy is in a cultural sense an expression of the liberal modern world that situates the individual as the moral center of politics and society. The mechanics of democracy rest on an electoral system that provides for contested elections among individuals and parties. It is in the regular functioning of the electoral system, its provisions established in constitutional documents that a culture of democracy will emerge. When sovereign individuals embrace inalienable rights that no authority may abridge or revoke, non-democracies evaporate. The idea of democracy as a culture is found in the work of Tocqueville and in recent times has been given the most subtle renderings in the writings of the American political philosopher George Kateb.[32]

It is the idea of the inalienable rights located in the individual, rights that need to be protected, nurtured, and allowed the fullest unhindered expression that makes democracy so morally distinctive from other cultural systems. From this liberal perspective, the common error about democracy is to view it as a majority system of governance. In a democracy based on individual rights, on the contrary, it is the protection of the rights of minorities and dissidents that reflect the different nature of politics within the larger context of democratic culture. Democracy produces a citizenry distinctively different than those in the culture of deference. The cluster of values distinguishing democratic culture from nondemocratic culture is qualitative. According to Kateb, "In its distinctive way of forming political authority, representative democracy cultivates distinctive ways of acting in nonpolitical life – of seeking and giving, of making claims for oneself and one's group and acknowledging the claims of others."[33]

There is an urgent need when discussing reform of Islam or Muslims to keep in perspective the culture of democracy as found in the United States and the notion of democracy simply as the mechanics of government. Political essayist Fareed Zakaria suggested the need to distinguish between "liberal" democracy and the "illiberal" democracy found in many developing countries.[34] Such a distinction suggests an eventual evolution from illiberal to liberal democracy. For such an evolution to be successful, however, a sufficient number of people in an illiberal democracy who believe in the culture of democracy and all of its freedoms must coalesce. The reality in the Muslim world remains different. Zakaria's illiberal democracy is similar to what Samuel E. Finer, a professor of politics and government, wrote about in *Comparative Government* as "façade democracy,"[35] a bowing of the head to the idea of democracy by the tiny elite of those in power as a means to enhance their legitimacy and perpetuate their authority. The October 1999 military coup in Pakistan and the apathetic manner in which the public greeted the ouster of an elected government, or the commonality of authoritarian governments in Arab states, are not anomalies but reflections of a cultural system operating on assumptions different from the democratic cultural system of the West.

What Can the American Experience Provide?

The U.S. involvement with the Muslim world since 1945, and the resulting Muslim perception of the United States, has been difficult for a number of reasons. The Cold War in the Muslim world, U.S. support for Israel, and historic U.S. preference for stability in the Persian Gulf has led Washington to support governments that lack popular approval by Muslims. All of this has less to do with American democratic culture than with U.S. foreign policy during a period of global politics when the United States assumed responsibility for maintaining freedom, democracy, and market economy in its confrontation with international communism. That America made mistakes during this period, that it overreached, and that there were negative consequences to some actions that could have been mitigated if not avoided are all part of the internal American debate.

The majority public opinion in the Muslim world has been shaped by the power of the United States abroad rather than by the nature of American democracy at home. The result is a grossly distorted image of the United States among Muslims, even among those who reside in America. Edward Said, for instance, observed that despite the fact of the United States looming large in the lives of Arabs and Muslims, there was no serious institutional effort to be found in the Arab-Muslim world to study the United States, and that not "even the celebrated

American universities of Beirut and Cairo teach American culture, society, and history in any systematic way."[36] When Ayatollah Ruhollah Khomeini, leader of the Islamic Revolution in Iran, denounced America as the "Great Satan," he gave voice to a popular opinion among a great many Muslims worldwide – an opinion frequently expressed in flag burnings, attacks on American assets and citizens abroad, and a readiness to believe both the worst about decadence and corruption in American society and that the United States, as Israel's patron, is an enemy of Islam and Muslims.

For Muslims, the requirement of seriously studying America carries the risk of the undermining the cultural assumptions by which they live. Their study of American democracy and of the lives and contributions of American men and women of diverse ethnic origins who make its democracy immensely rich, would force Muslims to discover how the core values of American society are profoundly moral, indeed religious, and how at critical moments of American history, as Seymour Martin Lipset, dean of American sociologists, wrote, "the hand of providence has been on a nation which finds a Washington, a Lincoln, or a Roosevelt when it needs him."[37] Poets possess an inward eye with which to gaze upon the world. Intuitively they give voice to the spirit of their age. Kateb noted, "Walt Whitman is a great philosopher of democracy. Indeed, he may be the greatest."[38] The Muslim world has not produced any poet like Whitman, and this absence, when poets and poetry have traditionally been an exalted facet of Islamic culture, reflects the absence of the democratic ethos among Muslims and by which the West is distinguished from the East.

It is urgent that Muslims set aside their blinkers, their self-perpetuating resentments, their anger and complaints against the United States, which reflect their own weaknesses and failures and ultimately erupted in the events of 9-11. They need to carefully, earnestly, and with humility begin to explore and understand what America represents as a democracy. There is some difficulty in this enterprise of exploration and comprehension due to the range of contradictory images that Americans float about their country through mass media, which is the only way most Muslims learn anything about the United States. The difficulties in sifting through the contradictory images only make it more urgent to engage in an effort of discovery as a corrective to those selective images and stories which fuel the existing resentment and anger of vast majority of Muslims.

The irony is that it is not Islam as transcendent truth about the unity of God but rather the historical-cultural system associated with Islam that now encloses Muslims and prevents them from hearing ever fresh the Word of God when they read the Quran. It is this cultural system, once proven to be remarkable for the achievements of its civilization that now weighs upon Muslims, and its inertia prevents them from once again being progressive and in harmony with the world around them. Textual interpretations may help individuals to reorient themselves to their world, but there is insufficient evidence from Muslim history to suggest that textual interpretation may bring about a reform of Muslims collectively as a people.

In concluding, the Quran informs that without reform or belief, civilizations in the past vanished, and warns, "O people, it is you that have need of God, and God is the Self Sufficient, the Praised One. If He please, He will remove you and bring a new creation (in your place)."[39] In the democratic age, God's message resonates through the voice of sovereign people. Muslims are standing at a fork of history in the early years of the twenty-first century. Their choice for reform will lead them on the path of Islam as democracy. Their refusal to embrace reform, however, will leave them stagnant within a cultural system incongruent with the spirit of the modern age of democracy while they indulge in identity politics, nostalgia, grievances, and resentment against a West they do not understand.

4

Three Muslim perspectives

In the wake of the September 11, 2001 terror attacks, historian Bernard Lewis crystallized the key question about Muslims by asking "What went wrong?"[40] Nor was Lewis alone, for a number of Muslim writers have authored books in response to it. Among the most prominent are Tarek Heggy and Tariq Ramadan, the former an Egyptian and the latter of Egyptian descent, and Akbar Ahmed, a Pakistani living in the United States. Heggy and Ramadan publish not only in English but also in Arabic and so transcend audiences. Ahmed's books, too, are widely translated, even appearing in Indonesian and Chinese. Significantly, all three live in the West. Such important and active debates are simply not possible in countries that still punish dissent and open intellectual discussion. By choice and circumstance, they find themselves dragomen and diplomats between two worlds. Their writings reflect the Muslim dilemma of how to separate Islam as a transcendent faith of universal appeal from the immediate history of Muslim societies. All three are well regarded in their home communities. Their works are widely read and followed, and their commentaries on the state of Muslim politics and society earnestly sought by a diverse global audience interested in Muslim affairs.

Individual Vs Society in the Islamic World

Tarek Heggy's *Culture, Civilization, and Humanity* is a collection of his essays providing insight into contemporary politics in the Arabic-speaking countries of the Middle East with emphasis on his native Egypt. Partly polemical and partly analytical, Heggy seeks to awaken Arabs to how extensive is their collective responsibility for derailing themselves from progressing as a civilization. Heggy does not offer any striking new perspective to explain how and why the Arab world has fallen so far behind the West. The United Nations Development Program's *Arab Human Development Report* for both 2002[41] and 2003 have provided a catalogue of reasons as to why Arab countries have shown such poor socioeconomic development compared to other late-modernizing societies such as South Korea, Malaysia, and even India. But what Heggy's essays lack in originality, they make up for in the frankness with which the author discusses the historical and cultural failings of Egypt and the Arab world which retards the human potential of nearly 300 million people in a region stretching from the Atlantic Ocean to the Persian Gulf.

In a culture preoccupied with form over content, and where collective honor trumps collective self-examination of the gap between rhetoric and reality, Heggy explains his purpose:

> I write to urge Egyptians to accept criticism and to engage in self-criticism because, unless they are willing to do so, they will not discover the root causes of the ills they complain of today…I write in defense of freedom of belief but not in the context of a theocratic culture that places our destinies in the hands of men of religion. No society should allow its affairs to be run by clerics who are, by their nature and regardless of the religion to which they belong, opposed to progress…I write to call for an end to the Goebbels-style propaganda machines operating in Egypt and the Arab world and their dangerous manipulation of public opinion.[42]

Heggy thus highlights the tension between the individual and the community. Egypt remains caught in a vortex of contradictory pressures in respect to individual rights, rationality, and democracy in a clash with tradition that venerates the past while holding the future at ransom. While important to voice, there is nothing new about such discussions within the Arab world. The late Oxford historian Albert Hourani chronicled this intellectual ferment in the Arab world in his important study, *Arabic Thought in the Liberal Age, 1798-1939*.[43]

Heggy does not limit himself to repeating the ideas of intellectuals of the past and is not afraid to critique socialism and Marxism, a subject to which he has devoted some of his writings. This is important because both Marxist ideology and the patron-client relationship between the

Soviet Union and Arab states influenced the late Egyptian president Gamal Abdel Nasser and the politics of Arab nationalism. Nasser borrowed not only his state-centered economic planning but also his political vision of a single party state from his Soviet patrons.

Heggy's most important contribution is to shed light on the mind set of a culture responsible for the attacks of 9/11. He describes a society in part held hostage to the "Big Talk" syndrome, a situation in which a society is beholden to exaggeration, inflated rhetorical flourishes and bragging as individuals and groups strive to outdo each other in verbal displays of superiority. While in the modern age, "there is no room for big talk, only for moderate language that tries as far as possible to reflect the unembellished realities of science and culture,"[44] Heggy observes that in the Arab world, "our culture…has a long tradition of declamatory rhetoric that places more value on the beauty of the words used than on their accurate reflection of reality."45 Such a cultural trait hampers critical assessments and contributes to a failure to understand lack of progress and defeats such as those suffered in the June 1967 Arab-Israeli war. Instead, the "Big Talk" syndrome promotes an indulgence in nostalgia to escape from the demands of the present and punishes individuals who break the collective code of honor. Heggy explains,

> Of all the nations of the world, we sing more loudly and frequently of our history, our past glories, and our superiority to others…This leads to the prevalence of subjectivity rather than objectivity and ultimately to the formation of judgments from a purely personal perspective.[46]

Politics under these conditions encourage demagoguery and extremism and repress moderation. Conspiracy theories thrive. Realists live in fear of the radicalism of those who view subjects in absolute terms. This makes for a society of despots and demagogues. In shedding light on the sensitive aspects of a people's culture, Heggy's book illuminates how problems of a stalled society in the Muslim world have contributed to politics uninhibited in the use of terror.

The Islamic Community in New Domains

Tariq Ramadan is a controversial Geneva-based academic and public intellectual, listed by *Time* magazine as one of the world's

100 most prominent thinkers for his efforts to interpret Islam in the West.[47] Since 9/11, Ramadan's views and writings have come under increased scrutiny. In July 2004, the U.S. Department of Homeland Security decided to revoke his visa to the United States, preventing him from teaching at the University of Notre Dame. In December 2004, Ramadan withdrew his visa application. Ramadan's recent book is important, if only to see how an individual who describes himself as a bridge between cultures retains Islamist ties that remain suspect in the West.[48]

The intellectual work of any individual is inseparable from his biography. Tariq Ramadan is not an ordinary academic. In the words of Fouad Ajami, professor of Middle Eastern studies at Johns Hopkins, "In the world of new Islamism, Mr. Ramadan was pure nobility."[49] Ramadan is the grandson of Hassan al-Banna, the founder of the Muslim Brotherhood. Beginning in 1928 and lasting until his 1949 assassination, Banna preached a dangerous mix of religion and violence. Though Banna's life was short, his influence cut across a wide swathe of Egyptian society and the Arab world. He is not just the founder of the Muslim Brotherhood, but he is also the source of modern fundamentalist politics in the Arab-Muslim world. His teachings evolved and mutated into the politics and terrorism of Osama bin Laden's Al-Qaeda and similar organizations. Ajami explains why Ramadan's lineage is so important:

> The genealogy of Tariq Ramadan was fundamental to his ascendancy to power and prominence: *Nasab* (acquired merit through one's ancestors) is one of the pillars of Arab-Islamic society. Cunning in his use of his grandfather's legacy, Mr. Ramadan could embrace his grandfather while maintaining, when needed, that the sins of his ancestors cannot be visited on descendants. But…pride in his grandfather suffuses his work. In a piece of writing in November 2000, the reverence for Banna was astounding. No, he would not, he said, disown his descent from a man who "resisted British and Zionist colonialisms, who founded 2,000 schools, 500 social centers, and as many developmental cooperatives," and who never ordered or sanctioned terrorist attacks.[50]

As Ajami rightly points out, such assertions stand in sharp contrast to reality. This was a period when Banna provided the potent mix of religion and politics to the rising tide of Arab nationalism eventually putting an end to Egypt's brief interwar flirtation with liberal politics.

Nasser forced Ramadan's father to leave Egypt in 1954. He found refuge in Geneva where he established an Islamic centre. Tariq Ramadan grew up in Geneva and in his adult years began to see himself as a bridge between his adopted home and the Egypt of his grandfather. He expressed this self-identity recently while responding to his critics: "Those so focused on my genealogy should examine my intellectual pedigree, which along with my grandfather and father includes Descartes, Kant and Nietzsche."[51]

Ramadan's *Western Muslims and the Future of Islam* is a sequel to an earlier book, *To Be a European Muslim*.[52] These books are Ramadan's response to the reality for Muslims in a globalized world where increasing numbers live outside of lands traditionally demarcated as *dar al-Islam* (abode of Islam). He writes,

> More and more young people and intellectuals are actively looking for a way to live in harmony with their faith while participating in the societies that are their societies, whether they like it or not. French, English, German, Canadian, and American Muslims, women as well as men, are constructing a "Muslim personality" that will soon surprise many of their fellow citizens. Far from media attention…they are drawing the shape of European and American Islam: faithful to the principles of Islam, dressed in European and American cultures, and definitely rooted in Western societies. This grassroots movement will soon exert considerable influence over worldwide Islam: in view of globalization and the Westernization of the world, these are the same questions as those already being raised from Morocco to Indonesia.[53]

In this world of flux for Muslims, Ramadan recognizes that traditional categories of Islamic thinking and practice require re-conceptualization for the modern age. For such an effort to succeed, he sees the need first to rediscover the essential timeless principles of Islam as a transcendent faith, and then to situate them within the boundaries of Islam but beyond the limiting context of customs and traditions.

In the traditional world of Islam, there was harmony between faith and customs for Muslims. North Africa and the Middle East were *dar al-Islam*. Beyond their boundaries lay the *dar al-harb*, or abode of war, a land of infidels and those who had not seen the revelation. But such terms, which are keys to both Arabic and European explanations of Islam through the twentieth century, have increasingly diminished in importance as pluralism has spread and as Muslim communities have established themselves throughout the world. As an example of re-conceptualization, Ramadan offers the phrase *dar ash-shahada* (abode of testimony) as a substitute for *dar al-harb* to designate lands beyond *dar al-Islam*. But the effectiveness of re-conceptualization is questionable if it means changing labels for terms and phrases without repudiating the thinking and politics of that stream of traditional Islam that mutated into an ideology that motivated the 9/11 attacks.

Ramadan is acutely aware that the central issue confronting Muslims in the West is one of loyalty. While the terrorist attacks of 9/11 and their aftermath accentuated this issue, its tension predates the destruction of the World Trade Center. For traditional Muslims, religion and politics are inseparable. In the religion's early years, an imam or caliph ruled over the *ummah*, or community of believers. But history made the reality of *ummah* redundant a very long time ago. Long before the age of colonialism, the Islamic world fragmented. The concept of the *ummah*, nevertheless, remains important among some Islamic thinkers who see it as an ideal point of reference for those who believe that reconstructing such an arrangement is a religious duty for the believers in the message of Muhammad. Ramadan's counsel to Muslims living in the West is to embrace the West's pluralist democracy in order to eliminate suspicions about Muslim loyalty. Indeed, the West can be a useful refuge, if only to protect the essential principles of Islam since "the West still appears to be a place where Muslims can live securely with certain fundamental rights granted and protected."[54]

But Ramadan cannot entirely shield himself from critics who charge him with relativism, arguing that in the attempt to find a common ground between Islam and the West, he descends a slippery slope of diluting Islam to the point of compromising its authenticity. Muslim reformers have invariably found themselves trapped in this conundrum and have consistently been undone by the logic of traditionalists.

What Ramadan does not do is to break the intellectual straitjacket that disallows any challenge to the traditionalists' definition of Islam, faith, and history. Traditionalists maintain any dissent from their collective judgment is misleading and an opening for error. The probable reason for his inability to make the break and engage in real reform is biography. Ramadan is bound by his own loyalties and shies away from the more demanding post 9/11 task of explaining how Islamists have gotten away with defiling Islam without generating apposite outrage among Muslims. To engage in such an accounting would require placing responsibility first on the practices of traditional Islam that laid the ground upon which Islamists nurtured, and second, on mainstream Muslims who have reacted with silence and refusal to banish Islamists from their midst, thus making them accomplices. The reality of the post-9/11 world is mutual suspicion between the West and Islam. Western Muslims, whom Ramadan addresses, will have to decide where their loyalty rests. Ramadan's experience in being denied entry to the United States should demonstrate to him that space for accommodating Muslims who are not unambiguous about their loyalty to the country where they wish to reside has greatly shriveled in the West.

Islam under Siege

Akbar Ahmed's writings are fine examples of an attempt to reconcile conflicting beliefs as an aid in understanding and explaining the turmoil of the Muslim world. An anthropologist by training, Ahmed does not hesitate to reflect on his own experience in order to examine the internal disorder of Muslim society. In *Islam under Siege*, he weaves a tapestry of explanations to unmask how and why a civilization that once shone a beacon of light on the world became a seedbed of terrorism, bigotry and war.

Ahmed's origin is in South Asia, a region that, beginning in the sixteenth century, was the seat of one of the great empires of Islam. Born in India, as a child he moved with his family to the newly established Islamic state of Pakistan. He joined Pakistan's elite civil service corps in 1966, working as a civilian administrator in the tribal areas of Pakistan bordering on Afghanistan, and eventually became his country's high commissioner in Britain. After resigning from the diplomatic service, he began a second career as an academic in the United States.

His personal story sheds light on the trajectory of the "decay of development" of Muslim societies in the post-colonial period. At the time when Ahmed began as a civil servant, many in the United States saw Pakistan as a successful model of a rapidly modernizing economy in the developing world.[55] But that promise turned sour when Pakistan fell apart as a result of a violent and costly civil strife in 1971. When Bangladesh succeeded, it shook Pakistan's selfimage as a nation where religion transcended ethnic identity. Pakistan never fully recovered and increasingly turned towards a form of militantly fundamentalist Islam to renew its identity.

Islam under Siege attempts to explain the 9/11 attacks as a product of the decaying political reality of the Muslim world. The siege, Ahmed argues, is primarily internal to the society. On one hand, there is a widening gap between Muslim societies and the rest of the world. On the other hand, there are rising expectations within Muslim societies, which have simultaneously experienced a demographic explosion and the declining effectiveness of governing institutions. The effects of accelerating global change and internal population pressures have undermined the traditional social and cultural cohesion of Muslim societies, setting them adrift in the modern world.

Ahmed, who holds the Ibn Khaldun Chair of Islamic Studies at American University, in fact leans heavily on Ibn Khaldun, the great North African scholar of the fourteenth century, to explain the breakdown of the Muslim world's social and moral order.[56] Using Ibn Khaldun's notion of '*asabiya* – "group loyalty, social cohesion, or solidarity" – he describes the making and breaking of a closed circle of authoritarian politics in the Muslim world. Ahmed, also, cites Ibn Khaldun's belief that "social organization is necessary to the human species." Without organization, Ibn Khaldun argues, "the existence of human beings would be incomplete. God's desire to settle the world with human beings and to leave them as His representatives on earth would not materialize." Ahmed elaborates: "Social order thus reflects the moral order; the former cannot be in a state of collapse without suggesting a moral crisis."[57]

When *'asabiya* weakens, relationships binding individuals together also weakens. Unless these are replaced and strengthened by a new set of relationships, individuals are driven to abnormal behavior. Ibn Khaldun theorized that there was a four-generation cycle where existing orders would rise, peak, and then collapse, only to be replaced by a new order. But in the modern world, Ahmed argues, loss of social cohesion is brought about by the speed and impact of a fastpaced globalization. This leads to bewilderment compounded by an inchoate desire of victims to punish those they view as responsible for their misery.

Traditional societies are bound by a sense of honor to some higher authority providing norms for behavior. Ahmed dwells on how traditional societies construct honor and conduct themselves accordingly. He suggests that in the process of globalization, when speed of communications shrinks the world and compresses the boundaries of traditional societies, the old meaning of honor disintegrates, and "people respond by an excessive emphasis on group loyalty – or hyper-*'asabiya* – and create conditions for our post-honor society."[58]

Ahmed seeks to explain elements that produced bin Laden's mentality, something neither Heggy nor Ramadan address. His approach, combining cultural anthropology and political history, is somewhat persuasive. He argues that the mentality of bin Laden and like-minded individuals is reflective of a traditional society and culture mostly in ruin as a result of its collision with the fast-paced, scientific, and technologically-minded modern world. But it remains a frustrating exercise because the description of the Muslim world caught in a vortex of "anger, incomprehension, and violent hatred"[59] does little to explain how it can break the cycle of decay in which it appears stuck.

Conclusion

After 9/11 and the unremitting series of Islamist atrocities from Bali to Beslan, Muslims have reached a cul-de-sac of their own making. They have nurtured their demons from the first generation of Islam, from the killers of Muhammad's companions and rightly-guided caliphs Uthman and Ali, whose brief leadership of the Muslim community after Muhammad's death ended with assassins' knives, to those who have made suicide-bombing a religiously sanctioned method of warfare. The demons are internal, and how Muslims deal with them will speak much more compellingly about who they are than their protestations about being victims of history or the nobility of their faith. Moreover, their effectiveness, or the lack of it, in confronting their demons and eliminating the conditions that nurture them is now a global concern.

The core issue most Muslim intellectuals leave unaddressed, or address with diffidence, is what happens when religion becomes a handmaiden of politics. Islam became a tool of men in power, and men in power bent Islam to their purpose and interests. In the process, politics squeezed religion of its spiritual content and made examples of those individuals, such as Mansur ibn Hallaj, an Islamic mystic who was nailed to a gibbet in tenth century Baghdad, who insisted on holding to Islam as faith and not bending to the demands of politics in its name.

The Muslim world is not alone in the whirlwind of globalization. People of other cultures, also, contend with the same forces of economics and technology as do Muslims. This is why it might be said that the words of the Qur'an, "Allah will not change the condition of a people until they change what is in their hearts," applies to Muslims and non-Muslims alike.

5

Sadat's Conversion and What the Qur'an Says About Jews in the Holy Land

In the middle of the commemorative parade marking the eighth anniversary of the October 1973 war launched by Egypt and Syria against Israel on Yom Kippur, also known as the Ramadan War, Anwar Sadat, President of Egypt, was murdered by a band of Egyptian soldiers taking part in the event. Twenty-five years later as we recall the legacy of Sadat – his journey to Jerusalem in November 1977, his reaching out to Menachem Begin, the Prime Minister of Israel, and the two of them forging together a partnership of respect and affection culminating in the Camp David Accord of September 1978 for which the two leaders shared the Nobel Peace Prize – it becomes unmistakably clear that the men who killed Sadat on October 6, 1981 were forerunners of those who flew passenger jetliners into the Twin Towers of the World Trade Center in New York City and the Pentagon in Washington on that fateful morning of September 11, 2001 unleashing a whirlwind of hatred and bigotry emanating from the deep toxic bowels of a medieval age that still clings to our world at the beginning of the 21st century.

This essay is a reflection on the meaning of Sadat's historic journey to Jerusalem and the speech he delivered at the Israeli *Knesset* on November 20, 1977 within the larger context of Arab and Egypt's modern history. I will also briefly dwell on what the Quran tells us about Jerusalem and Jews in the Holy Land.

Sadat's journey to Jerusalem marked a departure, politically dramatic and then fatal for him, from the course taken by the Arab states with Egypt at its head three decades earlier in repudiating the decision of the United Nations to partition Palestine under the British mandate into two states, one Arab and one Jewish. It was also a departure for Sadat from the politics and ideology of Arab nationalism of the previous half-century with which his generation was associated. In setting out for Jerusalem Sadat broke ranks with his fellow Arab leaders and, in seeking reconciliation with Jews and Israel, he practically signed his own death warrant. His journey from Cairo to Jerusalem was, in the first instance, conceived in strategic terms to wrest back territories by diplomatic means lost to Israel in the June 1967 war, and he drove a hard bargain in the subsequent negotiations at Camp David to recover Egyptian territories from Israeli occupation. Yet the nature of the journey with all the symbolical trappings carried within it the possibility of putting in place an entirely new Arab-Israeli and Jew-Muslim relationship that could heal the rift between the two branches of Abraham's family. We will never know how Sadat would have nurtured this relationship if he had lived longer.

Sadat's murderers belonged to the most rabid fundamentalist Muslim cells in the Egyptian society known as *al-Takfir wa'l Hijra* (meaning "Excommunication and Flight") and *al-Jihad* (meaning "Holy War"), and were offshoots of the Muslim Brotherhood. The theoreticians of these groups denounced Egypt as an apostate nation for not following in full what they considered the teachings of the Quran, most importantly the practice of *jihad* literally taken to mean engaging in violence and bloodshed in the cause of their faith and land and given equal importance as prayers, fasting, charity and pilgrimage that taken together represent the "pillars of Islam." The leader of Sadat's assassination squad was a lieutenant in the artillery, and after unloading his machinegun on the president he yelled out, "I am Khalid al-Islambuli, I have killed Pharoah, and I do not fear death."

I view Sadat's decision to visit Jerusalem and forge together with Begin, Israelis and Jews outside of the Middle East a new relationship of mutual respect and common interest as an act of conversion on a journey that never got fully consummated. The significance of Sadat's journey might only be appreciated if it is understood within the larger framework of modern Arab politics and history that shaped the thinking, attitude and behaviour of the generation to which Sadat belonged and those which have come after his.

Sadat came of age between the two world wars. Those were the years when the brief blossoming of liberalism in Egypt that coincided with the British presence in the country following Disraeli's purchase of shares in the Suez Canal

Company in 1875 began to fade. In the three decades before the guns of August ended the long twilight of the Victorian Age, Egypt became receptive to the flow of ideas from Europe which generated a movement of reform across the society. This period in Egypt's history is known as the *nahda*, an awakening or renaissance, when Egyptians experimented in arts and letters, in politics and religion, with the wish of reconciling its culture based on traditional Islamic values with the modern world of science and democracy as found in Europe. By the time Sadat graduated from Cairo's Royal Military Academy and got posted in the Signal Corp of the Egyptian Army in 1938 as a Second Lieutenant at the age of twenty, reformist liberalism was being rapidly replaced by a rising tide of nationalism combined with a militant rendition of Islam as an ideology opposed to Britain and France as victorious powers over the Ottoman Empire in the Middle East.

The First World War in the Levant was fought around the edges of Egypt, and Egypt was not directly affected by the partitioning of the Arab provinces of the Ottoman Empire between the Suez Canal and the Persian Gulf after the war. Egypt was nominally an independent country under a monarchy belonging to the sons of Muhammad Ali, an Albanian soldier who served the Caliph-Sultans in Istanbul but following Napoleon's successful military interlude in Egypt emerged as *de facto* ruler in Cairo. But since 1882 Britain came to control aspects of Egypt vital to her strategic interests in the area and beyond. Following the war Britain arranged a treaty with the ruling monarchy by which the security of Egypt and Sudan and the control of the Suez Canal area were retained by London. It was an arrangement that quickly became the focus of nationalist resentment ultimately culminating in the Suez crisis of 1956.

It was in this context of anti-British nationalist sentiments fueled in part by the new phenomenon of Islamism of the Muslim Brotherhood founded in 1928 by Hasan al-Banna that Sadat's generation came of age. Islamism might be described as the reduction and bending of a faith tradition for political purpose, and as an ideology fed by an increasing number of Muslim intellectuals Islamism grew alongside the other two modern secular ideologies born in Europe, Bolshevism or Communism and Fascism, as a bitter opponent of Liberalism. Nadav Safran, a historian of modern Egypt, writes of the ideology of the Brotherhood as a "simple creed, grounded more on faith than systematic thought, cast into the frame of a militant movement inspired and activated by negative nationalism, and reinforced by concern with the bitterly felt social misery."[60] The nationalist anger inside Egypt drew upon the sense of betrayal felt beyond its borders by Arabs newly liberated by the arms of Britain and France. Britain's decision to help Jews establish their homeland in Palestine announced by Balfour in his letter of November 2, 1917 to Lord Rothschild, and the revelations of the Sykes-Picot draft agreement from May 1916 about post-war settlements in the Middle East were taken as evidence of perfidious intentions of London and Paris to divide and hobble Arabs from achieving their independent goals. In time the theme of Arab betrayal became the axiom of Arab nationalist politics. These were also years when the Mufti of Jerusalem, an appointed position and in Hajj Amin el-Husayni's case his appointment made by the first British High Commissioner to Palestine, Sir Herbert Samuel who was a Jew, disclosed how the combined effect of nationalist resentment and Islamism led to a populist support of Arabs for Hitler and the German Nazis when the Mufti became a collaborator with the Third Reich.

In his autobiography, *In Search of Identity*, Sadat recalls these years and his own impression with the politics of the time. Sadat writes:

> I was in our village for the summer vacation when Hitler marched from Munich to Berlin, to wipe out the consequences of Germany's defeat in World War I and rebuild his country. I gathered my friends and told them we ought to follow Hitler's example by marching from Mit Abul-Kum to Cairo. I was twelve. They laughed and went away.[61]

But the adolescent impressions about Hitler remained with Sadat through the intervening years and after he graduated as an officer in the Egyptian Army. Again, here is Sadat in his own words describing his involvement in clandestine politics within the army:

> Meetings took place in my apartment in my father's house at Kubri al-Qubbah, in the Officers' Club, at cafes, and in the houses of our colleagues. Contacts were initially confined to fellow officers in the same corps, mostly my coevals, but, encouraged by Hitler's successive threats to the British in 1939-41, I widened the circle gradually. Many senior and junior officers were approached and actually responded to our call, namely, that we should seize the opportunity and carry out an armed revolution against the British presence in Egypt.[62]

At this time Sadat also made a secret acquaintance with Hasan al-Banna, and was positively impressed. A relationship began between Sadat and al-Banna, and though Sadat does not admit of formally joining the Brotherhood he writes about others who did and of how Brotherhood's ideology penetrated into the ranks of the Egyptian military influencing some who would join the Free Officers Organization led by Gamal Abdel Nasser, the future dictator of Egypt.

The Free Officers' coup of July 1952 ending the monarchy, later celebrated as a revolution, placed Sadat in the inner circle of the military officers who have held power ever since in Egypt. It became the model of other military seizure of power within the Arab world, and the political thinking and attitudes of the Free Officers would be in different degrees copied in Baghdad, Damascus, Tripoli, Algiers, Tunis, Khartoum and draw populist support in those Arab states where the traditional order as in Saudi Arabia held firm against pan-Arab nationalists. In Egypt the Free Officers suppressed the Brotherhood for being their rival competing for power, and similar measures were taken in Syria, Iraq, Libya, Tunisia, but the ideology of Islamism remained percolating through the ranks of those in power and those resentful of being denied power.

Arab nationalism of the variety that took hold in Egypt was an appeal to unite against outsiders, to achieve independence, provide for progress, development and regaining a past dolled up as glorious. It confronted Jews in Palestine, mobilized Arab states to war against Israel after repeated defeats found great difficulty in holding check the rising influence of Islamism grown more virulent in its hatred of Jews and opposition to the liberal-democratic West. Sadat as Nasser's deputy, and then following Nasser's death in September 1970 as a leader in his own right, was caught in the conflicting pulls of Arab nationalism and Islamism. For a while Sadat spoke about Egypt as the crossroad between Arab and Mediterranean cultures, of an Egypt with a history of several millennia prior to the coming of Arabs and Islam, of Alexandria connected to Europe, of an Egypt that is not entirely part of an Arab world as is Jordan or the Gulf emirates and hence an Egyptian-Arab identity that looks in both direction towards Europe and the East. This was pointedly an attempt to depart from Nasser's representation of Egypt as being at the centre of three concentric circles: Arab, African and Islam. Sadat's attempt to circle the conflicting pressures of history and ideology, to harness them on behalf of a clearly defined Egyptian national interest without completely rejecting the claims of Islamists eventually failed as he fell to the violence of those whose totalitarian impulse viewed anyone disagreeing with their pronouncements as enemies of Islam. But Sadat was part of the milieu that killed him, and the reason for his murder was his journey to Jerusalem seen as a betrayal of Arabism – the mix of nationalism and Islamism – of which he was a product. Sadat's Jerusalem journey, therefore, in its conception and execution signified a repudiation of what his generation's history had made of him until then. Before the journey, however, there was another war fought.

The October 1973 war was planned and launched to redress the humiliation of June 1967, to break the status quo in Israeli occupied Egyptian territory of Sinai, to open the blockaded Suez Canal, to harness U.S. support behind Arab claims and grievances, and to demonstrate to Israelis that the Arab states were not entirely without military recourse in meeting their objectives of regaining equilibrium in the Arab-Israeli face-off. At the end of the June 1967 war and ahead of the passage of the UN Security Council Resolution 242 in November the Arab states met in Khartoum, Sudan, in September and came out with the three "no": no peace, no negotiation and no recognition of Israel. For Sadat the October war was the means by which to cut through this stalemate and establish his own authority instead of being considered merely as Nasser's successor.

The October war designed as limited in scope and duration could only succeed if it caught the Israelis completely by surprise, and regain for Egypt and its Arab partners an initiative against Israel lost in 1967. From Sadat's perspective the October war fulfilled its purpose. The United States was drawn into the diplomatic pursuit of a negotiated disengagement between Egyptian and Israeli forces under Henry Kissinger's stewardship, the Suez Canal was re-opened, and Sadat emerged with the profile of a military-statesman in stature bigger than his predecessor who was held responsible for the debacle of 1967.

Sadat could have rested on the laurels of the October war. The world was prepared to tilt in favour of the Arab states as effects of the Arab oil-embargo and oil-price quadrupling in support of the October war sent chill through the global economy. One measure of this tilt was the passage in 1975 of the UN General Assembly resolution declaring Zionism "is a form of racism and racial discrimination." Sadat gradually awoke to the realization, however, that neither diplomacy nor military posture could break the impasse between Arabs and Israelis unless there was a prior change of thinking in head and heart among both parties after a painfully long, debilitating and ultimately meaningless cycle of conflicts denying hope for a better future to both the Arab and Jewish children alike.

In Sadat's view a "psychological barrier" imprisoned Arabs and Israelis, and this barrier needed to be scaled. This is how Sadat explained himself:

> By a "psychological barrier" I mean that huge wall of suspicion, fear, hate, and misunderstanding that has for so long existed between Israel and the Arabs. It made each side simply unwilling to believe the other…I have therefore tended to compare that barrier to the Australian Great Barrier Reef – which is so dangerous to navigation in the southern hemisphere. And if the apparent barrier goes back only thirty years, it really has far deeper roots in history. For if, as Begin alleges, the question has a religious dimension for the Israelis, it certainly has such a dimension for us. So I decided to look at the situation from a new angle and to embark on a fresh study that took all dimensions into consideration.[63]

What was then set into motion was the details of Sadat's Jerusalem journey on November 19-20, 1977. It took everyone by surprise. Sadat's foreign minister, Ismail Fahmy, tendered his resignation instead of boarding the jetliner prepared to carry the President of Egypt to visit with the Israeli leadership and address the *Knesset*. The date of Sadat's journey was also laden with symbolism. Sadat was visiting Israel on the eve of the Muslim feast of Abraham's sacrifice, and he wanted to pray in Jerusalem's al-Aqsa mosque on that occasion which fell on November 20. Sadat's Jerusalem journey moreover came on the sixtieth anniversary of the Balfour Declaration; it was also on the eve of the thirtieth anniversary of the UN partition resolution for Palestine passed on November 29, 1947, and just ahead of the tenth anniversary of the passage of the UN Security Council Resolution 242 on November 22, 1967.

Sadat's speech to the audience assembled at the Israeli parliament was revealing of the inner journey he had made to embark upon his outward journey that brought him into the heart of the Jewish state's capital. It was a carefully crafted speech, delivered in classical Arabic being the language of the Quran, to disclose his inner journey of mind and heart in order to advance the external requisites of peace. Sadat avoided getting stuck in the details of peace negotiations or in discussing the necessary diplomatic trade-offs that would be required for the eventual signing of an Egyptian-Israeli peace accord. Instead he invoked the names of Mahatma Gandhi, Abraham as the patriarch of both Jews and Arabs, and of Moses with whom God spoke on the soil that was part of Egypt's territory, as he described his vision of peace between two people who worship the same God. Sadat's speech was interlaced with words that touched upon the themes of becoming fully human and of common humanity, about God and of peace, about individual and national responsibility in seeking peace, and of peace to endure requiring justice that must not be denied nor abridged. Sadat drew support for his vision and journey from the prophets of the Old Testament held in common respect by Jews, Christians and Muslims, and quoted from Solomon's Proverbs: "Deceit is in the heart of them that imagine evil: but to the counselors of peace is joy" (Proverbs 12:20). "Better is a dry morsel, and quietness therewith than a house full of sacrifices with strife" (Proverbs 17:1). Then he read from King David's Psalms:

> Unto thee will I cry, O Lord.
>
> Hear the voice of my supplications.

When I cry unto thee, when I lift up my hands towards thy holy oracle.

Draw me not away with the wicked,

and with the workers of iniquity,

who speak peace with their neighbours,

while mischief is in their hearts.

Give them according to their needs

and according to the wickedness of their endeavours.

(Psalms 28: 1a and 28:2 – 4a)

Sadat's appeal to peace and to labour for peace was built upon the shared religious values of Arabs and Israelis, Jews and Muslims. Sadat called upon God to witness that he had faithfully delivered his message, and then he ended by reciting from the Quran the verse: "We believe in God and in what has been revealed to us and what was revealed to Abraham, Ishmael, Isaac, Jacob and the 13 Jewish tribes. And in the books given to Moses and Jesus and the prophets from their Lord, Who made no distinction between them" (2:136). Then Sadat departed after having traveled the distance to Jerusalem to embrace Jews in a manner that no Arab and Muslim leader in modern times until then even considered, nor since then has any Arab and Muslim leader equaled. It was a unique moment and a unique event in a history that became burdened with recrimination, violence and grief.

And so we ask what does the Quran, the sacred book of Islam whose words, according to Muslim belief, were first spoken to Muhammad by heavenly power the Archangel Gabriel has to say about Jerusalem and Jews in the Holy Land?

The striking fact on first reading of the Quran is how much of its message is Jewish. The Quran tells the story of Jews, of Abraham and Moses, of Jesus and Mary among others. The story is told for instructing Arabs and Muslims in a history of a people who received divine sanction in acknowledging the reality of One Supreme Deity as Creator of the universe and Lawgiver to mankind and forsaking idol worship. It is remarkable how Muslims, despite their daily readings of the Quran, tend to obscure this fact that the story of Jews is front and centre in their sacred text. And even more that it anticipates with favour the Zionist hopes for a re-born Israel.

The historian Max Dimont captured succinctly the meaning of the new history which erupted from the sandy waste of seventh century Arabia following the descent of heavenly message to a man born among pagan Arabs. Dimont wrote:

> In the same way as the Septuagint prepared the way for the teachings of Paul among the pagans in the Roman Empire, so a general knowledge of the Old Testament among the Arabs helped prepare the way for the coming of Islam. The stage was set for the hero in history to fuse the nature worship of the Arabs, the salvation doctrine of the Christians, and the monotheism of the Jews into a new God image. The hero was Muhammad; the creed was Islam; the motivating ideology was Judaism.[64]

Here is a capsule version of the history of which Thomas Carlyle, the Scottish essayist and historian of the Victorian age described as "if a spark had fallen, one spark, on a world of what seemed black unnoticeable sand; but lo, the sand proves explosive powder, blazes heaven high from Delhi to Grenada! I said, the Great Man was always as lightning out of heaven; the rest of men waited for him like fuel, and then they too would flame."[65] Muhammad was born in Mecca in 570 A.D. He died in Medina in 632 A.D. In his fortieth year, around 610, he began receiving heavenly revelations which comprise the Quran as God's messenger and later confirmed by these revelations as the seal of the prophets. In the twelfth year of his mission, 622, Muhammad fled Mecca for Medina when physical threats from his enemies among the idol-worshipping Meccans could no longer be discounted. This flight from Mecca to safety in Medina, located to the northwest of his native city, is known as *hijra* (the flight), and it marks the year one in the Islamic calendar. In Medina he found himself among various clans of Arabs, and among them were Jewish tribes. Here he eventually forged a new alliance, confronted his Meccan threats in three battles and various skirmishes, established a nascent form of some authority, administered justice, and eventually led the final campaign against his Meccan adversaries. He triumphed over his enemies, conquered Mecca, demolished the idols of the tribes in the Ka'aba, the sacred mosque of

Islam, and before his demise more or less unified the tribes of the peninsular Arabia by submitting them to Islam.

What is Islam? Islam in quintessence is the affirmation of belief in One God. The creedal statement of Islam expresses this in a formula of universal import: "There is no god but God" – *La illaha illalla* – "and Muhammad is His Messenger" – *Muhammad-ur-rasul Allah*. The formula is in two parts: the primary phrase is the central message of the Quran, and the rest is its explication in human history; the secondary phrase confirms the divinely guided mission of Muhammad. Then there is the *historical* Islam, the profane history of Muslims as any other people driven by the complex motivations of the plethora of human impulses across the spectrum of good and evil in the making of their somewhat distinct culture and civilization. This history was stamped at its outset by the tribal culture of desert Arabs among whom Muhammad was born, and while impressions of that tribal culture were refined during the imperial rule of the first Arab dynasties of an expanding Arab-Islamic empire this history has persisted into the present times. Muslims of subsequent generations, dissidents apart, came to view this period – the first two centuries of the Islamic calendar – as the template of Islam and Muslim history upon which rested the later developments of the Islamic civilization.

Following Muhammad's demise his successors, administering the quasistate the prophet established in Medina even as they were torn among themselves by blood-soaked internecine quarrels resulting from familial ambitions and tribal interests, directed military campaigns which eventually extended the boundaries of Islam beyond the Arabian heartland into North Africa and Asia. In 637 Jerusalem under Byzantine rule was conquered by Arab armies under the authority of Umar, the second caliph or successor of the prophet, and with this conquest of Palestine passed into the control of Muslims –except for the period of the Crusades in the 11th-12th centuries – until 1917 when British forces entered Jerusalem in the course of the campaigns against the Ottoman Turks during the First World War.

Since Palestine with claims on Jerusalem is at the heart of the conflict between Arabs and Israelis, Jews and Muslims, referring to the Quran is essential in verifying the legitimacy of Muslim position. The Quran was revealed to Muhammad prior to the Muslim conquest of Jerusalem in 637. This fact is critical, for either Arab-Muslim claim rests on the words of the Quran or it is based on rights as possession that came from the conquest of Jerusalem and Palestine by Arab-Muslim armies. In Muslim religious perspective, a claim legitimized by the Quran will be of timeless duration. But if it is based on mere conquest by arms, then it could only be maintained by force and lost to superior force; in other words, if force and conquest provide legitimacy, then defeat and loss make that legitimacy null and void.

Islam – the Quran repeatedly reminds Muslims and others who may read the text – is not a new religion but the primordial faith of man, the belief in and the witness thereof to the reality of One God as the source and origin of all things in the universe. This primordial faith gets repeatedly corrupted, yet God in His infinite mercy sends prophets and messengers to reform the corrupted faith and remind people how their sorrow in this world is a product of their corrupt ways as they deliberately or mistakenly wander away from the path rightfully prescribed. Islam is a reminder to each and every soul endowed with free will of its connection with God, of its responsibility and accountability on the Day of Reckoning, of the relationship of God and man in the divine scheme of things, and those who acknowledge this cosmological reality and submits to it in living out of obedience, faith, love, devotion – however one wants to explain the meaning of *submission* which is one of the cognates of the word "Islam" in Arabic – is then at peace within while outward reality of such a person would reflect God's mercy and compassion. The outward turmoil in an individual or a nation is the absence of inner peace and harmony, and nothing better reveals the wisdom of this message then the present state of Muslims and their nations so utterly in disrepair indicating how greatly absent is God's message as delivered to Muhammad from their lives.

Once Muhammad was instructed to preach God's message to his people and engage in devotion through prayers privately and in public, Jerusalem became the axis of religious orientation of the prophet and his early followers. The reason was simple. Again, according to the Quran, Islam was the primordial faith of the people in closest proximity to Arabs of the desert among whom Muhammad was born and to whom he preached. These people are the children of Abraham, the various tribes of the Jews, and then Christians who parted from the Jews in following Jesus, the son of Mary.

The direction in which a person stands and prays is a matter of orientation, of affirming the chain of connections or relationship in the divine plan to which an individual submits. Muhammad prayed in the direction of Jerusalem, and Jerusalem in the very early years of Islam was the *qiblah*, or the direction of prayers for the first Muslims in Mecca. This orientation was an affirmation that Islam was the primordial message of submission that prophets from Adam to Abraham, and then through Moses and David and Solomon to John and Jesus brought as God's favour to their people, and later this same favour was dispensed to Arabs through a prophet born among them.

Soon after Muhammad left Mecca and settled in Medina he was instructed to reorient his *qiblah* or direction of prayers towards Ka'aba, the mosque in Mecca originally built, according to the Quran, by Abraham and his son Ishmael. The specific verse of the Quran reads: "We have seen you turn your face to the heavens. We shall turn you to a Qiblah that will please you. So turn towards the Holy Mosque, and turn towards it wherever you are" (2:144). Since then Muslims have turned in their prayers towards Mecca, and not Jerusalem. In the divine scheme there is a message here that those with discernment might discover. My view is by turning Muslims away from Jerusalem meant any future claim on the City of Prophets by Muslims on religious grounds was taken away by a just and merciful God.

An event of much significance occurred just before Muhammad took flight from Mecca to Medina in 622. This was his Night Journey to the heavens. This journey is narrated in chapters 17 and 53 of the Quran, both chapters revealed in the early years of Islam in Mecca. Chapter 17 of the Quran is called *Bani Israel* or the Children of Israel, and Chapter 53 is called *An-Najm* or the Star. *Bani Israel* is the story of the Jews, and it opens with the following verse: "Glory to Him who took His votary to a wide and open land from the Sacred Mosque (at Mecca) to the distant Mosque whose precincts We have blessed, that We may show him some of Our signs."

It is instructive this Night Journey or *miraj* (ascent), of Muhammad took place from the distant Mosque that most commentators from the early years of Islam agreed was located in Jerusalem, and where at the presumed site the Dome of the Rock was subsequently built by the Muslim ruler, Caliph Abd al-Malik, in 691 some seventy years after the event the Quran narrates. This narration is part of the story of the Children of Israel, and thereby it is made clear the mission of the prophet is in the same line as the prophets of Israel, belongs to the same tradition and constitutes and completes the story in the divine scheme of things, places and people whose patriarch is Abraham.

These are the two instances reported in the Quran by which Muslims find their spiritual connection with Jerusalem. In one instance it is to do with the *qiblah*, when the Quran instructs Muhammad to change his direction of prayers from Jerusalem to Mecca. This instruction to Muhammad becomes the fixed orientation of Muslims as Mecca with its Ka'aba becomes the epicenter of Islam. Jerusalem is holy to Muslims, a place to be revered as the City of Prophets, but it is *not* the centre of Islam.

In the second instance, the Night Journey of Muhammad from presumably Jerusalem (accepting the interpretation given by earliest commentators of the Quran) established his intimate relationship with all the prophets in the tradition of Abraham who preceded him. This relationship is at the *spiritual* level, its occurrence precedes the subsequent events of Muslim history, and this spiritual connection stands outside of time and place in the secular history of Muslims, Jews and Christians and, hence, is incorruptible by what people do in the name of their faith traditions as in the sack of the holy city during the Crusades. This spiritual connection with Jerusalem for Muslims, following the relationship of Muhammad with the city built by David and Solomon and where Jesus preached, should remain unsullied by any secular politics, and its holiness revered. But this spiritual connection offers no basis for any claim on a city that the Quran clearly instructs is not the *qiblah* of Muslim prayers and obligatory pilgrimage and, consequently, the city sanctified by prophets of the Old Testament must not become a matter of contestation – specially by Muslims with Jews – among people who together revere Abraham. It might also be noted here that since its conquest in 637 by Arab-Muslim armies and its loss in 1917 by the Ottoman forces to the British army under General Allenby, with the exception of the hiatus during the Crusade years,

Jerusalem never served as a political capital of any Arab-Muslim dynasty. The religious-political capital of Islam in the classical period of the 7th through the 15th century moved from Medina to Damascus then Baghdad, and later was situated in Istanbul until the end of World War I.

The history by which the Quran illuminates the divine scheme and instructs Arabs of the desert is of the Israelites. Indeed, the Arabs of the desert and, in particular, the Meccan clans of the Quraysh – with the most illustrious among them being the family into which Muhammad was born – traced their descent from Abraham through his older son Ishmael born of Hagar. Muhammad's mission was returning his people back to the path which Abraham had walked as a *hanif* (believer in One God), and the Quran's narration of the Israelite story is an illustration of God's mercy and favour for a people most proximate to the desert Arabs who have remained faithful despite adversity to the One God that Abraham worshipped.

In this narrative of the Israelites, the Quran retells and confirms the story of Moses, of his tribulation and that of his people in the land ruled by the Pharoah, and of their flight to freedom and to the land promised for them to live and multiply in faithfulness to God's commandments. The land promised is Palestine, or the land of Canaan, and the words of the Quran cannot be mistaken. In *Bani Israel* (Children of Israel), chapter 17, verse 104, which opens with the Night Journey of Muhammad, the Quran states: "And We said unto the Children of Israel after him [Moses]: Dwell in the land; but when the promise of the Hereafter cometh to pass we shall bring you as a crowd gathered out of various nations." Then in a later Medina revelation, *Al-Ma'idah* (The Table Spread), chapter 5 and verses 20-21, the Quran declares: "Remember when Moses said to his people: 'O my people, remember the favours that God bestowed on you when He appointed apostles from among you, and made you kings and gave you what had never been given to any one in the world. Enter then, my people, the Holy Land that God has ordained for you, and do not turn back, or you will suffer.'"

The words of the Quran pertaining to the Jews and Palestine, of their right to live free and secure there where their prophets preached and their kings built the temple in Jerusalem, cannot be misunderstood.

misread or denied. It was always incumbent on Muslims, as it is today, as part of their faith tradition to acknowledge the rights of Jews in Palestine, while denying or twisting the words of the Quran to suit their contrary purpose amount to repudiating in effect the message contained in their sacred text. Muslims cannot have it both ways, venerate the Quran as divine revelation to Muhammad and then contradict those passages of the Quran, as in these instances where the words are amply clear and precise, because they find them distasteful or contrary to their tribal (nationalist) interests.

The leap Sadat made from making war against Israel to striving for peace in embracing Israel was driven as much by calculations of national interest as it required reaching back into his faith tradition to legitimate his journey to Jerusalem among his people. Sadat gave enough indication in his memoir that he had thought deeply about the journey he set out to make. Yet it is also clear that there still remained a distance for Sadat to travel in his own thinking to fully circle the politics of his people with the message of the Quran.

Sadat did not fully understand, nor did those after him, the extent to which nationalism of the illiberal variety tainted with anti-Semitism that drowned Europe in blood and ashes twice in a generation corrupted the faith tradition of the Arabs and pushed them into the sort of hostility against Jews that went against the words of the Quran. Yet it is not improbable to speculate that Sadat had slowly awakened to the fact that for Arabs and Muslims to be in harmony with the world around them, to make progress as a people striving to live in accordance with the values of Islam, required fully reconciling with Jews and accepting Israel as a legitimate partner and friend in the family of nations. Sadat's journey to Jerusalem in this sense symbolized the acceptance by a Muslim, however belated, that the rights of the Jews are bestowed by God of Abraham, Moses and Muhammad, and that these rights must be unquestioningly protected by Muslims if they are to remain bound by the truth of their sacred text, the Quran. In this respect Anwar Sadat's journey to Jerusalem was an act of conversion, of coming to terms with the marvel of God's message, and of dying in the work of repairing the broken triangle of relationship among Jews, Christians and Muslims.

6

Only Connect: Reconsidering Jewish-Muslim history

The need to reflect on Jewish-Muslim history in our post-9/11 cannot be overstated. Peace in our time – not Neville Chamberlain's peace that betrayed the Czechs in Munich in 1938, but a peace that recognizes our common humanity–hinges upon whether Jews and Muslims can find the insight and spiritual resources necessary to bridge their divide. As the Berlin Wall fell to signal the end of the Cold War, there was a brief moment of optimism that peace and progress might be achieved in the new millennium. This crumbled in the fire, the dust and terror of New York's twin towers and the attack on Pentagon.

Among the multitudes of voices heard at that time was one that spoke to me with great lucidity and hope. In 1991 Hans Kung, a German Catholic theologian and academic, published a small book called in English *Global Responsibility*. His prophetic words were a challenge to all: "No survival without a world ethic. No world peace without peace between the religions. No peace between the religions without dialogue between the religions."[66] With this Kung reminded us that our political world cannot be separated from our religious world, and that the most important political questions in our time are also religious questions.

Today it seems as though all possible roads toward mutually respectful relations between Jews and Muslims have reached dead ends. The failure of either of these two peoples to continue to work toward mutual respect, the failure to learn from both the distant and the immediate past is a prescription for unspeakable tragedy. If this tragedy should occur it shall not matter who was most responsible. Jewish-Muslim reconciliation is an imperative in and of itself, as was Jewish-Christian reconciliation before the *Shoah*. It is an imperative as well for global peace, for an end to Muslim terrorism and the war against Muslim terrorism, and for ending a history over-burdened with recriminations, each side denying the other's capacity to be fully human, with neither recognizing the other as oneself.

In recent history Jews and Muslims have become *strangers* to each other even when they have inhabited the same space. Too often because of personal choice and circumstance hostility has eliminated respect and affection, a hostility that imprisons both sides. The present has come to define the past. The past that was once a treasure held in common is now lost to most on both sides, thus deepening their *estrangement*. It is rare that we now recall how much our ancestors learned from and grew with one another in their shared history.

I must confess I did not always see this estrangement as clearly as now, nor have I always felt the tragedy of this history as acutely as I do now. Our understanding of the world is conditioned by our living, and thus writing is always partly biographical.

The events of September 11, 2001, Arab-Muslim terrorists hijacking and crashing jetliners into buildings in America's heartland made me rethink the basis of my thinking and living, writing and teaching regarding the politics of the Middle East, the world of Islam and its relationship with the West. That morning of 9/11, I along with so many of us was overwhelmed by the horror of the evil we witnessed. That night I went to bed unaware of how greatly changed would be my sense of the world on awakening. I soon realized that I was beginning to reclaim a history and meaning for my faith – Islam – that was obscured, if not deliberately erased by those in authority and those aspiring to replace them. A significant dimension of this history deals with Jewish-Muslim relations.

Once I began to focus on this it became clear to me that for Muslims a reconciliation with Jews is not only necessary to becoming reconciled with the modern world, it is required by their faith as well.

Regarding the former, Jews as individuals have legal recognition as full participants in the democratic nations of the world. The State of Israel, which is recognized as a particularly Jewish homeland has been accepted as a full participant in the global community of democratic nations. This should not and does not prejudice consideration of the rights and claims of the Palestinian people. How is it possible then for Muslims as individuals, and as members of states which are made up of a majority of people belonging to the Muslim faith, to fail to come to terms with Jewish individuals as fellow citizens and with the State of Israel as a fraternal partner in the family of nations? It is unthinkable.

Regarding faith it became clear to me that the pillars of Islam – the Prophet's example and the text of the Quran – assume and express a close relationship between Islam and Judaism, between Muslims and Jews. Both faiths thus require reconciliation between them. For me, as a Muslim, this continuing estrangement and enmity are unthinkable. Such rethinking prompted me to write the following during the Ramadan (month of fasting in the Islamic calendar) of 2004 in a column for the *Toronto Sun*.

> Muslims rarely consider that the Quran is a text rehearsing for them the story of Jews...Muslims need to consider their politics as inseparably bound and shaped by religion. They need, then, to reflect on religious grounds why so many of them wage wars on Jews, when the sacred words are indisputable. The Quran recites the story of God directing Moses and the Israelites out of captivity in Egypt. It states how Moses was commanded, *"Go into the holy land which God has ordained for you" (5:21).* Since Muslims believe the Quran is God's revelation to Muhammad, how can they reconcile the atrocities committed by their coreligionists in the Holy Land with their scripture's authoritative words? Jewish and Muslim calendars are lunar. This is the Islamic year 1425 and the Jewish year 5765. Many Muslims need to be reminded of over four millennia of Jewish history, and of how Islam's noontide also marked the golden age of Judaism in Muslim lands.[67]

Many Jews have also forgotten a rich part of the history they share with Muslims, a history that lasted over a thousand years before their estrangement – a phenomenon of recent origin and within the living memory of both peoples in the 20th century. Fourteen centuries of history is in peril of being lost because of events of the last one hundred years.

The Age of Islam from the seventh to the sixteenth century was also the Age of Judaism. This is true in more ways than we may imagine when the seeds of what would come after – European renaissance and enlightenment – were sown by people who understood their faiths as diverging streams emerging from the deep wells of shared spirit. Max Dimont, a hugely best-selling Jewish historian, wrote,

> The Jew in this age became statesman, philosopher, physician, scientist, tradesman, and cosmopolitan capitalist. Arabic became his mother tongue. This era also saw the philandering Jew. He not only wrote on religion and philosophy, but also rhapsodized about love. Seven hundred years passed and the pendulum swung. The Islamic world crumbled and the Jewish culture in the Islamic world crumbled with it.[68]

Seven hundred years is a long time. The Roman Empire became a memory in seven centuries. Britain's empire generously measured in time was acquired and lost in about two centuries. The dominant presence of the United States in our world is still young, not quite the span of a man's life.

The secret of this history was in the faith of a people, the nomads of a desert without any history, the Arabs of a vast and uninviting peninsula protruding from the land bridge connecting Eurasia with Africa, who were moved by a simple conviction that there is only One Supreme Lord of the Universe, *Allah* in Arabic, to make their exit from barbarity and embrace civilization. This idea was not an Arab invention, nor were they as Arabs the first people to make such an assertion. There has not been another comparable event such as the dramatic entrance of seventh century Arabs into world history. These Arabs lived at the edge of two great civilizations – Byzantine or the Eastern Roman Empire and the Persian Empire. They were seized by a simple yet ground-breaking conviction in the God of Abraham taught to them by a prophet in the tradition of the Old Testament. Their faith was expressed in Arabic of the creedal formula *La illaha illalla* ("There is no god but God"), and affirmed with the acknowledgement the formula carried, *Muhammadur rasul allah* ("Muhammad is the Messenger of God"). In less than a hundred years following the desert prophet Muhammad's death in 632 A.D., his people, the Arabs, arrived in Spain on the western extremity of the then known world, and the inner deserts of China and the mountains and river plains of India to the east.

The quality of the faith of a people is as varied as people themselves. But there is no faith which can move people to build a civilization if it lacks an ideal at its core. This ideal among desert Arabs as the first Muslims was a belief in an infinitely powerful God Who is ever just and ever merciful, Who creates and sustains the universe and all things in it in an orderly manner, and Whose mercy was manifest in the messenger He sent to them speaking in their language to guide them out of their ignorance into knowledge. Muhammad as the messenger, and the Quran as the sacred text containing words originally communicated to Muhammad by the Source of all things created, are the fundamental elements of Islamic civilization. A Muslim is anyone who of his own accord in submitting himself to the ever-present and all-embracing reality of God also embraces Muhammad and the Quran as signs of God's mercy.

Over time the original faith of Muslims was corrupted by power. But the pristine faith of Muslims unencumbered by the accretion of human failings is a reassertion in historic time and space, in the seventh century wasteland of peninsular Arabia and then carried forth into our modern world, of the primordial faith of Adam as man's archetype to which Abraham pledged himself and his progeny.

The Quran's core message, and the practice of Muhammad as messenger and prophet, is this: that Islam is not a new religion but the reaffirmation of God's original covenant made with man. In the inscrutable design of the Lord of the Universe as the Quran narrates, and so does the Bible, Abraham was elected from among his generation to broadcast the primordial faith of Adam. Jews were Abraham's people in freedom and in captivity, and whenever their faith dimmed and they became lost, God's mercy shone and He sent them a prophet from among their people to rekindle that faith and save them from destruction.

God is the unnamed, or in the Hebrew formulation *"I Am What I Am."* He made Moses, a man of obscure birth, to be raised by a daughter of the Pharaoh. He led Abraham's people out of the Egyptian exile. He made a virgin woman, Mary, belonging to the house of David, the King of Jews, conceive untouched by man the child Jesus. He made Jesus His instrument in bringing the gentiles accept the God of Abraham. He chose an orphan, Muhammad, among the pagan Arabs descended from the family of Ishmael born to Abraham from Hagar his bonds maid, and raised the child to be a messenger of the same primordial truth which secured for Jews their amazing survival through more than four millennia of history and the rise and fall of many civilizations.

Jews in sufficient numbers did not accept Muhammad as prophet, just as they did not accept earlier Jesus as the Saviour. But they did recognize, or the learned among them did, that the Quran's core message resonated the message God delivered to Moses. It was on the basis of this message, irrespective of Jews recognizing or not Muhammad's claim to be the seal of prophets in the Abrahamic tradition, that the Islamic civilization was built. In this respect, on matters of belief, the affinity between Jews and Muslims was felt to be greater than what separated Jews from the theology of Pauline Christianity.

The *Shema* in Deuteronomy among the Books of Moses opens with the proclamation affirming the primordial faith of Abraham and setting his monotheism apart from the beliefs of others.

> *Hear, O Israel, the Lord our God, the Lord is One* (Deuteronomy 6:4).

Histories of people differ in language, in customs, in modes of living conditioned by environment. But in the flux of all things created, as Abraham discovered, there is an Absolute centre. This centre, the Source of life, is singular, infinite and unbound by the limitations of human intellect. He is the God Who speaks to Moses, and then will speak to Muhammad giving him the same message for his people. The words transmitted to Muhammad echoes the opening lines of *Shema* and read,

> Say: "He is God, One,
>
> God the Everlasting Refuge
>
> Who has not begotten, and has not been begotten,
>
> And equal to Him is not any one" (Quran, 112).

It was in the *ambiance* of this message, in the civilization constructed by those who embraced this message as the core of their identity as a people defined not by ethnicity but belief, that Jews found both a reprieve from persecution and the space to reinvigorate their own traditions even as they made seminal contributions to the world of Islam. It was in Spain between the arrival in 711 of Tariq bin Zaid and the expulsion of Jews and Arabs in 1492, a heady mix of cultural learning took place. Here is how Erna Paris sets the stage of what came to be the al-Andalus of Jews, Christians and Muslims of Cordoba and Granada, of Toledo and Seville:

> [R]umors of something new and utterly astonishing are on everyone's lips. Tariq the Moor has sent advance couriers to announce that his new regime is offering unheard-of terms: anyone who wants to leave Toledo can do so, but Christians and Jews of the city who choose to stay will be free to open property and practice their religion, including governing themselves according to their own civil and religious laws. In return they will have to pay a head tax, refrain from public processions, and agree not to punish any coreligionist who has chosen freely to convert to Islam. The acceptance of other religions was set out in a verse in the Quran itself:
>
> *Say, O believers! I shall not worship what you worship. You do not worship what I worship. I am not a worshipper of what you have worshipped, and you are not worshippers of what I have worshipped. To you, your religion. To me, my religion.*
>
> After centuries of oppression, it is hard to imagine that the persecuted Jews and oppressed serfs of Visigoth Spain would not have welcomed a change of regime; in fact, the Jews were instantly accused of throwing open the gates of Toledo to the invaders, and the charge may have been well founded.[69]

It will not do to measure the past by present standards for the present, by the same standards, is bound to be judged harshly by the future. We must be cautious as we consider Jewish-Muslim history. We must avoid being seduced by the mindless apologetics of Muslim polemicists on the one hand, or driven to the other extreme of those Jews and their Christian counterparts who view limitations on Jews in the Islamic civilization as not substantially different from those imposed on Jews in Christian Europe. Here the sage counsel of Bernard Lewis, perhaps the most influential scholar in our time of Islam, Muslims, Arabs, Turks and the Middle East in history, should be heeded:

> If by tolerance we mean the absence of discrimination, there is one answer; if the absence of persecution, quite another. Discrimination was always there, permanent and indeed necessary, inherent in the system and institutionalized in law and practice. Persecution, that is to say, violent and active repression, was rare and atypical. Jews and Christians under Muslim rule were not normally called upon to suffer martyrdom for their faith. They were not often obliged to make the choice, which confronted Muslims and Jews in reconquered Spain, between exile, apostasy, and death. They were not subject to any major territorial or occupational restrictions such as were the common lot of Jews in premodern Europe.[70]

Until the end of the nineteenth century Jews were suspect in the liberal Europe of France, England and the Low Countries. From within the illiberal frontiers of the east Jews left in a steady stream from Russia and adjoining lands to either the relative safety in the New World, or to reclaim their history in Palestine. Bernard Lewis in *Islam in History* addresses the Jewish problem in passing. The Jews were suspect of harbouring pro-Muslim or pro-Turkish and anti-Christian sentiments detrimental to European interests. The case against Alfred Dreyfus, a French army officer, for treason came to symbolize the grip of anti-Semitism deeply entrenched in European societies. E.A. Freeman, an Englishman, a historian, and contemporary of the British statesman Benjamin Disraeli, is quoted by Lewis:

> "Throughout the East, the Turk and the Jew are leagued against the Christian...We cannot have the policy of Europe dealt with in the like sort. There is all the difference in the world between the degraded Jews of the East and the cultivated and honourable Jews of the West. But blood is stronger than water, and Hebrew rule is sure to lead to a Hebrew policy. Throughout Europe, the most fiercely Turkish part of the press is largely in Jewish hands. It may be assumed everywhere, with the smallest class of

exceptions, that the Jew is the friend of the Turk and the enemy of the Christian."[71]

The final years of the nineteenth and the early decades of the twentieth centuries were transitional years in Jewish-Muslim history. A breach unsuspected by Jews and Muslims was opening at this time that eventually would become so wide that the two people who were relatively intimate would become strangers. The lives and work of two Jews – Ignaz Goldziher and Shlomo Dov Goitein – from Central Europe during this period illustrate how the long phase of Jewish-Muslim history in the Islamic world now seem so remote and perhaps irretrievable in our lifetime.

Much of Jewish-Muslim history was recorded and narrated by Jews. If the Islamic civilization was the bridge connecting the ancient Greek philosophers and their writings to the world of European renaissance, Jews were the most prominent interlocutors between Islam and Muslims on the one hand, and Christianity and Christians on the other. Jews understood that what were the most prized ideals of Judaic culture found receptive soil in the lands of Islam. Moreover, the affinity they found of their faith's traditions with those of Muslims brought Jews to the study of Islam with a sense of respect and empathy that was missing among Christians until very recently. Whatever were the causes of religious hostility between Christians and Muslims these were exceeded by the hostility of Christians and Muslims belonging to the two expansive proselytizing faith traditions and as people organized within competing political systems on each other's frontiers.

Here is Raphael Patai, a Hungarian Jew born in Budapest in 1910 and the author of several books on the Middle East including *The Arab Mind* and *The Jewish Mind*, introducing one of the foremost Jewish scholars of Islam:

> I was not ten years old when, one day, my father took me along on a visit to Ignaz Goldziher. On our way back home, my father said to me: "Remember you shook hands with the greatest Orientalist alive."[72]

Orientalists and Orientalism were given a bad name by the late Edward Said, a Palestinian of Christian faith, and his followers who tended to reduce the invaluable contributions of scholars such as

Goldziher to mere polemics in the service of European imperialism in Muslim lands. We will recover from these tendencies, but it is doubtful we will again see the likes of Ignaz Goldziher picking up the threads of Jewish-Muslim history.

Goldziher's most formidable work available in English is *Introduction to Islamic Theology and Law*. Modern scholarship, as Lewis points out, has corrected some of the marginal flaws of Goldziher's reading of Islam in terms of Muhammad's biography or the exegesis of the Quran, but the substantive nature of his work in illuminating the classical tradition of Islamic thinking in terms of doctrine and law remains unsurpassed. Goldziher was born in Hungary in 1850 and died in 1921, some time shortly after the encounter which Patai so many years later eulogized. As a young man Goldziher spent some months in Damascus and Cairo and there acquired permission from the authorities of the al-Azhar mosque university to attend lectures. He was the first non-Muslim to so engage himself and given permission to join Muslims in their congregational prayers. Goldziher recorded in his diary those months in 1873-74 spent among Muslims were his happiest days providing him, as Lewis notes in his biographical preface to Goldziher's book, "deep feeling of sympathy with Islam, and of kinship with the Muslims."[73] In his diary Goldziher wrote,

> I became inwardly convinced that I myself was a Muslim. [In Cairo], [i]n the midst of the thousands of the pious, I rubbed my forehead against the floor of the mosque. Never in my life was I more devout, more truly devout, than on that exalted Friday.[74]

In another revealing anecdote of this Jewish scholar of Islam we learn from a Turkish historian of the time, Ahmed Refik, when asked on returning from Europe what was the most memorable thing or event he had witnessed there he replied: "The University of Budapest, where I found a Jewish professor expounding the Quran to a class of Christian pupils." Refik's observation illuminates a time not too long ago when Jews maintained the view that Islam and Muslims still had something of value to teach modern Europe.

Shlomo Dov Goitein was born in 1900 in a little village in southern Germany and died in 1985 while living in Princeton where he taught at the Institute for Advanced Study for many years. Eric Ormsby, of McGill University in Montreal, wrote a beautiful and elegant biographical essay, published in *The New Criterion*, about his teacher affectionately known and remembered as the "Schulmeister." Goitein belonged to Goldziher's tradition and his widely read book *Jews and Arabs: Their Contacts Through the Ages* illustrates his faith in the kinship between the two people and the three faiths at a time in mid-twentieth century when Jews and Arabs, Jews and Muslims, turned their backs on each other. Eric Ormsby comments, "In the 1960s every department of near Eastern or Islamic studies was torn apart by dissension arising from the Arab-Israeli conflict. By focusing so resolutely on the philological tradition as well as on the common humanity of Jews, Christians, and Muslims within a specific historic milieu and tradition – and not through some vague good will or fuzzy ecumenism – Goitein gave us a way of negotiating those awful divisions."[75]

But Goitein's most important contributions were his translations and commentaries on the documents of the Cairo Geniza, the record of Arabized Jews meticulously preserved from the 10th-11th century through the Middle Ages. Goitein's work revealed the process of cultural synthesis between Jews and Muslims, and since Arabic was the primary language of the Islamic lands around the Mediterranean the extent to which Jews contributed to the making of a Judaeo-Arabic, or Judaeo-Islamic culture. In theology, in law, in philosophy and literature, in science and in mysticism, Jews contributed as broadly to Islam and Muslims as they borrowed from them.

The towering figure from that period, as Goitein's work sheds light on his life and philosophy, was the Jew Moses Ben Maimonides known to his Muslim contemporaries as Musa ibn Maymun. Maimonides, revered by Jews as the second Moses, was born in Cordova in 1135, some ten years after Ibn Rushd (known in the West by his Latin name, Averroes) was born in the same city. Ibn Rushd is possibly the most important translator and commentator of Aristotle in the medieval era. They were acquainted with each other, were probably friends, and both had to leave their native city for North Africa when a rising tide of fanaticism and bigotry gripped parts of the Muslim communities of al-Andalus as a prelude to what came later and made the re-conquest of Spain by Christians less difficult than it otherwise could have been. It is instructive to note that

Maimonides travelled east to Egypt where he thrived as a court physician to members of the Ayyubid dynasty and its most famous son, Salah ad-Din, or Saladin to the Europeans, and died in Cairo in 1204.

Ibn Rushd and Maimonides were not strangers. For Goldziher and Goitein several centuries later Islam as religion and culture was still a presence that reflected for them an understanding of their own tradition that was increasingly being lost in the secularized West. Now we know there were other forces and ideas at work through this period of history when Europe became the colonizing and imperial power over Muslim lands. These forces, primarily nationalism and secularism, would seep through the barriers of culture and faith that formally separated Islam from the West and affect the Jewish-Muslim history in ways that Goldziher certainly, and Goitein to some extent, could not have imagined.

We now stand in more ways than we might want to admit on the ruins brought about by these forces of nationalism and secularism in the world of Islam at one end and the West at the other. We do not know how the relationship between Islam and the West, between Muslims and non-Muslims, might be repaired. The war on Muslim terror, or "radical Islamism," as a response to what produced 9/11 is one sort of effort with the hope that democracy may find roots in Iraq and elsewhere in the Middle East and drain the toxins of the region to let once again the promise of what al-Andalus represented in its time be renewed in the twenty-first century. But it can be said with some degree of certainty no such promise can be realized unless Jews and Muslims find the resources within themselves of being reconciled again as members of the Abrahamic family. And in this instance, in our time, at the beginning years of a new millennium, such effort at reconciliation must begin with Muslims unconditionally reaching out to embrace Jews.

We saw a glimpse of such reconciliation when Anwar Sadat, the President of Egypt, traveled to Jerusalem and embraced Menachem Begin, the Prime Minister of Israel, in November 1977.

The journey of Sadat from Cairo to Jerusalem was, in the first instance, a political journey conceived in strategic terms by a military leader of the most important Arab state at war with the Jewish state to wrest back by diplomatic means territories lost in the June 1967 war. Yet it carried within it the possibility of renewing and reconstituting under entirely new conditions Arab-Jew and Jew-Muslim relationship that could heal the rift between the two branches of Abraham's family.

Sadat's speech at the Israeli Knesset was loaded with allusions of the shared descent of Jews and Arabs, and of much that is common to their respective faith traditions. Sadat had traveled far from where he began as a young soldier in awe of dictators – Napoleon, Hitler, Ataturk – and in sympathy with the political ideology of Hasan al-Banna and his Muslim Brotherhood, to arrive in Jerusalem and make peace with Israel. Sadat knew the risks involved in his attempt to scale the walls of enmity which separated his people from Jews, and he was shortly thereafter murdered for his audacity by radicalized Muslim warriors who broke away from the Brotherhood and became the ideological precursor of Osama bin Laden's network of al Qaeda terrorists.

We will never know how Sadat, if he had lived longer, would have steered Egypt's relationship with Israel and demonstrated what it means in practical terms of forging familial ties between Jews and Muslims. But we know that in the reciprocal friendship of Begin and Sadat we were witnessing once again the sort of respect and generosity of feeling that Ibn Rushd and Maimonides held for each other, and the warmth of affection that once flowed naturally between Jews and Muslims of which Goldziher wrote from personal experience.

From this point in the twenty-first century we can see that Jewish-Muslim history was fatally ruptured by the events of the twentieth century. At the heart of Muslim-Jewish animosity is the question of Palestine, and the competing claims of Arabs and Jews to Jerusalem. But if Arabs had not become blinded by modern nationalism and had instead heard the words of the Quran uncorrupted by the politics of the time seething with anti-colonial anti-imperialist rhetoric, they undeniably would have learned their claims were not warranted by Islam and its sacred text.

At best Arab claims to Palestine and Jerusalem were based on squatters' right, and this right was not denied by Jews as they pursued their historic right of return for establishing home in the land of their prophets. Palestine was "liberated" from Ottoman Turkish rule by

Britain towards the end of World War One and then partitioned twice. In 1922 for the first time when Britain demarcated the land on the east bank of the River Jordan as Transjordan (later to become the Kingdom of Jordan); and then for the second time in November 1947 when the United Nations divided the remaining territory on the west bank into two states, one Arab and one Jewish.

In denying Jewish rights to a homeland in Palestine, Arabs departed from the path of righteousness and became mired in anti-Jewish bigotry. This is the "root" cause of the problem in the Middle East, the bigotry of Arabs and Muslims towards Jews, and over the years the problem has worsened with Arab refusal to acknowledge the wrong done by them to Jews through boycotts, wars, and terrorism with the aim of defeating and eliminating Israel. It was to the credit of Anwar Sadat that he recognized the futility of Arab enmity against Israel, and then sought to remove its root cause by making his journey to Jerusalem for reconciling with Jews.

Jews and Muslims as believers in the God of Abraham may only guess what might be His design for them. Yet for Muslims the Quran provides indication of God's purpose if they swallow their false pride and listen carefully to the sacred words retelling the story of Abraham and his people as instruction about His providence in history.

Some 1300 years after Muhammad had delivered to his people God's message revealed in the Quran, the return of Jews to their ancestral land held forth another lesson for Arabs and Muslims. Jews as contributors and participants in the making of the modern world of science and democracy could be the catalyst for the Arabs in their transition from the old world to the new.

Such a partnership in the making of a more humane, prosperous and peaceful world would not be unprecedented; it would only be picking up the threads of the vanished world of Spain before its Christian re-conquest. In doing so it would reclaim a past for a future with limitless possibilities for Jews and Muslims as they learned to share in common what was given to them in Abraham's name. The alternative for the Arabs and Muslims is to persist in their bigotry against Jews bringing greater ruin for themselves and their children; to watch from the sidelines of history as the distance between their world and the West as a result become increasingly remote.

7

Of Danish Cartoons, Muslim Rage and the Bedouin State of Mind

The furor in the winter of 2006 over cartoon drawings of Muhammad that appeared in Denmark was a repeat of the fury unleashed by Salman Rushdie's novel, *The Satanic Verses*, first published in 1988. Now, as then, Muslims, or a great many of them worldwide, expressed outrage over the irreverent drawings of the prophet of Islam published in the Danish newspaper, *Jyllands-Posten*, as they did with the fictional depiction of the prophet in Rushdie's novel. Now, as then, Muslim outrage was part spontaneous and part organized, and in varying measures seized upon by religious leaders, dictators, political opportunists, demagogues and rascals of all stripes, turned into a witch's brew and released into public space to go rampaging as demonstration of Muslim rage against those who profane what Muslims revere as sacred. Then, in February 1989, the dying Ayatollah Khomeini of Iran's Islamic Republic declared in a *fatwa* (nonbinding religious ruling), the offending author of *The Satanic Verses* and those associated with its publication and distribution should be killed. Governments were intimidated as was the government of Prime Minister Rajiv Gandhi in India, a non-Muslim majority state, and fearing public unrest Gandhi banned publication and distribution of the novel in the country of the author's birth. During this period a mob attacked the USIS office in Islamabad, the capital of Pakistan, and huge public demonstrations with ritualistic burning of Rushdie's novel were orchestrated from the streets of Dhaka, Bangladesh, to the streets of Bradford, England. Similarly now, mobs raged across the streets of Cairo, Tehran, Kabul and other such Muslim cities, and the mob in Damascus torched the Danish and Norwegian embassies and set fire to the Danish consulate in Beirut.

How should we explain such furor over cartoons, or works of fiction, that so readily seize Muslim sensitivities, and then spill over into the streets with appalling consequences? What is to be made of the cartoon controversy, and the earlier controversy surrounding Rushdie's novel? And what is the implication, if any, of such conduct on the part of Muslims for the West?

Before proceeding any further I need to clear a definitional problem that persists in confounding discussions of issues relating to the Muslim world. Here is how Bernard Lewis described the problem pertaining to the word *Islam*:

> ...the word itself is commonly used with two related but distinct meanings, as the equivalents both of Christianity and of Christendom. In the one sense it denotes a religion, a system of belief and worship; in the other, the civilization that grew up and flourished under the aegis of that religion.[76]

Marshall Hodgson of the University of Chicago suggested in his study of Arab-Muslim history, *The Venture of Islam*, the use of the word "Islamdom," analogous to Christendom, to avoid the confusion which results from conflating religion and civilization in the singular usage of the word "Islam." Hodgson's suggestion has not been followed, and confusion remains perhaps because "Islamdom" does not sound right, or the traditional use of "Islam" with its ambiguity prevails as a matter of long standing habit, or the deference shown to the insistence of Muslim traditionalists and fundamentalists alike that Islam allows for no separation of religion and politics. I will restrict the use of Islam to mean civilization, as Lewis indicated, that emerged first among the Arabs and spread to other lands and peoples following the success of Muhammad in converting pagan Arabs from idolatry to monotheism in the first third of the seventh century in the Christian era.

***

In explaining events of such magnitude as the Danish cartoon controversy one needs to account for both proximate and underlying causes. The proximate cause was the cartoons published in a not well-known newspaper were shown by Muslim activists residing in Denmark to Arab leaders and among them was the religious leader Sheikh Yusuf al-Qaradawi, an Egyptian linked to the Muslim Brotherhood residing in Qatar with his own television program on al-Jazeerah broadcast across the Middle East. This media savvy religious leader issued a *fatwa* demanding retraction and public apology by *Jyllands-Posten* that was echoed in the demand of the member states of the Organization of Islamic Countries during a December 2005 meeting of Muslim leaders in Mecca, Saudi Arabia. The cartoons were published on September 30, 2005; some twelve weeks later, by early January 2006 the issue had stirred Muslim opinion and Muslim rage became a concern in capitals around the world. On January 30, 2006 *Jyllands-Posten* posted on its website an apology to Muslims for causing them pain, but the matter by then was no longer a local affair as Muslim countries initiated boycott of Danish products, and non-Muslims wondered where to draw the line between religious-cultural sensitivities and protecting values of an open secularliberal democracy.

The reason for Muslim outrage was explained by Tariq Ramadan, grandson of Hasan al-Banna, the founder of the Muslim Brotherhood in Egypt. Ramadan is based in Geneva, Switzerland and has been an adviser to the British home secretary on matters relating to Islam and Muslims. He wrote in the English newspaper *The Guardian*,

> In Islam, representations of all prophets are strictly forbidden. It is both a matter of the fundamental respect due to them and a principle of faith requiring that, in order to avoid any idolatrous temptations, God and the prophets never be represented. Hence, to represent a prophet is a grave transgression.[77]

What Ramadan did not, and could not, provide was scriptural authority for his position. This is because there is no injunction against images or representation in the Quran for supporting such prohibition. Ramadan's view and that of the religious leaders mostly belonging to the dominant-majority Sunni sect in Islam represented a traditional consensus on the matter. The consensus was reached in the early years of the post-prophetic period when Islam became an empire and Arabs came in contact with Jews and Christians in the Levant and, as Islam acknowledges Moses's Decalogue, the early theologians and jurists of the expanding empire adopted Jewish prohibition against graven image as part of their heritage. The only prohibition as an absolute principle of Islam, which makes it most strictly monotheistic, is not to join anything as equal to God or ascribe to Him any partner (Quran 6:152).

In the first recorded biography of the prophet, compiled and narrated by Ibn Ishaq (704-767) and available in English translation by Alfred Guillaume as *The Life of Muhammad*, there is the following anecdote from the incidents surrounding the conquest of Mecca in the year 630, or on the 8th year of the Islamic calendar:

> When the apostle prayed the noon prayer on the day of the conquest he ordered that all the idols which were round the Ka'ba should be collected and burned with fire and broken up...Quraysh had put pictures in the Ka'ba including two of Jesus son of Mary and Mary (on both of whom be peace!)...The apostle ordered that the pictures should be erased except those of Jesus and Mary.[78]

Ibn Ishaq was born 75 years after the death of the prophet in Medina, the city where the prophet lived the last ten years of his life and was laid to rest. He acquired his knowledge about the prophet from the second generation of traditionists who either witnessed the prophet themselves or learned about him from those who werewith him. All subsequent historians of Islam, the most famous from the classical period being Abu Ja'far Muhammad b. Jarir al-Tabari (839-923), were indebted to Ibn Ishaq even as partisan hacks in the context of widening schisms and fratricidal warfare among Arabs sullied his name. But Ibn Ishaq's authority given his proximity to the prophet is greater than that of any Tariq Ramadan or Sheikh al-Qaradawi and their likes in the Muslim world, and his anecdote provides us with a deeper understanding of Islam's prohibition than the politics of those who unleash mobs in quest of their own ambitions. We find preserved in museums within the Muslim world, in Topkapi, Istanbul and in Bukhara and Samarkand, Uzbekistan, portraiture paintings done during the middle age depicting Muhammad in various situations, while depictions of other Biblical prophets were common, and portraits of Ali ibn Abi Talib (cousin and son-in-law of the prophet, fourth caliph of Islam and the first Imam of the Shiites) including his sons Hasan and Husayn (the second and the third Shiite Imams) are readily found in present day Iran.

Fleming Rose, the culture editor of *Jyllands-Posten*, following the official apology of his newspaper explained to his readers his views on the matter of the cartoons he had published in a column as follows:

> Has *Jyllands-Posten* insulted and disrespected Islam? It certainly didn't intend to. But what does "respect" mean? When I visit a mosque, I show my respect by taking off my shoes. I follow the customs, just as I do in a church, synagogue or other holy place. But if a believer demands that I, as a nonbeliever, observe his taboos in the public domain, he is not asking for my respect, but for my submission. And that is incompatible with a secular democracy.[79]

Respect or submission – the former may not be demanded and the latter can only be a result of compulsion – are the two polar elements involved in the furor unleashed by Muslims over the Danish cartoons. Ramadan's view was the more polished expression of Muslim position that has elicited empathy among non-Muslim multiculturalists in the West. It spoke to that segment of educated opinion which has come to believe that though secular-democracy must maintain a clear line of separation between religion and politics, especially when that religion happens to be Christianity, it should accommodate in public sphere the prohibitions and sacred symbols belonging to non-Christian traditions, while making allowance for religious-based personal laws within immigrant communities. It sought submission in the guise of respect without showing any deference to the fact that secular-democracy has also evolved over time on a foundation of principles that is near-absolute to the extent permissible within the bounds of a written constitution as, for instance, in Canada, France and the United States.

The counter-position to Ramadan was framed by Ibn Warraq, a pseudonym of the author of *Why I Am Not A Muslim*, born in India, raised in Pakistan and settled in the United States. Ibn Warraq reminded the West of John Stuart Mill's essay *On Liberty*. Mill wrote as if anticipating the West's dilemma over Danish cartoons: "Strange it is that men should admit the validity of the arguments for free discussion, but object to their being 'pushed to an extreme', not seeing that unless the reasons are good for an extreme case, they are not good for any case. Strange that they should imagine that they are not assuming infallibility when they acknowledge that there should be free discussion on all subjects which can possibly be *doubtful*, but think that some particular principle or doctrine should be forbidden to be questioned because it is so *certain*, that is, because *they are certain* that it is certain."[80] Firmly staking his position on Mill and the enlightenment tradition that gave birth to secular-democracy, Ibn Warraq observed,

> The cartoons in the Danish newspaper *Jyllands-Posten* raise the most important question of our times: freedom of expression. Are we in the west going to cave into pressure from societies with a medieval mindset, or are we going to defend our most precious freedom – freedom of expression, a freedom for which thousands of people sacrificed their lives?[81]

Danish cartoons, as did Salman Rushdie's novel, unwittingly placed on edge two contrasting views held by two contrary civilizations, one modern and the other pre-modern, in collision. The irony in this situation is the view of the adherents of pre-modern civilization, demanding submission to its taboos by adherents of the modern civilization, emanates as much from within the boundaries of the modern civilization as it rages across its own pre-modern terrain. This is why there exists a degree of uncertainty in any answer to the question posed by Ibn Warraq.

***

The underlying causes in understanding the controversy surrounding Danish cartoons, or Rushdie affair, are more complex than explaining the proximate cause, since Muslim rage is symptomatic of a terrible malady within Islam. It reflects the irreparable breakdown of the civilization's centre that held together its constituent parts which at one time in history was co-equal, if not briefly superior, to Christendom. The question why did Islam, once dynamic and creative, stall, retreat, and then collapse from the pressures brought about by an expansive and far more creative West, has fascinated for sometime historians and philosophers both Muslims and non-Muslims alike. A recent speculation is to be found in Bernard Lewis's *What Went Wrong?* Among Muslim thinkers there have been many of as diverse background as Muhammad Iqbal (1876-1938) born in India, Malik Bennabi (1903-73) from Algeria, or Fatima Mernissi (b.1940) from Morocco, who have reflected upon the causes of Islam's decline. But there is none among Muslims who meditated about the apparent cycle of civilization's rise and fall as did Ibn Khaldun (1332-1406). He wrote with a keen sense of Islam's disintegration as Arab-Muslim power around the Mediterranean crumbled and Christendom in Europe, seen from the perspective of its advance in Spain at the expense of Arabs, began to edge ahead of Islam. In his book *Al-Muqaddimah* he proposed a pattern might be discerned from the study of history revealing the character of a people and the nature of society they construct or bring to ruin.

The causes for the decline of civilization are primarily internal. And when the collapse occurs, recalling W.B. Yeats's 'The Second Coming', "anarchy is loosed upon the world." Yeats meant by anarchy more than mere disorder, as did Ibn Khaldun some seven centuries earlier. In Yeats's poem when things fall apart the centre can no longer hold the caged beast which preys upon civilization, and when this beast is let loose, as Ibn Khaldun witnessed, night descends on common humanity until some other power can slay the beast or return it to its cage.

The beast within Islam has been prowling for a very long time. Islam as a religion was also a civilizing force in Arabia as it brought for a while some discipline to its native population, the Bedouins of the desert. But the Bedouins are, as Ibn Khaldun wrote, "a savage nation, fully accustomed to savagery and the things that cause it... Such a natural disposition is the negation and the antithesis of civilization. All the customary activities of the Bedouins lead to wandering and movement. This is the antithesis and negation of stationariness, which produces civilization."[82] Ibn Khaldun, unconstrained by political correctness of any sort, observed how the Bedouins, if they were not caged by superior civilizing power, got loosed and preyed upon civilization to its ruins. He wrote:

> It is noteworthy how civilization always collapsed in places the Bedouins took over and conquered, and how such settlements were depopulated and laid in ruin. The Yemen where Bedouins live is

> in ruins, except for a few cities. Persian civilization in the Arab Iraq is likewise completely ruined. The same applies to contemporary Syria.[83]

Bedouin is a state of mind, a psychology of a people, if we abstract from Ibn Khaldun's sociology, and not merely a description of an ethnic group. The state of mind thrives on anarchy, seeks anarchy where it is non-existent, and celebrates anarchy for the feast it is in preying upon the decaying corpse of civilization. This state of mind cannot build for it has not the capacity to be stationery, as Ibn Khaldun observed, and make investment in energy and resources required for sedentary living as prerequisite for the making of civilization. Hence, this state of mind relishes in bringing ruin where order prevails. History, Ibn Khaldun concluded, is driven by the tension between the forces of civilization and the forces of its ruin, and this for him constituted the cycle of history.

But what is most remarkable about Ibn Khaldun's writings is that he conceived the idea of civilization in the singular. On reflection, however, this is not surprising. Ibn Khaldun was a Muslim, and he plumbed deeply into the message of the Qur'an even as he read Greek philosophers. The central message of Islam is the concept of unity, *tauhid*, indicating that all of creation bears the stamp of a single author, God, as unique and supreme creator. From this axiom Ibn Khaldun did not require a philosophical leap to see that behind and beyond diversity and plurality of cultures is to be found the essence of human enterprise in history, its self-discovery of its common origin and its singular destiny. Thus in Ibn Khaldun's majestic speculation history of mankind is a movement from ignorance to knowledge, and knowledge in its most elevated sense is a common, shared resource of humanity. In civilization knowledge is of the higher sort, of knowledge organized, progressively cultivated and transmitted among people who commonly appreciate arts and sciences.

Islam before its decline began possessed plasticity to adapt what it borrowed from others – Persians, Hindus, Jews, Chinese, Greeks and Romans – and innovate as it improved upon the borrowings before transmitting them to others. By the time Napoleon made his entrance into the Middle East arriving in Egypt in 1798, or some decades earlier Robert Clive set in motion the conquest of India by defeating the massed army of Nawab Siraj-ud-Dowla of Bengal at the battle of Plassey in 1757, Islam's plasticity had hardened and Muslims as a people were ready to be colonized and ruled by Europeans. Ibn Khaldun had seen the beginning phase of Islam's cycle of decay, and he understood, as Yeats would under somewhat similar circumstances several centuries later that in the decline of civilization the caged beast would find itself let loosed unless it got held in check by a rising new power given to renewing civilization. And, indeed, this is what occurred.

As Europe's star rose in civilization's firmament, European power expanded into Asia and Africa and kept the beast caged within Islam's decadent boundaries. But when Europe reached its peak as civilizing order in the early decade of the last century exporting its enlightenment values and new political arrangements based on ideas of nationalism and democracy, the cycle of decline set in. Europe emasculated itself in two world wars, and with the civilization's ebb tide gaining momentum it began to retreat from Asia and Africa, more particularly from the lands of Islam, with unseemly haste. The post-colonial order Europe left behind among Muslims in the second-half of the twentieth century was mostly a pathetic caricature of European culture. Nowhere this caricature was more evident than in the post-Ottoman Turkey of Mustafa Kemal. Ottoman rulers of Islam once terrified Europeans, then when decay set their realm was dismissively referred to as the "sick man of Europe." Following the defeat of 1918 a truncated country of Turks emerged on the Anatolian peninsula with a tiny grasp of Europe remaining in its fist, and it has displayed ever since a divided identity of being neither any more Ottoman nor sufficiently European to be recognized by other Muslims as a model of a reformed and democratic Muslim country.

Elsewhere the beast within Islam grew bolder and more invigorated as the artificial façade of a mongrel European order resting on decrepit foundations of pre-modern culture began to peel off. The effort to keep the beast in Islam caged is part of a long history of civil wars among Muslims. These internal conflicts remained mostly incomprehensible and distant to non-Muslims; occasionally Europeans, and then Americans, heard far away rumblings of battles that made little sense to them. In more recent times news about the hanging of an elected president, Zulfikar Ali Bhutto of Pakistan, or the tumultuous revolt of a people overthrowing a monarch, Mohammed Shah Pahlavi of Iran, or the public killing of a military-president Anwar Sadat of Egypt, raised concerns in the West and intellectuals or worldly-wise journalists got together to make sense of such events in London, Paris, and New York. But still these events and the civil wars within Islam, despite infrequent attention, remained remote to the Western public. The West during these years was preoccupied with the Cold War against its Bolshevik-Communist nemesis in the Soviet Union. When reversals as in Vietnam or the shock of oil-price quadrupling resulting from the Middle East conflict occurred, these were explained away as peripheral costs of the Cold War. Then the Cold War ended luckily without a nuclear Armageddon, and the West, particularly the United States with the restoration of the Democrats in the White House, took holiday from history as deserving after the mighty exertions during the previous four decades due to the Cold War. As Bill Clinton and his party-goers, like the French Bourbons of whom was said they never learned much nor forgot much, indulged themselves during the final decade of the last century in frivolous escapades, the beast within Islam smashed through its retaining walls and went on rampage beyond Islam's domain. The attacks on New York and Washington on September 11, 2001 brought the long simmering Islam's internal conflicts into America's heartland, and into Europe. These conflicts whose primary victims have been Muslims are no longer merely a matter of local or regional interest since Islam's internal struggles have snared the West into the conflict which is the first global war of a new sort – some might call it the first post-modern war – of the 21st century.

The origin of the civil wars in Islam is located in the conflicting claims over authority in the immediate years following the demise of the prophet in the year 632. Usurped power, and the demand placed on religion with acquiescing religious leaders in the service of such power, shaped the features of Islam as civilization. Bedouin disposition of raging against civilization was also instrumental in the shaping of Islam. The modern faces of this disposition, or the beast set loose, are those of Osama bin Laden and his coterie of terrorists in the al Qaeda network; the mob in the streets of the Muslim world serves the beast as retainers; and Muslim intellectuals and religious leaders such as Tariq Ramadan and Sheikh al-Qaradawi serve the beast as apologists and propagandists.

***

Ibn Khaldun did not indulge in romanticism, unlike Jean-Jacques Rousseau's depiction of the savage as noble, when describing Bedouins and their culture as anti-civilization. Bedouins are crafty as they must be to survive in the hostile environment of the desert. In modern times the founding ruler of the Saudi dynasty, Abdul Aziz ibn Saud (1880-1953), displayed amply the craftiness of Bedouin chiefs to acquire and maintain power in Arabia that is prone to challenge by competing Bedouin tribes. The intriguing aspect of modern-day Bedouins, exemplified by the House of Saud, has been their capacity to straddle the increasing tension between the modern world of science and democracy and their own disposition against modernity defining contemporary civilization.

Osama bin Laden being true to his Bedouin heritage has over-ridden this tension by seizing products of the modern world and turning them into his weapons against civilization. But the al Qaeda chief could have been captured or slain, as the Ottoman rulers did with the marauding bands of Bedouins, if the rulers of the Muslim world were committed in destroying the beast that has brought ruin to Islam. The bewildering fact is, however, that so many of Muslim rulers and their people sympathize with the beast and share its rage against the modern world and its dominant powers, particularly the United States. In delving into this rage for explanation the curious fact surfaces – in retrospect not surprising – the extent to which Muslim sympathy for the beast draws support from the internal opposition within the West to secular-liberal democracy and the West's economic success in terms of capitalism.

A civilization that loses its inner plasticity, the Algerian writer Malek Bennabi noted, has lost "its aptitude to progress and to renew itself" and, hence, "little by little the Muslim world came to a stop like a motor that had consumed its last litre of petrol."[84] The place of creative thinking in such society, which requires openness and tolerance for criticism, gets substituted by politics of resentment and grievances. In a seminal essay published by the *Atlantic Monthly* in September 1990, Bernard Lewis explained 'The Roots of Muslim Rage' resulting from a mood of hostility and rejection "due to a feeling of humiliation – a growing awareness, among the heirs of an old, proud, and long dominant civilization, of having been overtaken, overborne, and overwhelmed by those whom they regard as their inferiors."

This mood is infectious, addictive and, ultimately, provides a crutch for a people unable and unwilling to be creative and taking responsibility for their history instead of blaming others. In a long list of intellectuals and writers who fed this mood, even as the beast roamed and plotted among sympathetic crowds, there were two Palestinian-Americans, Edward Said (1935-2003) and Ismail Raji al-Faruqi (1921-1986) who proved to be specially gifted in packaging the politics of resentment.

Edward Said was a professor of contemporary literature at Columbia University in New York, and he devoted his talents to give respectability to this mood with his polemics against the West and its perfidy at the expense of Islam by indulging Jews, supporting Zionism and defending Israel. His book *Orientalism*, much celebrated among third world students and intellectuals with their Western sympathizers, is a polemic masquerading as scholarship providing Arabs and Muslims a stick with which to beat the imperialist West for the impoverishment of the Orient, particularly the Middle East, and the alleged systematic exploitation of its resources. Said blamed Western scholars, in particular those of Anglo-American background, specializing in the study of the Orient of enclosing and representing the Orient and its people, Arabs and Muslims specifically, in an essentialist manner by dehumanizing them and in depicting them as the "other" of the civilized Europeans. In such representation Said found, "On the one hand there are Westerners, and on the other there are Arab-Orientals; the former are (in no particular order) rational, peaceful, liberal, logical, capable of holding real values, without natural suspicion; the latter are none of these things."[85] The study of the Orient, of acquiring knowledge about it and representing it amounted to a "Western style for dominating, restructuring, and having authority over the Orient."[86] The relationship between the Occident and the Orient, Said theorized, is "a relationship of power, of domination, of varying degrees of a complex hegemony."[87] He then concluded, "It is therefore correct that every European, in what he could say about the Orient, was consequently a racist, an imperialist, and almost totally ethnocentric."[88] In a reverse reductionism Said explained the West to the Arabs and Muslims, representing the tremendously diverse Occident with its writers, historians, painters variously involved in learning and knowing other cultures in an essentialist manner, no different than what he accused the West in portraying the Orient negatively. Danish cartoons simply confirmed to Arabs and Muslims across the vast realm of Islam, from Morocco to Indonesia, the inherent racism of Europe as Said had shown by deconstructing the Orientalist discourse as racist.

Ismail Raji al-Faruqi was a professor of Islamic Studies at Temple University in Philadelphia, and he devoted his considerable energy to popularizing his idea of "Islamization" as cure-all for Muslims and Islam. In 1982 al-Faruqi published his manifesto called *Islamization of Knowledge*. He began as follows:

> The world-*ummah* of Islam stands presently at the lowest rung of the ladder of nations. In this century, no other nation has been subjected to comparable defeat or humiliation. Muslims were defeated, massacred, robbed of their land and wealth, of their life and hope. They were double-crossed, colonized and exploited; proselytized and forcefully or bribefully converted to other faiths. And they were secularized, westernized and de-Islamized by internal and external agents of their enemies. All this happened in practically every country and corner of the Muslim world. Victims of injustice and aggression on every count, the Muslims were nonetheless vilified and denigrated in the representations of all nations. They enjoy the worst possible 'image' in the world today. In the mass media of the world, the 'Muslim' is stereotyped as aggressive, destructive, lawless, terrorist, uncivilized, fanatic, fundamentalist, archaic and anachronistic. He is the object of hatred and contempt on the part of all non-Muslims, whether developed or underdeveloped, capitalist or Marxist, Eastern or Western, civilized or savage. The Muslim world itself is known only for its inner strife and division, its turbulence and self-contradictions, its wars and threat to world peace, its excessive wealth and excessive poverty, its famine and cholera epidemics. In the minds of people everywhere the Muslim world is the 'sick man' of the world; and the whole world is led to think that at the root of all these evils stands the religion of Islam. The fact that the *ummah* counts over a billion, that its territories are the vastest and the richest, that its potential in human, material and geo-political resources is the

> greatest, and finally that its faith – Islam – is an integral, beneficial, world-affirming and realistic religion, makes the defeat, the humiliation and the misrepresentation of Muslims all the more intolerable.[89]

Such thinking over-flowing with self-pity found a captive audience in the streets and capitals of the Muslim world, for Said and al-Faruqi had taken Frantz Fanon's *The Wretched of the Earth* – which Jean-Paul Sartre celebrated by noting "the Third World finds *itself* and speaks to *itself* through his voice"[90] – and Islamized its sentiment. Fanon's heated polemics excused the violence and its excesses of the colonized against the colonizers, for his wretched of the earth could do no wrong in righting all the wrongs done by the Europeans to him and his people. In Iran Muslim intellectuals turned radical, such as Ali Shariati (1933-1977), were greatly influenced by Fanon. This mood found its fulsome expression when Ayatollah Khomeini as the father of the Islamic Republic of Iran approved the storming of the U.S. embassy in Tehran and taking American diplomats as hostages, and thereby repudiated all accepted norms and protocols of international politics and diplomacy. It is the same mood of repudiation that exults in burning flags and effigies of Western countries and their leaders, or torching their embassies. The beast within Islam, the Bedouin psychology that once found thrill in bringing ruin to Muslim civilization, now set loose finds itself invigorated by this mood among a large segment of Muslims and is encouraged to strike with impunity countries most representative of contemporary global civilization that so many Muslims find unbearable.

This mood brimming with humiliation, suffused with resentment and burdened with grievances, should be recognized for what it is, a symptom of Islam broken down. It is not a mood that is inherent in Muslims as a people, or a mood that is an attribute in some manner to the religion of Islam. On the contrary, Muslims like any people of any other faith-traditions have a great sense of hilarity in their literature, art, poetry and music. Amir Taheri, the Iranian political writer and columnist, wrote:

> The truth is that Islam has always had a sense of humor and has never called for chopping heads as the answer to satirists...Both Arabic and Persian literature, the two great literatures of Islam,

> are full of examples of "laughing at religion," at times to the point of irreverence…those familiar with Islam's literature know of Ubaid Zakani's "Mush va Gorbeh" (Mouse and Cat), a match for Rabelais when it comes to mocking religion. Sa'adi's eloquent soliloquy on behalf of Satan mocks the "dry pious ones." And Attar portrays a hypocritical sheikh who, having fallen into the Tigris, is choked by his enormous beard. Islamic satire reaches its height in Rumi, where a shepherd conspires with God to pull a stunt on Moses; all three end up having a good laugh.[91]

It is true, however, that this self-pitying mood has had a dampening effect within the Muslim world, and Muslim fundamentalists have succeeded through violence and support from unelected leaders, for example military dictators in Pakistan, in intimidating Muslims to comply with their literal-minded, bigoted and witless interpretations of the Quran and the *shari'ah*, the legal norms constructed by religious scholars in the first two centuries of Islam.

***

In his *Atlantic Monthly* essay Bernard Lewis introduced the phrase "a clash of civilizations" in explaining the quarrels of Muslims against the West. Samuel Huntington borrowed Lewis's phrase and used it as a title for his 1993 *Foreign Affairs* essay, and later his book. Lewis wrote,

> It should now be clear that we are facing a mood and a movement far transcending the level of issues and policies and the governments that pursue them. This is no less than a clash of civilizations – the perhaps irrational but surely historic reaction of an ancient rival against our Judeo-Christian heritage, our secular present, and the worldwide expansion of both. It is crucially important that we on our side should not be provoked into an equally historic but also equally irrational reaction against that rival.[92]

Lewis cautioned the West against being provoked, but the beast set out to deliberately provoke. Then the provocations of September 11, 2001 amounting to acts of war required response adequate to the challenge the beast had mounted. It is in the context of the war on terror or, more appropriately, Islamist terror, we need to assess the implication of the Danish cartoon controversy. The war on Islamist terror is not a clash of civilizations, rather it is a war against a mood striving for some ideological coherence that needs to be purged, and the beast exploiting this mood killed or caged.

Islam as a civilization crashed a long time ago as Malek Bennabi noted, the fuel driving it exhausted. The question for Muslims is how they will reconcile themselves with civilization based on secular-democratic values and modern science in the 21st century recognizing, as they must, mixing religion and politics means remaining confined within authoritarian politics tending towards totalitarianism and a corrupted religion. For the West, the question is how to prevent the detritus of Islam still extant and its rampaging beast still breathing fire from undermining the values of freedom and democracy at the centre of its history.

Through the Cold War decades we heard from a body of opinion in the West that shared in the goals of its communist adversary in the Soviet Union. This body of opinion is skeptical of democracy, and opposes freedom as the fundamental liberal value. Jean-Francois Revel, the French public intellectual and author of *The Totalitarian Temptation*, explained, "The totalitarian phenomenon is not to be understood without making allowance for the thesis that some important part of every society consists of people who actively want tyranny: either to exercise it themselves or – much more mysteriously – to submit to it. Democracy will therefore always remain at risk."[93] This body of opinion takes refuge in the ideology of multiculturalism, romanticizes culture and history of the peoples of Asia, Africa and Latin America, seeks support for its anti-capitalist ideology in the politics of resentment and grievances, and readily denigrates the culture which served as the cradle for enlightenment, modern science and democracy. The Danish cartoon controversy showed this body of opinion being in sympathy with the Muslim outrage arguing for abridgement of the freedom of expression in open society, a right protected by constitution in liberaldemocracies, as a demonstration of solidarity with people at odds with modern civilization. This body of opinion ironically has a greater capacity to do harm to liberal-democracy and the open society than any outrage of Muslims orchestrated to extract concessions from non-Muslims. It has an enervating effect on those in Europe and America on whose conviction and strength rests the defense of modern civilization. It feeds upon an excess of white guilt about past sins and, as Shelby Steele has observed, "this guilt makes our Third World enemies into colored victims, people whose problems – even the tyrannies they live under – were created by the historical disruptions and injustices of the White West."[94] This is the paradox of our time, and for liberals the perennial dilemma to contend with while remaining true to liberal ideals.

8

Pakistan As It Turns Sixty

Poets reputedly possess an inner eye which sees what is obscure to others. One of the more loved poets of his time in Urdu, the language of Muslims in north India, was Faiz Ahmad Faiz (1911-84). He was born in Sialkot, Punjab, a province divided in August 1947 between two independent successor states to the British Raj, India and Pakistan. On the eve of that division Faiz wrote with anguish about the coming of freedom for the land of his birth in a poem that speaks about the agony of Pakistan since its making. He wrote, "This dawn that's marked and wounded, this dawn that night has nibbled on – It's not the dawn we expected; it's not the dawn we were looking for…The lamp still waits for the morning breeze, the night weighs on us still. This is not the moment of our freedom. Keep moving, keep moving! We have not arrived."[95]

In March 2004 Dina Wadia, daughter and only child of Pakistan's founder, Muhammad Ali Jinnah, traveled to Lahore from her residence in New York City with her son, Nusli Wadia, to watch a cricket match between Indian and Pakistani teams. It was only the second time Jinnah's daughter visited the country he founded; the first time was when she came to attend his funeral in September 1948. Dina Wadia had refused to accompany her father from Mumbai (Bombay) to Karachi in August 1947, and instead settled in the United States. As a frail old woman born in August 1919 to Jinnah and his Parsi-born wife, Ruttie Petit, Dina Wadia once more visited Karachi to place a floral wreath at her father's grave turned into a mausoleum for the founder of the country. There she wrote the following words in the visitor's book: "This has been very sad and wonderful for me. May his dream for Pakistan come true."[96]

Between the poet's anguish and the wishes of a daughter for her father's dream, Pakistan is a tale of an imagined "nation" concocted out of fears and loathing among an elite that once ruled a vast land of diverse population before Europeans arrived and then dreaded their departure in the wake of a rising tide of anti-colonial movement. To make sense of Pakistan – a country with nuclear arms that cannot feed its people while exporting terrorism abroad – it is vital to understand the deeply flawed nature of its conception and birth.

The basis of partitioning India by Britain in 1947 was a concession made to the argument that Hindus and Muslims as two people with irreconcilable interests could not live together in an undivided India. This was the idea devised by the land-owning Muslim elite of north India and propagated as "two nation theory" by the Muslim League under Jinnah. Apart from religion Hindus and Muslims as the two largest religiously defined communities shared much in common. Both remain ethnically diverse communities, and neither can be defined as a "nation" in the sense of a people bound by a common ethnic identity, history or language. India was, contrary to the specious theory of "two nations," a land of vastly diverse people with multiplicity of languages and regional cultures given a semblance of administrative unity by Britain as an imperial power. It was in this sense a composite "nation," a political community in the making under colonial rule that could have been divided by Britain into many smaller states along linguistic boundaries, or its administrative unity protected by leaving India undivided in 1947. In partitioning India and providing Muslims with a state of their own, a war-exhausted Britain accepted Jinnah's argument and a country emerged entirely on the basis of religion, Islam, meant to provide national identity to a people.

Muslims are not an ethnically homogenous people, and Islam as a religion with universal appeal cannot be reduced to providing national identity for a people without distorting it for political purposes. The flawed theory of Jinnah and his Muslim League was shown for all its worth when Pakistan fell apart in 1971 as a result of ethnic politics that brought the military to unleash a blood-bath in the eastern half of the country, now Bangladesh. The break-up of Pakistan and the continuing inability of its rulers, predominantly men in army uniform, to provide the country with government representative of and elected by the people illustrate how an imagined "nation" has remained an internally divided society and a political community lacking consensus about its governance.

Nationalism is a secular ideology opposed by those Muslim religious leaders who supported the demand for Pakistan. For them the making of Pakistan was a guarantee to save their version of traditionally-bound Islam being undermined in a secular democracy an independent India was meant to become, as envisaged by the leaders of the Congress-led nationalist movement. Pakistan was demanded on the basis of Islam and, hence, Pakistan was meant to be an Islamic state in the opinion of religious leaders who pushed to make Jinnah's twonation theory a reality. But when Jinnah spoke to the members of the Constituent Assembly for Pakistan in Karachi a few days ahead of the independence on August 11, 1947, he declared in the new country "Hindus would cease to be Hindus and Muslims would cease to be Muslims, not in the religious sense, because that is the personal faith of each individual, but in the political sense as citizens of the State."[97] Jinnah's words confirmed the worst fears of traditional-minded religious leaders about secularism as a political idea requiring the separation of religion and politics, and also indicated the confusion about what sort of country Pakistan as a modern state might become when the basis of its establishment was Islam. In the years since Jinnah spoke on the eve of Pakistan's birth confusion has persisted in the unsettled nature of the country's politics.

How to define Islam, or reform it, consistent with the needs of a modern state has not been met by Pakistanis and, consequently, traditional-minded views of a doctrinaire Islam effectively opposed any advancement of the country along modern lines of liberal democracy. The version of Islam – literal minded and fundamentalist, patriarchal-bound, punitive in practice, heavily-influenced by

Saudi Arabia's Wahhabi doctrine at odds with the principle of gender equality and intolerant of non-Muslim minorities – become dominant since mid-1970s when General Zia ul-Haq was the military ruler has exacted a heavy price by undermining democratic evolution of the country.

For more than half of Pakistan's history the country has been ruled by military dictators. General Pervez Musharraf is the fourth military ruler to seize power from a civilian-led government. The excuse for open military rule, and not disguised influence on political power, is corrupt politicians who endanger the security of the country. In justifying military rule generals need an external enemy and internal allies to support their claim on power. Pakistan under the generals has fought several wars with India over Kashmir, lost half of the country, made itself a frontline state in the war against the former Soviet Union's occupation of Afghanistan, supported Taliban rule in Kabul until the events of September 11, 2001 when circumstances compelled the military rulers to offer the country as a strategic ally of the United States in the war against terrorism.

Pakistan's national obsession with India provided justification for both military dictators and politicians to pursue the objective of acquiring nuclear capability in maintaining nuclear parity in South Asia. But in quest for nuclear power Pakistan became somewhat isolated from the West, particularly its relationship with Washington suffered once the Afghan war ended with Soviet withdrawal. The secrecy surrounding the nuclear-program, and the requirements for funds to support it, also led Pakistan into becoming a full-fledged participant in the nuclear black-market selling its acquired expertise to Iran, North Korea, Libya and possibly other countries seeking to acquire nuclear capability. The public confession on February 4, 2004 in the state-run television of Dr. Abdul Qadeer Khan, revered by Pakistanis as the father of the country's nuclear bomb, in the presence of President Musharraf that he was alone responsible for operating in the nuclear black-market was a staged event. It was done to placate the United States so the country could continue being a strategic ally of Washington even as its conduct was that of a rogue state engaged in nuclear proliferation.

The internal allies of the military rulers have been religious leaders and their entire network of religious-based schools (*madrassas*), political parties such as the Jamaat-i-Islami, charity funded organizations, and supporters in league with or paid by land-owning rural elites. This religious network propagates the most regressive social and political views in the name of Islam, and its schools have functioned in producing a vast army of semi-literate students incapable of productive work in a modern economy. From this pool of unemployed or underemployed students have come the foot-soldiers of "jihadis" or Muslim warriors who went to Afghanistan as freedom-fighters against the Soviet Union, have supported the Taliban regime in Afghanistan and remain favourably disposed to al-Qaeda's ideology of "jihad" (holy war) against the United States, Israel, India and their allies. This segment of Pakistani society has never been able to win sufficient electoral support in any of the fairly open elections held, and even in the rigged election of 2002 religious parties together barely polled over a tenth of the votes cast. But these parties have received support from the military as they have supported military dictators for implementing their version of Islam.

Pakistan is a declared nuclear weapon state. But it is also a "failing state" and is listed in the top ten of the second annual "Failed States Index" compiled by The Fund for Peace and the Carnegie Endowment for International Peace.[98] According to this index a failed or failing state is "one in which the government does not have effective control of its territory, is not perceived as legitimate by a significant portion of its population, does not provide domestic security or basic public services to its citizens, and lacks a monopoly on the use of force. A failing state may experience active violence or simply be vulnerable to violence."[99] The case of Pakistan as a failed state poses a nightmare scenario in a part of the world that is most strategically important for Europe, North America and Japan and greatly vulnerable to political instability.

The most pressing social reality of Pakistan is the demographic catastrophe in the making with profound political consequences locally and globally. The population has more than tripled over the past three decades and is presently estimated around 160 million. During 1990s the population grew at an annual rate of just under three per cent, and at this pace by the middle of the present century Pakistan's population will probably reach 400 million. The capacity of the country to feed, clothe, shelter and educate its people has barely been adequate with a per capita income of less than two dollars per day. As the country is unable to meet basic needs of the people social unrest will increase and so will repression. There is long simmering ethnic unrests in the tribal areas of Baluchistan province and along the borders with Afghanistan in the North-West Frontier Province. The continuing violence in Afghanistan more than four years after the overthrow of the Taliban regime, and despite the efforts of multilateral forces to stabilize the country under President Hamid Karzai's rule, is directly connected with the situation inside Pakistan where military rulers are unwilling to fully cooperate in the war on terrorism by denying Taliban fighters sanctuary in the tribal border areas.

A failed state breeds resentment among its people, and magnifies the politics of grievances. At the pace in which Pakistan's population is growing its only recourse will be in the short term to encourage people to leave. This is a prescription for its people becoming carriers of the sort of politics most vulnerable to "jihadi" influence, or providing the global network of terrorists an endless supply of recruits. For the West in general, as it is for the United States since 9/11, the dilemma Pakistan poses is how to provide a failing state with material support that it does not collapse when what it increasingly represents is undeserving of support.

Since Pakistan's break-up in 1971 its military and civilian rulers sought to position Pakistan into close partnership with the Gulf countries of the Middle East, and with Libya and Saudi Arabia as strategic allies. Funds from these countries enabled Pakistan to make its secretive bid for nuclear power, and in return Pakistan offered its services as a clearinghouse of Islamic militancy. In the process Pakistan's military, and particularly those officers who run the Inter-Service Intelligence (ISI), became intimately linked with the "jihadi" global network during the Afghan war, providing training and logistical support to "jihadi" recruits while supporting the aims of global "jihad."

Any hope for Pakistan to recover from its present situation requires the country be returned to elected government and the army be returned to its military barracks. Only by nurturing democracy the bitterness of a people repressed and betrayed by unaccountable military dictators might be dissolved, and a politics governed by the priority of meeting the long denied needs of the people might replace a culture of graft and exploitation of the weak. For even a minimal success of Pakistan turning away from the conditions of a failing state, it will need to address the foundational basis for its establishment nearly sixty years ago by asking what Islam means for its national identity and survival as a decent state for Muslims. Any meaningful answer will make allowance for the reform of Islam enabling Pakistan to reconcile itself with the reality of the modern world, and for Pakistanis to meet their basic needs without causing further injury to others or themselves. In the absence of democratic renewal Pakistan's future is dismal and an immense threat to global peace and security in the coming decades.

9

Muslim on Muslim Violence: What Drives It?

Since Samuel Huntington's widely read *Foreign Affairs*' essay published in the summer 1993 issue of the journal, the idea of "the clash of civilizations" has come to be the most handy explanation of the troubled relationship between the Muslim world and the West. Huntington's phrase, "Islam has bloody border," was provocative and yet not inaccurate. Islamic or, more appropriately, Muslim militancy has fuelled a mindless and bigoted conflict, civilizational in nature, that sort of peaked with the terrorist attacks on New York and Washington on September 11, 2001.

But what Huntington's essay, and later his book on the same theme, and other writings of similar kind does not mention, and the subject remains largely unexplored, is the bloodier conflict within the Muslim world. The phenomenon of Muslim violence against Muslims demands attention, for it is primarily this inner conflict which periodically spills over beyond the borders of the Muslim world. More Muslims have been killed by Muslims, more Muslims continue to be victimized by Muslims, and more Muslims are in danger of dying at the hands of Muslims than non-Muslims. This is a subject that demands a wider examination and attention than has been given by Muslims and non-Muslims alike.

Of Muslim violence against Muslims, we are concerned here primarily with the politically organized violence of those in power against those who are contesting that power, and the appeal to Islam is made in common by all parties in the conflict. In writing about this subject, we do not need to look at the record of Muslim violence against Muslims in the archives, for the subject continues to be part of the experience of contemporary Muslims and in many instances is part of their living memory. In my case, I was both a victim and a witness to organized violence of a Muslim majority state against its own population with the result that one out of seven people, nearly ten million, were forced from their homes to take refuge in a neighbouring country as refugees and over half-million were killed.

I am referring to the actions of the military government of Pakistan against the people of former East Pakistan, now Bangladesh in 1971. This was a politically catastrophic event of genocidal proportions in the modern history of the Muslim world. A brief description of the culture and politics surrounding the founding of Pakistan in 1947, and the manner in which it broke apart 24 years later, can well illustrate that aspect of Muslim history – Muslim violence against Muslims – that has received insufficient notice in the writings about Muslims and Islam.

Here I will merely provide a brief overview of Pakistan within the larger context of Indian history or, more appropriately, the history of Islam and Muslims in India. The more interesting aspect of the subject of this paper is explaining the nature of Muslim on Muslim violence that makes a mockery of Islam.

The case of Pakistan is not unique in Muslim history. The violence that has characterized much of its history is quite common and persistent within most Muslim societies since the very early years of Islam. In recent times, in the three decades following the violent break up of Pakistan in 1971, we may cite from a long list of similar violence a few examples of Muslims engaged in brutal conflicts within a state, or inter-state conflicts of two or more Muslim majority states. Within Pakistan sectarian violence has continued since 1971; the politics of Islamization under the military dictator General Zia ul-Haq added another dimension to this violence with the execution of an elected president, Zulfikar Ali Bhutto, in 1979. Other examples of similar kind are: state directed violence and counter-violence of Muslim extremists in Egypt; the killing of Anwar Sadat; the repression of Palestinians inside Jordan in 1970-71; the sectarian strife in Lebanon during the 1970s; the seizure of the holy mosque in Mecca in 1979 and the violence that followed; the violence in Iran since 1979 between followers and opponents of the late Ayatollah Khomeini; the nearly decade long Iran-Iraq war; the civil war inside Syria culminating in the Hama uprising of 1982 and its severe repression by Hafez Asad; the civil war in Algeria since at least early 1992; the unsettled situation in Afghanistan following the brutal rule of the Talibans; the genocidal violence against the people of Darfur by the Khartoum supported militias in Sudan. And then there is the case of Iraq.

In all of the violence and counter-violence among Muslims, between those who control the state and those who are in opposition, the one common element has been the appeal to Islam as Muslims have engaged in the killings of Muslims. The abuse of religion in such a manner is not confined to Muslims only; Christians have their own history of violence. But the intensity and persistence of Muslim violence against Muslims – the intra-Christian violence is now an exception when it occurs and not the norm – requires an explanation. Muslims need to confront their record on this matter, if they are going to break out of this cycle, by acknowledging the problem, understanding what are the sources of such violence, and then engaging in that brand of politics which will guide them into a democratic future and allow them to construct an alternative vision of Islam than the one that has been so destructive and counter-productive in the making of their history.

I return to the example of Pakistan. Any description of Pakistan's history will need to take account of its making; of the prior history of Muslims and Islam in India; of the failure right at the outset in constitution-making and the transformation of Pakistan into a praetorian state; of its ethnic divisions; and of the causes leading to the break up of the country. What followed was the subsequent history of internal strife, the program of Islamization, sectarian violence, the war in Afghanistan and the Talibanization of Pakistan.[100]

A detailed description of these events is beyond the scope of this paper. Here I will limit myself to the proposition that the record thus far of Pakistan as a Muslim majority country, its state of unsettled politics with accompanying violence of Muslim against Muslims, is bound by the history of its founding.

Muhammad Ali Jinnah's vision for Pakistan was based on his "twonation" theory that Muslims of India constitute a nation, separate and distinct from non-Muslim Indians. It was an unprecedented innovation in Muslim history. This invention of a *nation* caught hold of the imagination of a sufficiently large number of Indian Muslims and the religious nationalism that followed led to the division of India.[101]

Jinnah's demand did not go unchallenged by those Indian Muslims who viewed the idea of a separate Muslim state as impractical, and its consequences hugely tragic for Muslims and non-Muslims alike. A majority of Indian Muslim scholars, Maulana Abul Kalam Azad belonging to the Indian National Congress being most prominent among them, repudiated Jinnah's nationalist claim as being contrary to the traditional teachings of Islam and argued that the history of Muslims in India did not warrant such a division of a country that had been their *watan* (home) for over a thousand years.[102]

Jinnah prevailed, and those Muslims who followed him turned their backs on a history of Hindu-Muslim coexistence that represented for Muslims of India an alternative to the politics of exclusion and separation within a religiously defined nationalism. The politics of Muslims opting for Pakistan had a broader implication for Muslim history beyond the Indian subcontinent; such separatism suggested that for Muslims the idea of coexistence as a minority with a non-Muslim majority was untenable – that Muslims as a minority population preferred separating from non-Muslims within an existing larger political territory to form a majority in a smaller political territory – when the global reality is Muslims are a minority in the world at large as they were within India, and the main challenge confronting them politically and culturally remains that of coming to terms with the modern world in all its complexity.

The demand for Pakistan was accompanied with the battle cry that "Islam is in danger within a Hindu majority India." The politics of "two nation" theory was laden with emotionalism, and the partition of India erupted in an unprecedented explosion of communal carnage. Once the dust settled, the question of what sort of state Pakistan would be, an Islamic state or a secular-national Muslim majority state, emerged as a highly divisive issue.

Jinnah interestingly observed in a speech delivered a few days before the date of formal independence of Pakistan, that in the new state "Hindus would cease to be Hindus and Muslims would cease to be Muslims, not in the religious sense, because that is the personal faith of each individual, but in the political sense as citizens of the state."[103] Jinnah's thinking was remarkable given the carnage his "two nation" theory had wrought, but he died a year later and those who had been mobilized in the name of Islam were not prepared to see their sacrifices denied. The struggle to make Pakistan an Islamic state began with the first sitting of the Constituent Assembly.

The initial confrontation between defenders of Jinnah's legacy and proponents of Islamic state took place over the demand made by religious parties, most notably the Jamaat-i-Islami of Maulana Maududi, to declare Ahmadis, a relatively new sect in Islam, as non-Muslims. The anti-Ahmadiyya movement became violent and led to the imposition of martial law in Lahore and the adjoining areas of Punjab in 1953. It was the precursor of what would follow in terms of sectarian violence and ethnic conflict leading eventually to the crisis of 1971.

The word "Pakistan" interestingly means "the land of the pure." Pure here signifies Muslims being pure in their monotheistic faith. The subtext of the Pakistan movement was the many-layered meaning of "Islam is in danger." It meant the Muslim community in a Hindu majority India was vulnerable to the creeping impurity of polytheism undermining their faith. There were moments in the long history of Muslims in India when the cry of "Islam in danger" was used by Muslim rulers to consolidate their power against rivals as Aurangzeb, the Mughal prince and later emperor, did in his bid for power against his brothers; or such a cry was raised by religious leaders against a Muslim ruler who seemed to be too accommodating of Hindus as was Akbar, the Mughal emperor, renowned for his openness to all faiths in his empire.[104]

Once Pakistan was attained, the demand for an Islamic state also meant to keep the country "pure" and uncontaminated by alien impurities. The anti-Ahmadiyya movement was indicative of this mind-set, and eventually the Ahmadis were declared non-Muslims. The same sort of thinking went into describing one group of Muslims being ethnically purer than another on the basis of geographical location or origin, of ethnicity being close to or distant from Arab lands. In this scheme of purity and impurity, the faith of Bengalis was held suspect since their language was Sanskrit in origin and did not belong to the family of languages, Arabic-Persian-Urdu, considered Islamic, and the ethnogeography of Bengali Muslims was furthest in the Indian subcontinent from Arab lands.[105] Hence the military campaign in East Pakistan was justified by Pakistani authorities in religious and racial terms, that the faith of Bengali Muslims was Salim Mansur 83 doubtful since they were converts from Hinduism, and they were racially inferior as a people to those Pakistanis who claimed belonging to the martial races as descendants of Arabs, Persians, Turks and Afghans.[106]

The violence surrounding the effort to make Pakistan an Islamic state, whether initiated by religious parties challenging the authority of those who viewed themselves as heirs to Jinnah's quest to make the country a modern nation-state, or resulting from the effort of those in power as in the case of General Zia ul-Haq's program of Islamization, is indicative of an absence of consensus on what is meant by an Islamic state. One of the most fascinating records of probing into the thinking of those demanding an Islamic state is provided in the *Report of the Court of Inquiry into the Punjab Disturbances of 1953*, also known as the *Munir Report* after Justice Munir who headed the inquiry. The Court of Inquiry engaged in questioning all the leading religious leaders involved in the agitation against the Ahmadis, and in its Report concluded that on the question of what constitutes an Islamic state, of how it would be instituted and governed, there existed much confusion among those who were its most determined proponents. Justice Munir wrote: "If there is one thing which has been conclusively demonstrated in this inquiry, it is that provided you can persuade the masses to believe that something they are asked to do is religiously right or enjoined by religion, you can set them to any course of action, regardless of all considerations of discipline, loyalty, decency, morality or civic sense." These words were remarkably prescient of things to come in Pakistan, and elsewhere in the Muslim world.

How are we to explain Muslim violence against Muslims within the framework of Islam and Muslim history? The task is not difficult, but there is peril in pursuing such an explanation. The task of re-reading Muslim history, especially the earliest years of the post-Prophetic period, is not one of retrospectively reading our standards into what was narrated in the formative period, but finding clues in that narrative to explain the subsequent development of Muslim politics into our time. The peril in this endeavour is in running afoul of those Muslims, a great majority, who view the history of early Islam and Muslims as sacred and closed to any further interpretation apart from that provided by Muslims most proximate to that period.

But the earliest narrators of Arab-Muslim history were not reluctant to record events surrounding the lives of the Prophet and his companions and of the difficulties and conflicts encountered in their effort to establish Islam among their people. These narrators – most notable among them, for instance, are Ibn Ishaq (d. 761), Bukhari (d. 870), Muslim (d. 875) and al-Baladhuri (d. *c.* 892) – provided the raw material for those who came later and sought to systematize the historical record and provide commentaries of their own on the earliest developments of Arab-Muslim history and Islamic civilization. The voluminous writings of al-Tabari (d. 923) remain an unequal resource for all subsequent historians – for instance, the celebrated philosopher of history, Ibn Khaldun (1332-1406) – in their efforts to understand and interpret the formative period of Islam between 632, the year of the Prophet's demise in Medina, and 680, the year of the martyrdom of Husayn (the Prophet's grandson) at Karbala in Iraq.

The record of this earliest period of Arab-Muslim history is troubling to most Muslims, and the best they can do is gloss over it, remain silent, or offer no judgment. But without unraveling the record of this period and making an effort to critically understand what it tells us, Muslims will remain stuck in apologetics or, worse, denial. The recent work of Wilferd Madelung, based on the earliest available records and later commentaries, in analyzing the violent nature of the succession struggle that followed the demise of the Prophet is a most welcome effort in shedding light on that period with tools of modern historiography.[107]

The history of Pakistan is indicative of the causes of Muslim violence against Muslims. In the first instance there is the appropriation of religion for politics, of bending faith for power, and then the rest follows. In the ascribing of ethnicity in politics we may note the flavour of tribalism; in the arguments over purity of faith among Muslims we may discern the custom of establishing genealogical connections among believers of their respective closeness and distance to the Prophet; and in the securing or denial of authority to rule we find the appeal to Islam and the preparedness to use violence against opponents as the one constant theme of politics in Muslim history right from the beginning of the post-Prophetic period.

The Prophet of Islam's death was barely announced when the struggle to succeed him as the temporal leader of a community defined by faith emerged among his followers. Muhammad had renewed the faith of Abraham in One God among Arabs of the desert. In the process of rekindling the faith of Abraham to be known as Islam, Muhammad had established a state and made of Muslims a political community.

While returning to Medina from his farewell pilgrimage to the *ka'aba* in Mecca, Muhammad addressed his followers for the last time and told them, as narrated by Ibn Ishaq, the earliest biographer of the Prophet from the 8th century, "Know that every Muslim is a Muslim's brother, and that the Muslims are brethren." The message was unambiguous, that Islam had cut loose the tribal bonds of the age of ignorance (*jahiliyya*) and replaced them by a new fraternity of a universal faith. Then he halted at a place called Ghadir al-Khumm and taking Ali, his cousin and son-in-law by hand, he gathered all his companions and prayed, "O God, be the friend of him who is his friend, and the foe of him who is his foe." Once again the message was clear, that the Prophet was indicating to his followers his affection for the one he considered to be nearest to him and that he felt the need to make a public show of this affection because of some dissatisfaction towards Ali he had observed. Then some time later in Medina the Prophet fell ill, requested Abu Bakr to lead the public prayers in his place, his illness took a turn for the worse and he died while being tended by his wife A'isha.

Right at the beginning of the post-Prophetic period in the history of Islam and Muslims there was a fork on the road, and the manner in which the path to go ahead was chosen by electing Abu Bakr as the successor of the Messenger of God, *Khalifat Rasul Allah*, was burdened with grief and discontent. The events at the portico of the Banu Sa'idah – where the *Ansars*, Helpers, who had welcomed the Prophet to their midst in Medina when he fled from Mecca into exile, made a bid for electing one of their own to authority and then were defeated by the claims made by Umar and Abu Bakr on behalf of the *Muhajiruns*, Emigrants from Mecca, that appointed Abu Bakr as the *khalif* – laid the seeds of Muslim violence against Muslims by dividing the community of believers the Prophet had brought together.

An axiom of Muslim belief is that the Prophet's life is a resplendent example for believers to emulate. It means taking every aspect of the Prophetic conduct as a lesson to be reflected upon and followed. During his lifetime all the wars the Prophet engaged in were between believers put under duress by nonbelievers, and he set the modality of settling differences among believers through consultation and mediation. He consulted widely among his companions, and the message of Islam forbade a believer from killing another believer at the risk of eternal damnation as a punishment for the transgressor. He united Arabs of the desert under his divinely guarded leadership, yet the question remains: was this unity the foundation for a state as we understand it – of authority in Islam representing the joining of religion and politics (*din wa siyasa*) as it was constructed in the post-Prophetic period by his immediate successors – or was this unity a unique function of the Prophet limited to his person. The striving of his successors to emulate him in authority could only be emulation, and not an article of faith for posterity. Moreover, there is the tantalizing possibility that the Prophet indicated the realm of religious quest for God stands physically apart from the realm of politics by his decision to return to Medina after the conquest of Mecca, instead of establishing Mecca – the City of God and the spiritual centre of Islam – as the political centre of Islam by once again taking residence in the city of his birth and of his ancestors.

During the first fifty years of the post-Prophetic period in Muslim history, bracketed by the events in the portico of Banu Sa'idah even as the Prophet awaited burial (632) and the brutal killing of Husayn, son of Ali and the grandson of the Prophet from his daughter Fatimah at Karbala in Iraq (680), the template of Muslim politics that remains dominant in practice was fashioned.

In this period the extraordinary departure took place from what was forbidden and scrupulously followed during the lifetime of the Prophet, the ban on Muslim violence against Muslims. There followed the wars or campaigns against apostasy; the first civil war after the murder of Uthman, the third *khalif*; the disputed leadership of Ali, the fourth *khalif*, and his murder; the political triumph of the clan of the Abdu Shams to which Abu Sufyan belonged, over the clan of Hashim, to which the Prophet belonged; the transformation of a consensus-based leadership of the Muslim community into a Roman-Byzantine type dynastic rule, and its most significant first victims were Husayn and his family, the direct descendants of the Prophet.

All of this took place even as the message of the Prophet, Islam, was glorified and the physical boundaries of Islam were rapidly extended beyond the confines of Arabia into Palestine and Syria, into Africa, and into Persia. But there was a huge disconnect between the expansion of Islam and the evolving nature of leadership among Muslims. The tribe prevailed over the fragile bonds of fraternity based on faith that the Prophet spoke about in his farewell message, and what emerged and became consolidated over the years was politics of the tribe. The fusion of religion and politics was in effect having religion provide legitimacy to tribal authority. Rulership over Muslims required reference to Islam; consequently, there emerged an "official" Islam legitimating function of the tribal ruler and, inevitably, an "Islam" of the opponents of those in power.

Muslims in general have refused to critically examine this period to understand how the evolution of their history was shaped by events of those fifty years. Instead a culture of denial took shape, and the majority of Muslims have continued to live in a traditional world of politics where tribal instincts of clan solidarity prevail and politics is predominantly a calculus of honour-shame that binds one clan, one tribe, one nation against another. In tribal politics an individual's worth is inconsequential, and the highest regard is placed for maintaining the collective reputation of the tribe in respect to other tribes. This politics of denial and group solidarity that allowed the murder of Husayn and his family go unanswered might be labeled as the Karbala Syndrome.

Ibn Khaldun wrote his penetrating works on the philosophy of history some 700 years after Karbala. In *Al-Muqaddimah* he offered his theory of *'asabiya* (group solidarity) to explain the rise and fall of Arab dynasties. In Aziz Al-Azmeh's reading of Ibn Khaldun there is a teleological destiny of *'asabiya* to establish rule of the group, the clan, the tribe over others: "the subjugation to its will of an ever-widening circle of groups with a progressively more obscure and higher tie of kin to the central group which is exercising leadership, a subjugation as if by suction into a vortex whose centre is progressively elevated from headship to kingship to the state."[108] This is a fine description of the *'asabiya* that surrounded Saddam Hussein and his Tikriti clan that squeezed Iraq and its people for all their worth.

In Ibn Khaldun's view the transformation of the office of the successors to the Prophet, the *khalifat*, into kingship occurred as a natural decline in the quality of faith among believers and the compensating increase of *'asabiya*. Ibn Khaldun wrote: "A change became apparent only in the restraining influence that had been Islam and now came to be group feeling and the sword...Then, the characteristic traits of the caliphate disappeared, and only its name remained. The form of government came to be royal authority pure and simple."[109] The Quran is, however, categorical about the nature of faith among the Arabs of the desert (49:14). The Quran declared that the desert Arabs merely submitted to the reality of power, since faith had not penetrated into their hearts.

Those among believers who understood Islam as an inner journey towards God gradually distanced themselves from the world of power and politics. They came to be known as *sufi* by reference to their simple garments of wool (*suf*), and through their efforts Islam was carried deep into the lands of Asia and Africa.[110] The spread of Islam in India, for instance, was more the work of the *sufi* orders than men who wielded swords.

The nature of rulership that emerged in the early post-Prophetic period, despite the terribly bloody history of the first fifty years following the demise of Muhammad, became the norm for all later generations of Muslims. Islam became politicized and corrupted to serve the needs of rulers unaccountable to Muslims, except those whose support was essential in the maintenance of *'asabiya*. A politicized Islam became a prescription for Muslim violence against Muslims. The history of Pakistan is indicative of this problem persisting into modern times.

The Karbala Syndrome prevents Muslims from confronting their unpleasant past, and this, in turn, prevents them from reforming their group behaviour so as not to repeat the errors of the past. Reform hinges on a critical understanding of the past, but the Karbala Syndrome is the group behaviour of denying the unpleasantness of the past, of escaping responsibility for history by blaming others.

In the years since 1971, no official effort of any public sort has been made in Pakistan to explain and understand the reasons for the break up of a country, nor any official apology have been given to the people of Bangladesh for the atrocities committed by the Pakistani military and its surrogates. The refusal to publicly acknowledge the events of 1971 is indicative of the Karbala Syndrome at work in the Pakistani society. The far more consequential harm to politics in the country from such practice of group denial is the continuing inability of the people to reform their society in keeping with the demands of the modern world.

In conclusion, Muslim violence against Muslims is a symptom of politics whose origins might be traced back to the earliest years of the history of Islam and Muslims. This history became a closed cycle of group solidarity and tribal politics, and its victims continue to be Muslims. An escape from this history is possible if Muslims can imagine what the alternative history of Islam and Muslims might have been if the successors to the Prophet had chosen a different path than the one that led from the portico of Banu Sa'idah to Karbala.

10

A Sufi saint's response to Khomeini

North America has provided a haven to Muslims from all corners of the world. Here in the United States and Canada Muslim immigrants find a secure and free environment to prosper while maintaining their faith-tradition. Indeed, North America is the real and grander version of the Muslim nostalgia for al-Andalus, or Moorish Spain, prior to the Christian re-conquest of the peninsular Iberia towards the end of the fifteenth century. Muslims view Spain once under Arab-Muslim rule as the lost ideal of Islamic civilization that tended towards some mix of what in contemporary times has come to be promoted in the West as multiculturalism. Yet that ideal, irrespective of how much of it was real and how much of it myth-making, never got copied even remotely in any of the independent Muslim country since the end of European colonialism at the midpoint of the last century.

The inability or unwillingness of Muslim immigrants to embrace the United States and Canada where they settled as their al-Andalus, and giving their adopted countries unreserved loyalty and devotion, never entered into public discussion or became a matter of reproach against Muslims before the events of September 11, 2001. But even as North Americans came to learn the extent to which some Muslims nurtured ill-will toward their adopted countries, and some proceeded to plan or engage in acts of war as did those nineteen Arab-Muslim men in hijacking airplanes and flying them into buildings in New York and Washington, there was no official policy adopted by governments to place Muslims under surveillance, or to abridge their rights as citizens of free and open societies.

The "war on terror", or more properly speaking, the war against radical Islam or Islamism, puts Muslims on notice. As this war unfolds and becomes increasingly ugly, as atrocities mount, as terrorism through suicide-bombings spread fear and havoc amidst the civilian population in the West, there will be declining tolerance for Muslims reluctant to publicly dissociate themselves from politics in their home countries and less acceptance of Muslim apologetics. North Americans have shown incredible patience in the face of insults and threats directed against them by Muslims who are generally considered to be a small band of fanatics, and they have maintained the widely held view that Islam is one of the great monotheistic religions that should not be judged in terms of how Muslim fanatics abuse it. This generous display of reason and tolerance has limits, and as the war against Islamists continues the limit will be reached. Then anger of the majority of North Americans may quickly turn into negative assessment and condemnation of Islam, and for Muslims this continent as al-Andalus may become unwelcoming to their presence. Such a scenario is hypothetical, perhaps also improbable. Muslims nevertheless bear great responsibility in recognizing, acknowledging and keeping safe North America as al-Andalus, and this requires an unreserved display of genuine affection for and loyalty to their adopted countries.

The situation Muslims find themselves in North America was not entirely unforeseen. Muslim immigrants, unlike the earlier traffic of immigrants from Europe to the United States and Canada including Jews, come from outside of the cultural matrix of North America and the western civilization. Muslims are outsiders in North America, though not alone in this respect. But unlike, for instance, Hindus from India or from Indian communities in Africa and the Caribbean basin, Muslims in general have seen themselves in an uneasy relationship with the West. This is due in part to the manner in which Muslims view their faith-tradition, derive their identity from it, invest in its public glorification, and increasingly see the public profession of their faith as an expression of their politics that reinforces their ties with the countries of their origin while preventing them from unconditionally embracing their adopted countries. Daniel Pipes, an astute observer of Muslims in North America, has noted,

> Muslims are confident that they have the best religion...Far from being embarrassed about Islam being temporally the last of the

> three major Middle Eastern monotheisms, Muslims believe that their faith not only preceded Judaism and Christianity but also improves on both. They see Judaism and Christianity as but defective variants of Islam, God's final, perfected religion. This inner sense of confidence helped imbue Muslims with an unparalleled loyalty to their religion.[111]

This confidence of Muslims in their religion that frowns upon any critical assessment of Islam and Muslim history can lend itself to chauvinism and hostility towards non-Muslims and Muslims. Such development among Muslims has been frequent, and while practitioners of other faith-traditions have also shown similar traits in certain moments of their history, Muslims have displayed an unusually high incidence of militancy in their practice of Islam. Muslim history is riveted with tension, often bursting into great violence, between those who take Islam to be an inner journey of individual seekers of truth[112] and those who demand the practice of Islam is inseparable from the politics of the community and its Salim Mansur 91 proclaimed leader. The seekers of knowledge and union with truth take to heart the verse of the Quran declaring "there is no compulsion in religion."[113] Others, the majority among Muslims, irrespective of which of the two branches – Sunni Muslims being the majority, and Shi'i Muslims being the minority – of Islam they adhere to, take for their guidance the verse of the Quran stating "obey God, and obey the messenger and those of you who are in authority."[114]

The dominant, official and institutionalized face of Islam from its earliest history in the post-Prophetic period following the demise of Muhammad, the founder of the religion, in 632 C.E. is politicized religion. Even though there is no Vatican-type centre in Islam the codified body of Islamic laws, derived from the Qur'an and the *hadith* literature of the Prophetic tradition during the classical period of the first three centuries of Islam by religious scholars under the authority of power-holders when Islam emerged as the religion of the ruling elite of a rapidly expanding empire, became the *de facto* and *de jure* centre of Islam. This closed system of Islamic laws known as the *shari'ah* – Sunni and Shi'i schools or branches of Islam while maintaining their differences in terms of interpretations and the mechanics of interpretation of this system agree on its existential validity[115] – has provided Muslims with a sense of religious-political centre binding them into a separate corporate entity and placing them apart from non-Muslims.

Muslims take Islam to mean peace that comes from the surrender or submission to God (*Allah* in Arabic). Ignaz Goldziher, the Hungarian Orientalist and possibly the most sensitive, if not the greatest, non-Muslim exponent of Islam provided the following explanation:

> *Islam* means submission, the believer's submission to Allah. The word expresses, first and foremost, a feeling of dependency on an unbounded omnipotence to which man must submit and resign his will. It expresses, better than any other, Muhammad's idea of the relation between the believer and the object of his worship. Submission is the dominant principle inherent in all manifestations of Islam: in its ideas, forms, ethics, and worship. Submission is the distinguishing feature that determines the specific character of the education of man that Islam intends to accomplish. Islam is the most cogent example for Schleiermacher's thesis that religion is rooted in a sense of dependency.[116]

But Islam as a politicized religion has come to mean in practice that *submission* to God demanded and coercively enforced by power-holders arrogating to themselves the authority to speak in the name of Islam, and supported by religious scholars as keepers and enforcers of *shari'ah*, is of an entirely different nature than the *voluntary* submission of those who believe in God. The political reality of the Muslim world is one of fragmented power, of power-holders as rivals, and this reality has made itself felt on Muslims as a corporate entity; power-holders have demanded with the support of religious scholars within their political realm that submission to God as an act of faith be consistent with submission and acknowledgement of those who rule. The culture of Islam has been shaped by this political arrangement masquerading as religion wherein Muslims accept as a given that in Islam religion and politics are inseparable. The result of such an understanding of Islam places those Muslims who are in a minority situation among a non-Muslim majority, as in North America, in a quandary when the demands of religion and the requirements of politics are at odds.

The largest portion of Muslims residing in North America (also in Europe) happens to be economic migrants. They left their home countries in search of economic prosperity which they more or less secured by arriving in the United States and Canada. But in terms of their psychology, these Muslim immigrants did not cut their emotional ties with their native lands and their adopted countries did not make such demand. This arrangement works well so long Muslims are not required by events, or by elements within their immigrant communities, to indicate publicly where their political loyalties belong in keeping with their faith and culture. The events of September 11, 2001 and after have placed Muslims under immense pressure of indicating where their loyalties reside; is it with political leaders and majority opinion in their adopted countries, or in supporting politics of their native lands where radical Islam, or Islamism, has declared war on the West?

In 1992 John Esposito, an American academic, posed the question whether Islam was a threat to the West.[117] The answer Esposito provided was that despite the long-standing rivalry and conflict between Islam and Christianity, there was no basis for Islam and the West to be threatening to each other in the contemporary world. Esposito described the internal upheavals in Muslim lands through the second half of the last century as an integral part of reform and renewal within Islam, and he viewed this process as distinct from the response of Muslims in the struggle for independence from European colonialism. David Pryce-Jones, an English writer and observer of the Middle East, offered a contrary view.[118] Pryce-Jones indicated,

> The primary characteristic of the custom of the Islamic world is a social and political order that endows a ruler with absolute power. Power-sharing is excluded and, as a result, sophisticated institutions cannot be formed to permit the peaceful mediation of conflicting interests.[119]

The result of Muslim world's internal dysfunction bred hostility among Muslims, and this pushed Islam into unavoidable conflict with the West. A reform of Islam would require Muslims to work out an arrangement for themselves that followed or imitated the reform of Christianity separating religion and politics, and eventually such reform would bring Muslims into harmonious relationship with the non-Muslim world.

But the Muslim world was seized less by reformist zeal than spreading militancy as Muslim societies stalled in their developmental efforts. Militant Muslims spread their message of being in a state of siege in the modern world, and that what was needed for Muslims to succeed was a complete repudiation of the West by returning to the original impulse of Islam untarnished by any un-Godly attributes of non-Muslim and un-Islamic cultures. Repudiation necessitated waging war against the West and its agents among Muslims in Muslim lands. The fury of Muslim militants got displayed on September 11, 2001.[120] For some time before this fury exploded in the attacks on New York and Washington, Muslim militants took to arms declaring *jihad* (war) against infidels of the West and their allies, the Jewish state of Israel and the Hindu-majority state of India. The waging of war, Muslim militants preached, had spread Islam beyond the primitive confines of the Arabian deserts, and so once again by raising the alarum for *jihad* they felt release from the frustration of watching the non-Muslim West taking a commanding lead in every aspect of civilization over the Muslim world. Militant Muslims viewed *jihad* would turn out to be the great equalizer by forcing the West into playing defence, by reorganizing Muslim societies along Islamic principles sullied through defeats suffered during the period of colonial rule by European powers of Muslim lands, by reclaiming Muslim territories such as Palestine and Kashmir under non-Muslim control, and even holding forth the possibility of spreading Islamic power beyond Muslim lands into Europe and North America as a repeat of the great Muslim conquests during the early centuries of Islam.

Islam may not be a threat to the West as John Esposito counseled, or to America as Daniel Pipes suggested, but radical or militant Islam is another matter. The Islamic revolution of 1979 in Iran led by Shi'ite clerics with Ayatollah Khomeini at their head occurred on the eve of Islam's fifteenth century, and it marked the seizure of political power by militant Muslims of a country strategically located at the heart of the Arab-Muslim world in the Middle East. Iran's Islamic revolution was uncompromisingly anti-West, anti-United States and anti-Israel. Khomeini dubbed the United States for its meddling in Iranian affairs since the Second World War as the "Great Satan" and Israel as the "Little Satan." In November 1979 revolutionary students swearing loyalty to Khomeini seized American diplomats at the U.S. embassy in Tehran and held them as hostages for over a year until the January 1981 inauguration of Ronald Reagan as the 40th President of the United

States. Iranians declared the American hostages were spies. Khomeini in his public speeches concurred with the students, and in his statement addressed to Muslim pilgrims gathered for the annual pilgrimage to Mecca in September 1980 declared,

> America is the number one enemy of the deprived and oppressed people of the world. There is no crime America will not commit in order to maintain its political, economic, cultural, and military domination of those parts of the world where it predominates…Let the Muslim nations be aware that Iran is a country effectively at war with America, and that our martyrs – the brave young men of our army and the Revolutionary Guards – are defending Iran and the Islam we hold dear against America.[121]

The Islamic revolution in Iran seized the imagination of a generation of Muslims come of age since the end of European colonialism and yearning for a dramatic engagement with their history in the name of Islam. Iran offered a model to the Muslim world of revolutionary change that took for its inspiration and guidance Muslim history viewed from the Shi'ite perspective of resistance and martyrdom. Muslim warriors traveled to Afghanistan during the decade after the Iranian revolution to wage war against the Soviet occupation of that landlocked Muslim country of immense poverty, and they would claim victory for Islam by forcing the withdrawal of the Soviet Union before its eventual collapse. Radical Islam was on the march and militant Muslims felt invincible.

But there are currents of opinions within Islam that question or do not take kindly the preaching of radical Muslims. The *Time* magazine in its issue of April 28, 1980 published a piece under the heading "Is the Ayatullah a Heretic?" The *Time*'s article was a report of what Muslim scholars and leaders were stating about the hostage crisis in Iran in terms of the traditional teachings of Islam, and among those cited there was the opinion of one that stood out sharply in being critical of the Iranian leader. The *Time* reported,

> When the Iranians understand the Koran, states Sri Lanka's ascetic M.R. Bawa Muhaiyaddeen, a teacher in the mystical Sufi movement, now living in Philadelphia, "they will release the hostages immediately." Muhaiyaddeen has sent Khomeini three

fervent epistles, urging him to free the captives and repent of his vengeance lest Islam be further disgraced before the world.

The epistles of Bawa Muhaiyaddeen to Khomeini, which the *Time* mentioned, were unusually strong and condemnatory letters from one Muslim religious leader to another. Bawa Muhaiyaddeen was not merely a simple and humble teacher of mystical Islam as he presented himself to the public at large who gathered around him and as the *Time* reported; he was a charismatic Sufi saint blessed with a remarkable gift of communicating the message of Islam in harmony with the ancient and esoteric wisdom of other great religions and prophets named in the sacred texts of the East. He was of an uncertain age when he arrived in the United States from Jaffna, Sri Lanka in 1971 on invitation of young American seekers of truth, and settled in Philadelphia. He died in 1986, his tomb is located in a quiet farm some miles outside of Philadelphia, and his message lives on through the work of the fellowship he founded in North America.

Bawa Muhaiyaddeen told his story allegorically in a book titled *The Tree That Fell To The West.*[122] In this story he likened himself, or the message he brought to North America, as fruit of the tree that once a long time ago was planted in the East. In time this tree decayed from within as a result of being untended and abused by people to whom it provided food and shade, and crashed with its top half bearing fruits landing in the West. In this allegory Muslims are people in the East caught in an endless quarrel of their own making over the dried and withered trunk of once life-nourishing tree of Islam, while new seeds from fruits of this same tree have taken roots in the West. He indicated in his discourses a renaissance of Islam and Muslims could only occur in modern times in a place where freedom is enshrined and protected by the rule of law. It was this belief that set him on his journey to the United States in the final chapter of his life. His mission was to bring the message of Islam as one of peace to Americans as much as awaken in Muslims an understanding of the centrality of the United States in the providential design for a worldwide spiritual renewal in a new millennium that followed the opening of a new Islamic century.

Bawa Muhaiyaddeen taught how to live in accordance with the teachings of Islam.[123] The main thrust of his teachings was acquiring the right conduct of love, charity, humility and knowledge through submission to God. He demonstrated what inclusiveness means when Muslims embrace those around them without distinction or discrimination in keeping with God's message:

> To each of you We have given a law and a pattern of life. If Allah had pleased He could surely have made you one people (professing one faith). But He wished to try and test you by that which He gave you. So try to excel in good deeds. To Him will you return in the end, when He will tell you of what you were at variance.[124]

It was providential that Bawa Muhaiyaddeen was residing in Philadelphia when the revolution in Iran broke out and the crisis over the taking of U.S. diplomats as hostages unfolded. In his public statements and in his letters to Khomeini he held out the face of the other Islam, of those who are lovers and seekers of truth, and not beholden to power-holders. Here are a few extracts from the letters of Bawa Muhaiyaddeen to Khomeini:

> [November 30, 1979]...You are in Islam and we are in Islam, but Islam has now become a disgraced word in the world. In the current state of affairs we feel we must write this letter...No one should rule with the arrogance of a dictator...The Shah, as a political figure, could have done this for political gains. But you were given the designation of Imam Ayatollah... so there should be a vast difference between the two of you.
>
> [December 11, 1979]...Imam Ayatollah Khomeini, I feel compelled to write this because I see that your actions are pointing toward destruction... Please release the hostages immediately... You shout, "*Allahu akbar!*" and you say you are fighting a holy war. This is not the way of Islam. In the days of the Rasulallah (*Sal.*), they fought only in defense of their right to accept Allah. You, on the other hand, fight for the sake of titles, land, gold, and wealth. There is a vast difference between the two.
>
> [March 11, 1980]...You are a sheik, your name is Ayatollah Khomeini, you have the title Ruhullah, you have such a resounding name, but today you have destroyed the splendor of Islam...you had better acquire a little understanding of what Islam is, quickly. You are not the only one who is Islamic, and the thirty-five million people in your country are not the only people who are Islamic.

> There are approximately eight hundred million Islamic people in the world, and Islam goes beyond that. People in all countries are listening to what you say. Since you came to power, not one word of yours or your revolutionary council has been the truth...What difference is there between you and the shah?...What you are doing is a great disgrace to Islam and to all religions...You must stop all this shouting and howling immediately...You have to honor your word, protect the honor of the Quran, of *sabur*, *shukur* and *tawakkul*, of the three thousand gracious qualities of God, of unity and brotherhood. That is Islam – behaving honorably... but none of your actions now are even approximately related to Islam.[125]

While writing to Khomeini, Bawa Muhaiyaddeen also at the same time addressed a few letters to Americans and to Muslims in America. Here are a couple of extracts from those letters:

> [February 6, 1980]...Since its beginning 200 years ago, America has emerged as a great nation...Every person in this country must realize this in his or her heart. Each must realize that the praise of a country is the praise of its people, the danger which comes to a country is a danger to its people...Why? Because all of you have a right to your own wealth, you have a right to speech, and you have a right to vote...None of these things would be available to you if you lived in a Communist country...Everyone in this country must reflect: What is freedom?

> [March 25, 1980]...This country is called the United States. Those who experienced difficulties and danger in their own countries came together here...Everyone who comes here has the right to live, the right to freedom, the right to vote...People have many rights in the United States. Even so, some are more eager to help their ancestral countries when those countries are in danger...The name United States exists on the outside, but many people do not have a bond to the United States in their hearts...Everyone who has come to this country and everyone who was born in this country must reflect...There are people who do not protect the dignity and freedom of this country, who nevertheless feel they have to protect their ancestral countries. This is a wonder, is it not? They can safeguard their own races, religions, and scriptures, but they cannot safeguard America...I first came to this country from Sri Lanka

> approximately ten years ago... I have partaken of the water and... the food of America, and it has become part of my body, my blood vessels, and my nerves. I am grateful for that, and I am grateful for having a place to stay.[126]

These words of Bawa Muhaiyaddeen were prescient. In his public letters to Khomeini, the Sufi saint rebuked the Iranian leader for perverting the message of Islam, and reminded him the splendor of Islam is inseparable from the conduct of Muslims as people in peace within themselves and with the world around them through their voluntary submission to God. And in letters to Americans and Muslims making home in the United States, the Sufi saint reminded them of the importance of being grateful and of publicly demonstrating this gratitude in return for receiving benefits of a free society, and to treasure freedom as the necessary condition for acquiring peace that is the same as living in Islam. In the post-9/11 world of Islamist politics Bawa Muhaiyaddeen's words and example offer Muslims an exit out of the black hole of their failed societies run by corrupt and tyrannical power-holders and perpetrators of Islamist terror.

11

Keeping faith in the age of Islamist terror

The world at the time when the Berlin Wall was torn down in November 1989 seems to be greatly removed from the world where we have arrived at in the early years of the third millennium. There was much anticipation of a New World Order then as the Berlin Wall got demolished and a divided Europe was once again joined together. We had survived a century of global wars, of megadeaths and the fear of mutual assured destruction (MAD) if our leaders were foolish enough to engage in a nuclear war. It was a century that future historians, if they are fortunate to have a functioning world in which to live and write and make love and prosper, may well describe as a "mad" century that survived human folly through sheer good fortune.

The tearing down of the Berlin Wall and all that it represented suggested, in the words of Vaclav Havel who would go on to be elected president of the new Czech Republic, "History has accelerated."127 And at the time there was a sense of rising excitement which seemed to ride the slipstream of history in acceleration, the giddying thrill catching hold of people witnessing and being a part of politics shaped by democratic ideals widely cherished. Mikhail Gorbachev, the Communist leader of the former Soviet Union, called for *glasnost* and *perestroika*, for an opening and thawing of politics and human relationships put in the deep freeze during the Cold War years, and a restructuring of the Soviet system; but the Soviet empire that Stalin built on a mountain of lies and human bones could not survive the reformist touch of Gorbachev, and it disintegrated before our eyes.

Amidst this expectation of history accelerating for the good, there were setbacks as warning of the perils that lurked ahead. There was the Gulf War, and Saddam Hussein holding his court in Baghdad was a reminder of the readily forgotten fact that evil persists and the journey out of the valley of tears is strewn with the burden of the sins of omission and commission. Then there were the Balkan wars, ethnic cleansing on the European continent fifty years after the Holocaust, Rwandan genocide and mounting casualties of local conflicts and regional wars from Indonesia to West Africa reminding us in the West that we cannot seal ourselves in comfort from the agony of the world beyond our seas. There were also indicators that sustained our frail optimism. The Madrid Conference in 1991 for the Middle East laid the ground for the Oslo Accord of 1993 between Israelis and Palestinians, and Northern Ireland showed signs of bringing to an end generational conflict between Protestants and Catholics. But in the final months of the 20th century our horizon darkened even as we continued to believe the promises we held for ourselves were secure, and the new millennium would open doors to the New Word Order of unlimited possibilities given our technological and scientific abilities to find answers. We had landed man on the moon, mapped our solar system as we did with the inner structure of an atom, vanquished diseases and decoded the book of life, cloned sheep and resisted cloning man only out of our own obsolete sensibilities as we pretended to become, in Freud's words, "a kind of prosthetic God."[128]

Then we witnessed the events of September 11, 2001. On a bright, autumnal morning evil struck leaving New York and Washington savagely wounded, the gaping charred holes where the Twin Towers of the World Trade Center stood reminding us, as Shakespeare would, about "the evil that men do" and which a great many of us would prefer not to know. We are now caught in the mesh of a war not of our making, yet the consequences of this war will be with us for a long time as our optimism in the future to make our world a more prosperous, more democratic and more peaceful place has been greatly undermined.

There is an inscription from an ancient temple wall in India which reads, "Coincidences, if traced far enough back, become inevitable." This inscription is consistent with the teachings of Hinduism about *karma*, the law of cause and effect, and *samsara*, the cycle of life and death. But the inscription might also be read as the distilled wisdom of the ages telling us that the past weighs heavily upon the present, and while evil cannot be excused or air-brushed through apologetics it also cannot be entirely disconnected from the chain of causality binding us together by the law of *karma*.

"Keeping faith" in our world and with our world in the face of evil requires something more than resoluteness in our values, religious or secular, to arm us in defeating evil. It requires openness to the world beyond our immediate surroundings, an embracing of others on the ground that we are incomplete without the other. It requires of us not to lose entirely the sensibilities of our ancestors, of keeping alive within ourselves that capacity to discern in the leaf of a grass or on the face of the moon the signature of God as our Father, as the Lord of Mankind, as the Moving Spirit on Water, as the Jehovah and the eternal Brahman, and these being merely our way of expressing the truth about the Infinite Intelligence that sustains us in our finite form and limited understanding of our sojourn on the planet Earth.

***

In the multitude of voices heard on the subject of peace since the end of the Cold War, there is one voice that stood out. It is the voice of the German Catholic theologian and academic, Hans Kung. In 1990 Kung published a small book appearing the following year in English titled *Global Responsibility*. In it Kung put forward the proposition, "No survival without a world ethic. No world peace without peace between the religions. No peace between the religions without dialogue between the religions."[129] Kung's words were a challenge to all of us, a call to reach deep within ourselves, and ask once again the perennial questions about who we are, where we are headed, what is our responsibility. Kung reminded us that our political world cannot be separated from our religious world, and the most important political questions of our time, or any time, are also religious questions.

But the modern world banished religion from public life. It declared, following Nietzsche, God is dead. The world of *modernity* belonged to science, and its achievements are staggering in altering within a few hundred years the entire edifice of human understanding and explanation of our world and the universe beyond it. Huston Smith, an American scholar of comparative religions, in *Why Religion Matters* explored the relationship of modernity with *tradition* and *postmodernity*. Smith noted that modernity's great achievement was discovery of the controlled experiment, otherwise known as the *scientific method*. Smith writes, "What the controlled experiment adds to generic science is proof. True hypotheses can be separated from false ones, and brick by brick an edifice has been created from those proven truths."[130]

The world of tradition was a world of *metaphysics*, a world in which the big picture or worldview, according to Huston Smith, was central to human understanding of itself and the universe. The answer religion provided – for religion is to tradition what science is to modernity – was to paint a big picture, to construct a worldview, in which the longings of the heart were reconciled with the thinking of the head. This was an "enchanted" world as Max Weber, the great German sociologist, described in which unseen realities were of equal, if not greater, importance than the real world of matter, and the most important of these was God being the greatest unseen reality holding everything together.

The modern world of science made for a "dis-enchanted" world. The world of metaphysics could not be measured, weighed, dissected, probed, or like a watch its inner mechanics pried open and then put back together again by the tools of modern science. It meant the *un*seen was *un*real, and therefore of no importance. The religious imaginings of people got dismissed in the modern world as defective knowledge, and the modern man instructed in science found little use in traditional metaphysics.

The modern man emptied himself of his heart, and placed all the weight of his existence on his head. Modernity opened a chasm between the head and the heart, between the world of *facts* and the world of *values*. He took pride in his knowledge of matter and his ability to manipulate matter to his needs and desire, and this filled him with the sense, as Freud wrote, of being god-like. And yet, Freud observed, the "present-day man does not feel happy in his Godlike character."[131] The reason is simple; happiness and unhappiness is not merely a state of the mind, or a matter of intellect, but also a condition of the heart and a matter of feeling. Emptying of the heart was thus limiting human capacity to feel, to be alive to the knowledge of the world and beyond *intuitively*. The modern scientific man, the prosthetic God, can decipher nature, but he is numb to the feelings aroused in the hearts of his ancestors as they beheld in awe the wonder of nature. William Blake expressed this wonder as only poets may:

> To see a World in a Grain of Sand
> And a Heaven in a Wild Flower,
> Hold Infinity in the palm of your hand
> And Eternity in an hour.

Max Weber described the condition of the modern man scathingly. Weber wrote about modern men being "Specialists without spirit, sensualists without heart; this nullity imagines that it has attained a level of civilization never before achieved."[132]

***

In banishing religion from public life modernity corrupted politics by insisting only facts which can be subjected to the scientific method are real and of importance. It came to mean that in the world of politics *power* measured in terms of hard, tangible assets and capabilities took precedence, and the pursuit and cultivating of power distinguished a successful "prince." This was "real politics" or *realpolitik* in German, "power politics," "geopolitics," or *realism* as variously labeled to distinguish it from the "unreal politics" of those who decried power and of those who held to some *ideal* view of politics which did not rely on the scientific method to buttress its validity.

Realism is not a flawed or evil ideology masquerading as science, and realist thinkers are not proponents of evil. But the smell of death from the concentration camps and gulags of the last century informs us that realists bear responsibility in sowing dragon seeds, and the result is the raging of monsters in our midst doing evil.

The flaw at the heart of realism is moral blindness. Our ideas of freedom, equality, human rights, justice are derived from a moral view of the world and our place in it. Philosophers and scientists did not independently arrive at this moral view; it has been provided to us through religious teachings and, hence, its origin is outside of human experience and history. The traditional world understood and affirmed the connection of moral ideas with religious teachings. This world has been left behind. We cannot bracket modernity and return to tradition. We need to embrace both in our forward journey. The *postmodern* world, as Huston Smith suggests, is concerned with individual and social *justice* issues since the defining characteristic and focus of *postmodernity* deal with *society*.[133]

The postmodern concern with and search for justice cannot be met adequately solely with the tools of modernity, or the scientific method. The issue of justice is not merely a legal matter of balancing competing interests, of laying down the rights and wrongs we hold in society even as we stand on shifting grounds of evolving tastes, opinions and knowledge, and of intellectual arguments without reference to any higher authority except ourselves. Justice is equally, if not more, a matter of the heart, of justice seen and done where mercy and compassion are joined together with intellect. There is no justice in the absence of mercy and compassion, and justice derived entirely on the basis of analytical reasoning tends to be display of power unchecked and unaccountable. Shakespeare intuitively understood what justice must mean as he described it in the speech he had Portia deliver in the *Merchant of Venice* thus:

> His scepter shows the force of temporal power,
> The attribute to awe and majesty,
> Wherein doth sit the dread and fear of kings;
> But mercy is above this sceptered sway;
> It is enthroned in the hearts of kings,
> It is an attribute to God himself,
> And earthly power doth then show likest God's
> When mercy seasons justice.

The founding fathers of the American Revolution understood well that ideas of justice, freedom, equality and human rights being moral in substance are religious in origin and derived from a higher principle. These ideas could not be located in terms of origin merely within the faculty of human intellect. It is then not a surprise to read the Declaration of Independence and find its author, Thomas Jefferson, in crafting one of the most important documents of secular authority locate its ground in God and not in the acts of men. Jefferson wrote, "We hold these truths to be self-evident, that all men are created equal, that they are endowed by their Creator with certain unalienable Rights, that among these are Life, Liberty and the pursuit of Happiness." The greatness of the American Revolution was not merely in its democratic impulse, but that this impulse and this well-spring of ideas brought Americans to seek a "more perfect Union," and the words of the Constitution to "establish Justice, insure domestic Tranquility, provide for the common defence, promote the general Welfare, and secure the Blessings of Liberty to ourselves and our Posterity," meant engaging in a deeply religious enterprise with an abiding faith in the goodness and wisdom of God. President Calvin Coolidge speaking in Philadelphia on the occasion marking the 150th anniversary of the Declaration of Independence concluded his address by declaring,

> No other theory is adequate to explain or comprehend the Declaration of Independence. It is the product of the spiritual insight of the people. We live in an age of science and of abounding accumulation of material things. These did not create our Declaration. Our Declaration created them. The things of the spirit come first. Unless we cling to that, all our material prosperity, overwhelming though it may appear, will turn to a barren scepter in our grasp. If we are to maintain the great heritage which has been bequeathed to us, we must be like-minded as the fathers who created it. We must not sink into a pagan materialism. We must cultivate the reverence which they had for the things that are holy. We must follow the spiritual and moral leadership which they showed. We must keep replenished, that they may glow with a more compelling flame, the altar fires before which they worshipped.[134]

It is this religious impulse in the political striving for the ideal of freedom and justice that makes for the positive advancement of society in history. The intellectual challenge in the postmodern world is awakening to this truth and closing the gap between tradition and modernity; it is to acknowledge the limits of the scientific method in politics and the persistent value of the traditional worldview. It is, moreover, to take the words of Hans Kung to heart and act on his advice. On the contrary, remaining dogmatically attached to the assumptions of modernity in the postmodern world with the unfolding of its history that begins with the dismantling of the Berlin Wall is to remain willfully disregarding of how denial of a higher reality makes for a blinkered view of the human condition. In contemplating this situation, Vaclav Havel wrote,

> ...we still don't know how to put morality ahead of politics, science and economics. We are still incapable of understanding that the only genuine core of all our actions – if they are to be moral – is responsibility. Responsibility to something higher than my family, my country, my firm, my success. Responsibility to the order of Being, where all our actions are indelibly recorded and where, and only where, they will be properly judged.[135]

The restoration of religion in public, however, cannot mean simply reinstituting tradition unreconstructed, and uninformed by the gains of modernity. While traditional worldview remains in a certain limited way meaningful, the traditional understanding and practice of religions need reform if religions are to have once again valid and constructive role in politics. We have to rescue Buddha, Jesus and Muhammad from the partisanship of their respective followers and see the world afresh with their eyes if they were walking in our company.

***

I mention here only Buddha, Jesus and Muhammad since their names are readily associated with the three faith-traditions, or religions – Buddhism, Christianity and Islam – which are by doctrine and practice universal in their appeal to all people. Their respective followers see them as the enlightened one, as the divine incarnation, and as the seal of prophets. Their teachings, despite differences in their institutionalized settings, share a common purpose of guiding men and women to overcome suffering, and reconcile life with death through reconciliation with an impersonal higher truth or an eternally living God.

All religions hold life as sacred, for life is viewed as the breath of God and reconciling with God is viewed as acquiring infinite bliss. The ancient and sacred Vedic texts of India speak of this unearthly reality in words of great beauty. In the *Taittiriya Upanishad* we read,

"Who denies God, denies himself. Who affirms God, affirms himself." And further, "Joy comes from God. Who could live and who could breathe if the joy of Brahman filled not the universe?"[136] Then there is the story of Bhrigu Varuni who asked his father to explain the mystery of Brahman, or God. And Bhrigu, as his father advised him to seek out the mystery through prayers and meditations eventually discovered the highest meaning of Brahman. The sacred text narrates, "And then he *saw* that Brahman is joy: for FROM JOY ALL BEINGS HAVE COME, BY JOY THEY ALL LIVE, AND UNTO JOY THEY ALL RETURN…This was the vision of Bhrigu Varuni which came from the Highest; and he who sees this vision lives in the Highest."[137]

Enlightened souls, or prophets and messengers of God, had visions and were sustained by them. Moses's encounter with God as the burning bush is one such example. Buddha's vision under the Bo tree is another. Jesus had his vision while being baptized, of the heavenly doors opening and the "Spirit of God descending like a dove, and lighting upon him." Muhammad's vision lifted him from the precinct of the sacred mosque at great distance from Mecca to the highest heaven and into the presence of God. These visions were transformative, and the bearers of these visions returned experiencing bliss to guide others to the same destination they were privileged to visit.

Different religions are not only different paths to the same eternal truth, they also are different in their grammar of verbalizing the encounter and experience of enlightened souls with God. But these differences while incongruent on the surface cannot subvert the meaning of the eternal truth beheld and related in different languages. Religions are oysters protecting the secret of the encounter of man with God, and with God language becomes superfluous since bliss is in the experience and not in reporting it to others. *Bhagavad Gita* was Mahatma Gandhi's favourite sacred text, and there we find the following explanation of the redundancy of language and grammar when encountering God:

> As unnecessary as a well is
> to a village on the banks of a river,
> so unnecessary are all scriptures
> to someone who has seen the truth.138

The modern man, however, came to detest religions not by disproving the visions of the enlightened souls but by watching the quarrels of their followers. If the visions were of bliss, why did the adherents of the various visions engage in such destructive quarrels as history of religions record? The answer to this ageold question given by Sarvepalli Radhakrishnan, philosopher-politician and the second president of the modern Republic of India, is instructive. He wrote,

> The view that God has entrusted his exclusive revelation to any one prophet, Buddha, Christ, or Mohammad, expecting all others to borrow from him or else to suffer spiritual destitution, is by no means old-fashioned. Nothing is so hostile to religion as other religions. We have developed a kind of patriotism about religion, with a code and a flag, and a hostile attitude towards other men's codes and creeds. The free spirits who have the courage to repudiate the doctrine of chosen races and special prophets and plead for a free exercise of thought about God are treated as outcasts. No wonder that even the sober are sometimes tempted to think that the only way to get rid of religious fear, conceit and hatred is to do away with all religion. The world would be a much more religious place if all religions were removed from it.[139]

Radhakrishnan had it right, and the postmodern world is quite capable of promoting this harmony of "free spirits" embracing the visions of enlightened souls without the rancour and quarrel of those who reduce religions into garments worn by scoundrels as flags. Postmodern emphasis on social justice needs to be rewired to the awareness that justice is a moral idea anchored in religion. An aversion to religion born of the narrow-minded quarrels among men holding to different accounts of the eternal vision as bliss paradoxically ends up in the barrenness of modernity. We are now possibly more acutely aware of the tragic consequences of modernity's politics as realism after having survived the "mad"-ness in the Cold War, and then losing the initial giddiness that came with the dismantling of the Berlin Wall as history accelerated. Hence, we are now possibly more awakened to an understanding that our effort to secure peace with justice cannot bear fruits without a religious vision guiding us. Keeping faith in the post-September 11, 2001 world of terror promoted by men of a particular faith tradition – Islam – means ironically refusing to trash religion, any religion, for that leads to the denial of the vision inherent in that religion and then all religions. Keeping faith then means engagement with all religions as Hans Kung counseled as the requisite for the effort in making and securing peace, since every religion carries in its language the resonance of God's breathe as eternal bliss.

12

A Bedouin state of mind

The port city of Annaba is on the coast of Algeria, near the eastern border with Tunisia. I set out for Annaba with a copy of St. Augustine's *Confessions*, hoping to understand something of Algeria's present – and of the Arab-Muslim world of which it is a part – by making a journey into its past.

The first sight for any traveller approaching Annaba by land or sea is the Cathedral of St. Augustine on top of a hill overlooking the Mediterranean. It was built in the late 19th century by the French, above the ruins of the ancient Roman town still visible after some 2,000 years. Annaba was founded by Phoenicians in the first millennium before the Christian era, and around the third century before Christ it became the favourite city of Numidian rulers allied with Rome against the power of Carthage.

After the Punic wars, when Carthage was destroyed by Rome, Annaba became a Roman city named Hippo Regius and an early centre of Christianity in North Africa. Here Augustine served as bishop from 396 until his death in 430, around the time of the Vandals' siege of Hippo. Some three centuries later, Arabs arrived here, bringing Islam and their language to make North Africa since then a part of the Arab world.

Augustine is Algeria's most famous son, revered by the Catholic Church as one of her pre-eminent thinkers and theologians, yet he's barely remembered today in the land of his birth, where the population is almost entirely Muslim. He was born in 354 in Thagaste, now generally recognized as the town of Souk Ahras south of Annaba. He was canonized by Pope Boniface VIII in 1303 and his work, in particular *The City of God*, continues to provide inspired insights into the human condition afflicted by material desires and spiritual doubts. In *Confessions*, Augustine narrated his journey from Manichaean religion to Christian belief.

Almost exactly 1,000 years later, the famous Arab historian and philosopher Ibn Khaldun (1332-1406) was born a short distance away in Tunis, travelled in the region and beyond, and died in Cairo. I travelled to Annaba, meditating on the lives and writings of St. Augustine and Ibn Khaldun as two North Africans who witnessed the decline of the great powers of their respective times.

In Milan, and later in Hippo, St. Augustine reflected on the causes of Rome's eventual ruin, hastened by the corruption and debauchery of its rulers and invasions by barbarians from beyond the empire's frontiers. Similarly, Ibn Khaldun – his family having fled earlier into exile from Muslim Spain (al-Andalus) riddled with conflict between Arabs and Berbers – contemplated on the characteristics of peoples as they construct civilizations or bring about their collapse.

Since the terrorist attacks in New York and Washington on September 11, 2001, the Arab-Muslim world and Islam have dominated news. The western effort for a better understanding of Islam as faith and culture has been driven after 9/11 by the practical necessity of containing and defeating terrorism increasingly, if not entirely, associated with Muslims.

During the 1990s, Algeria – a case study of a society besieged by Arab-Muslim terrorists – was turned into a killing field by radical Islamists preaching jihad (holy war) as an article of faith, to be fought indiscriminately against those Muslims viewed as corrupt and non-believers in Islam. The Algerian government, dominated by the military, responded to Islamist jihad with a ruthless campaign to crush terrorism, which it did. But the scar of that savage decade's killings is visible everywhere in today's Algeria, and the recovery will be haltingly slow and painful.

But why did Algeria plunge into terrorism? The explanations contemporary experts seek are in the mix of socioeconomic and political factors. What is missing, or barely touched upon, is the nature of man who indulges in terrorism or justifies it. This is where the writings of St. Augustine and Ibn Khaldun shed greater light on terrorism and its causes than any recent writings of experts in the subject.

Man, St. Augustine wrote, "is a great abyss," and "the moods and attractions of his heart far outnumber the hairs of his head." If there is evil in him, it is because he is insufficient in goodness, for evil "does not exist of itself." "True holiness," or goodness, "is an interior disposition," an inward awakening to the reality of where God resides in the heart of man. A man awakened to his inner reality could do no evil – for instance, be a terrorist – since, filled with goodness, there would be no evil in him.

Islamist and Muslim terrorists have closed shut their "interior disposition." For them, belief is reduced to outward rituals of conformity, in pursuit of power over other men, rather than an awakening to the infinity inside of them, filled with God in whose image they have been made. Hence, they do evil for they are insufficient in goodness, despite their insistence on calling upon God according to their faith tradition.

Ibn Khaldun wrote of Islam as a civilizing force among Arabs of the desert, the Bedouins. But Bedouins are "a savage nation, fully accustomed to savagery and the things that cause it...Such a natural disposition is the negation and antithesis of civilization."

Bedouin, if we abstract from Ibn Khaldun's sociology, is a state of mind. Islamists, as modern-day Bedouins, are unable or unwilling to fathom the workings of modern civilization, to accept its rationality as a means of changing their situation, trapped in the vortex of pre-modern backwardness. They have chosen instead to make war upon it.

In Algeria, Islamists engaged themselves in a conflict of self-destruction. They were driven to this by their nature reflecting the abyss within themselves. Elsewhere, for instance in Lebanon, Iraq, Afghanistan or the Palestinian territories, Muslim terrorists wage war on their opponents, indicating their incapacity to engage with the modern world rationally and in keeping with universal rules, rather than denying them by insisting on their savage disposition to oppose civilization.

From a great distance of time, two North African sages speak to us wisely about understanding why men are seized with evil intent and do harm. Even as we must resist and defeat the evil of Muslim terrorism in our midst, we must remain reminded of St. Augustine's admonition to act with love of mankind and hatred of sins lest we are consumed by that against which we fight.

14 August 2006, *Western Standard* (Calgary)

13

Where Mao meets Muhammad

Some months after the events of September 11, 2001, the former Conservative prime minister of Britain, Margaret Thatcher, wrote about Muslim terror and its ideology, Islamism, as the new form of Bolshevism threatening the free world. She observed, "The enemy is not, of course, a religion…Nor is it a single state, though this form of terrorism needs the support of states to give it succour. Perhaps the best parallel is with early communism. Islamic extremism today, like bolshevism in the past, is an armed doctrine. It is an aggressive ideology promoted by fanatical, well-armed devotees. And, like communism, it requires an all-embracing long-term strategy to defeat it."

Thatcher had it right, and so did President George W. Bush. Following the arrests on August 10 of 24 suspects in Britain for plotting multiple suicide bombings of 10 transatlantic airliners headed for the U.S., Bush remarked that "this nation is at war with Islamic fascists." Still, much of the free world, particularly those among the liberal left, remain in denial.

Islamism is not Islam, however confusing this might be to most people. Islamism is the ideology of a modern totalitarian movement in the guise of a religion with a confused program of reconstituting a first millennium political system – an empire based on *shari'ah* (Islamic law devised by men a thousand years ago), run by medieval-minded clerics with their politico-military gnomes in command – at the beginning of the third millennium. Islamists drool over past glories of a dolled-up Muslim history, unlike old Bolsheviks imagining a utopian classless future. But like Bolshevism, Islamism propagates a universal appeal – unlike Nazism based on a limiting ideology of race supremacy.

Again, like Bolshevism, and unlike Nazism, Islamism presents itself as a movement of the oppressed against oppressors, identified as worldwide capitalism with America at its head and international Jewry as its local client in the heartland of the Arab-Muslim world. This provides Islamism with some political appeal, especially to the self-loathing left in the West, closet anti-Semites, alienated, angry or resentful individuals in search of a political cause, and those seeking group bonding by converting to Islam and pursuing holy war (for instance, John Walker Lindh, the American Taliban, or Richard Reid, the British shoe bomber).

Then again, like Bolshevism, which eventually split into rival camps between post-Stalin Moscow and Mao's Beijing, Islamism is also split into warring camps. One camp has a physical centre in Tehran, headed by the Shi'ite clerics loyal to the Islamist ideology of the late Ayatollah Khomeini. Its primary line of influence runs through the heart of modern-day militant Shi'ism (Islam's largest minority sect) in Iraq and Lebanon.

Islamism among Sunni Muslims—Islam's largest sect, by a ratio of four to one – has no one centre. All the Sunni Muslim majority states – irrespective of whether they are monarchies, such as Morocco and Jordan, or some sort of authoritarian or quasi-democratic republics, such as Egypt and Turkey – are formally opposed to Islamism, or at least feign opposition to it, as in the case of Saudi Arabia and Pakistan. But many Muslim nations (Somalia, Sudan, Bangladesh, Yemen, Afghanistan, et cetera) also exist as something between being failed states and rogue states. Public support for Islamism as an opposition movement in those places is often in direct proportion to the failure of politicalmilitary- intellectual elite to build a minimally decent society.

Islamism is an ideology crafted by Muslim intellectuals. It has many fathers, but its founding theoreticians were Egyptians Hassan al-Banna (1906-49) and Sayyid Qutb (1906-66), Maulana Maududi (1903-79) of Pakistan, and Iran's Ayatollah Khomeini (1900-89). Islamism, in common with Bolshevism and Nazism, is an ideology seeking power to implement a program totalitarian in scope and brutal in means for achieving its medieval ends.

Mao Tse Tung, as his recent biographers Jung Chang and Jon Halliday have pointed out in their meticulously researched study of the communist tyrant, was "responsible for well over 70 million deaths in peacetime, more than any other 20th-century leader." Yet his portrait still hangs like the benign face of a modern-day Buddha overlooking Tiananmen Square. Similarly, Islamist leaders and their rank-and-file followers bear no scruple in killing by whatever means available (suicide bombings have proven to be an unanswerable weapon of choice against opponents with superior conventional arms) while they are uninhibited by any ideological consideration or ethical constraint in their readiness to commit genocide for a cause espoused in apocalyptic terms in the name of religion.

The recent war in Lebanon, started by the Shi'ite Hezbollah's Islamist warriors against Israel, illustrates how these new Bolsheviks behave much as the old Bolsheviks did. Hezbollah organizers, as quislings of the Islamists in power in Tehran, unleashed a war, as communists did on the Korean peninsula in 1950, in pursuit of a strategy to widen the regional influence of Islamism and consolidate Islamist control of a putatively independent Lebanon. Much as the communists succeeded in dividing Korea, Hezbollah has succeeded in its objectives, emerging in the aftermath of the war as the de facto power in Lebanon.

Interestingly, old Bolsheviks under Stalin, and even Mao, were prepared to pause and abridge their international movement for the sake of "socialism in one country," and to avoid direct confrontation with advanced western democracies. It was a pause that placed their fifth column in the West under cautionary notice, and provided the "useful idiots" (as Lenin called them) living in free western societies ample disinformation to sing praises of Marx's utopia. It would take Stalin's army arriving in the heart of divided Europe as a result of the Second World War, and later armed with nuclear weapons, for a sufficient number of people in the West to realize the global threat of Bolshevism.

But Islamists are on a roll, contemptuous of those – the so-called decadent "infidels" of North America and Europe – against whom they make war. Meanwhile, their own fifth column has become deeply embedded in the multicultural West. They have taken to heart the old Bolshevik tale that the greedy capitalist will sell the rope for his hanging, or in its Islamist rendition, the West will finance its own defeat by its insatiable addiction to Middle Eastern oil. The question that hangs over us all like the sword of Damocles is whether the West will awaken in time from its stupor, or whether Islamists will set the term for its surrender.

11 September 2006, *Western Standard* (Calgary)

14

The Ways of God and Man

Pope Benedict XVI's recent speech at the University of Regensburg in his native Bavaria sparked uproar in the Muslim world. Yet his talk was a dense meditation on the troubled relationship between faith and reason in the modern world. He took issue with the dominant value of scientific positivism that permeates western civilization.

Positivism assumes that valid knowledge can come only from the scientific method, verifiable experimentations or logical tests. It denies the existence or intelligibility of things that cannot be measured scientifically. Hence, says the Pope, "this method excludes the question of God, making it appear an unscientific or pre-scientific question. Consequently, we are faced with a reduction of the radius of science and reason, one which needs to be questioned."

The result of such thinking is writ large across the history of the 20th century, in particular the history of Europe – turned twice in one generation into a charnel house of human bone and ash by secular political ideologies. Reason circumscribed by positivism is dismissive of faith and leaves matters of religion to the individual alone. When religion is so reduced to individual subjectivity, then, warns the Pope, "religion and ethics lose their power to create a community," and society at large becomes incapable of making moral distinctions between good and evil, and particularly incapable of distinguishing between faith traditions devoted to peaceful persuasion, and those prepared to use violence to expand their influence.

The Pope made only a passing reference to Islam, but that caught the attention of the Arab-Muslim world. Its streets filled with entirely predictable rage that once again demonstrated – following the earlier controversy and violence over the Danish cartoons of the Prophet Muhammad – the unwillingness or incapacity of contemporary Muslim leaders to engage in a sober discussion on faith and reason, and especially on Islam and its history with non-Muslims. The Pope's reference to Islam and its prophet was not central to his purpose. It was simply suggestive of the problem contemporary Europe confronts from followers of a faith tradition – Muslims – who willingly use violence to advance their arguments. For anyone with an institutional memory as long as the Pope's, this is a perennial problem: Christian Europe has been at war on its borders with Islam repeatedly for the past 1,400 years.

The substance of Pope Benedict's meditation was the courage required "to engage the whole breadth of reason" – including theology – "and not the denial of its grandeur." This concerns everyone, including Muslims. It is not solely a Christian teaching that God can be apprehended by rational thought. It is also the Qur'an's teaching, because it appeals to man's rational faculties to see in nature the evidence of God's omnipotence.

The Pope raised the issue of Islam with an arcane reference to an ancient conversation between Byzantium's erudite emperor Manuel II Paleologus and a Persian Muslim. About the Persian, we are told only that he was educated on the subject of Christianity and Islam. Their conversation apparently took place in 1391, when the emperor was quartered in his winter barracks near Ankara.

The Pope quotes the emperor asking the following of the Persian: "Show me just what Muhammad brought that was new, and there you will find things only evil and inhuman, such as his command to spread by the sword the faith he preached." We are not told the Persian's response, since the emperor, the Pope says, probably "set down this dialogue during the siege of Constantinople, between 1394 and 1402; and this would explain why his arguments are given in greater detail than the responses of the learned Persian." We are left to speculate on the probable reply of the learned Persian. Such speculation by Muslims, in response to the Pope's comment, would have been useful and proper, advancing dialogue between members of two great monotheistic faiths. Instead, "evil and inhuman" rage and threats of vengeance against the Pope have poured forth from the Arab-Muslim world.

What could the Persian have said to the Byzantine, while Christians and Muslims were at war? As a learned man at the end of the 14th century – a time historians call the Golden Age of Islam – the Persian was most certainly well read in the writings of his contemporaries, from Baghdad, Damascus, Cairo, Tunis and the cities of Moorish Spain at one end of the Arab-Muslim world, and from central Asia's Bukhara, Khiva and Samarkand at the other. He would have known the works of Muslim scholars, translating Greek and Hindu philosophers, astrologers and mathematicians. He would have known of Cordoba-born Ibn Rushd (known in Latin as Averroes, 1126-1198), the great commentator on Aristotle. He would have known of the Persian philosopher-physician Ibn Sina (or Avicenna, 980-1037), the poet-mathematician Omar Khayyam (1048-1122), and Tunis-born historian Ibn Khaldun (1332-1406), who also conversed with an emperor – the Mongol conqueror Timur or Tamerlane. The Persian also would have read the Sufi or mystical writings of the Persians al-Ghazali (1058-1111) and Jalaluddin Rumi (1207-1273). Rumi was revered as Maulana, or the Master, and his magnum opus, *Mathnavi*, is spoken of as the Quran in Persian.

The Muslim would have been equally or even more learned than the busy Christian emperor in contemporary arts and sciences. And his response would have had great merit. The operative part of the emperor's request was, "Show me what Muhammad brought that was new." The Persian's reply would likely have been: "Muhammad never claimed to bring anything new to his people, the idolworshipping Arab pagans." This might have startled the emperor, so the Persian would have elaborated.

Muhammad was, as the Quran names him, a messenger and a reminder to his people to worship the one God of Abraham. The message he brought is expressed in the simple creedal statement of Islam, *la illaha illalla*, "There is no god but God." This message was neither new nor unique. It had been borne by all the prophets of the Old Testament, as in the proclamation found in Deuteronomy (6:4), one of the Books of Moses: "Hear, O Israel, the Lord our God, the Lord is One." The Quran, the Persian might have said, is the story of Abraham and his people, the Hebrews or Jews, closest in history to the pagan Arabs. It was revealed to Muhammad so that his people might abandon their idol worship in favour of submission to the one God.

The biblical stories retold in the Quran illuminate a message that is primordial, yet regularly corrupted by fallen men. Because God is infinitely merciful, that message is made fresh again by a chosen few, for the benefit of man and his accounting on the day of reckoning. "So what of the violence?" the emperor might have insisted. The Persian would then have reviewed Muhammad's life and his first 12 years as the messenger, patiently, peacefully speaking God's words to his people. He was met by violence and driven out of his native city, then repeatedly attacked to prevent him from establishing the worship of God. He was then instructed to take up arms in defence of his heavenly mission and guided through the warfare imposed on him, defeating the pagans and establishing worship of the God of Abraham in Arabia.

Muhammad's mission ended with him. Others could not assume it. The violence in the name of Islam that came after him had no heavenly mandate. It was the violence of men, spurred by politics. And this mixing of politics and faith became the ruin of both. The earliest victims of this confusion were members of Muhammad's own family, his cousin Ali and grandsons Hasan and Husayn. The Persian would have invited the emperor, "Let us speak of politics and not of faith, for both of us know how politics has corrupted both Christianity and Islam." If such a response of the Persian to the Byzantine emperor had been recorded, Pope Benedict XVI might well have pondered another dissonance between reason and faith in our times, history made by fallible men obscuring the pristine message of God, the same everywhere and for all as his warning and mercy.

The Persian lived at a time when Muslims were still engaged with the dilemmas of faith and reason in interpreting the Quran – whether God's words were to be taken literally or allegorically. Even as Christian Europe was beginning to liberalize, literal-minded holy warriors, precursors of today's Muslim fundamentalists, prevailed over the philosophers and ended the Islamic Golden Age. Ironically, Pope Benedict's speech bears greatly upon Muslims, for the inescapable choice they face today is between clinging to the medieval past, shaping their understanding of Islam, and reconciling their faith with reason, to live in the modern world.

November 2006, *Western Standard* (Calgary)

15

A Portrait of Courage

In her memoir, *Infidel*, Ayaan Hirsi Ali poses the questions towards its end, "How many girls born in Digfeer Hospital in Mogadishu in November 1969 are even alive today? And how many have a real voice?" The answers are likely few and none.

Hirsi Ali's journey to freedom from the traditionally preordained life of a Somali woman, or for that matter most women in Africa and other parts of the developing world littered with the ruins of failed state and society, is an astonishing story of grace and courage. If Hirsi Ali had limited herself to recounting this journey – of the immense obstacles as a girl growing into a woman she confronted in her escape to freedom from Mogadishu via various sojourns in Saudi Arabia, then Addis Ababa (Ethiopia) and Nairobi (Kenya) to Holland – the story would have remained gripping and inspiring, and it would have opened a window for readers in the West to glimpse the doubly-wretched condition of one half of the population of wrecked states such as her native Somalia.

But Hirsi Ali's story is much more than an escape to freedom from poverty, ignorance, civil strife and violence against women to security, peace and self-fulfillment. It is a story of a Muslim woman whose struggle to be free became eventually a confrontation with her religion, whose experience of genital mutilation and physical violence unmasked the extent of misogyny within Muslim societies that she eventually came to view as inherent to Islam, and whose escape to freedom culminated in abjuring the faith-tradition into which she was born.

This second aspect of her journey to freedom is the part of Hirsi Ali's life which coincides with the events of September 11, 2001 and the subsequent global war against Islamist terrorists. Hirsi Ali's story as an activist and public intellectual, as an elected member of the Dutch parliament and partnership with the film-maker Theo van Gogh in scripting and producing a documentary titled *Submission* that portrays violence against women within Muslim society, as a woman under threat for life after the murder of van Gogh in November 2004 in retaliation for the making of the documentary by a 26-year old Islamist (Muhammad Bouyeri) of Moroccan origin, and once again as an exile departing from Holland and its politics for a new life in the United States, has become unintentionally yet inextricably bound with 9/11 and what has followed since then.

The change in Hirsi Ali's view of the world around her came gradually, prompted by her experience and her university studies in Leiden. Then she saw on the CNN the second hijacked plane flown into the World Trade Center and her self-questioning became more urgent and radical. Finally, she reached her conclusion and one night some months after the terrorist attacks in New York and Washington Hirsi Ali "looked in the mirror and said out loud, 'I don't believe in God.' I said it slowly, enunciating it carefully, in Somali. And I felt relief."

It might be assumed that Hirsi Ali did not at first fully grasp the level of anger she would provoke among Muslims in Holland by taking her views into the public. Hirsi Ali's words on Islam, on the Qur'an and prophet Muhammad, were polarizing. She spoke from her own experience shared by millions of women in the Arab-Muslim world, and she was implacable, unrelenting and unwilling to be censored or silenced. In one interview for the Dutch media Hirsi Ali called the Prophet a pervert saying, "By our Western standards, Muhammad is a perverse man, and a tyrant."

Hirsi Ali might have been somewhat naïve not to consider in speaking out as she was doing she would be inviting the sort of censorship – death – pronounced by the late Iranian leader Ayatollah Khomeini in February 1989 on Salman Rushdie for his novel *The Satanic Verses*. But when Theo van Gogh was killed and his murderer pinned a note on the corpse that threatened Hirsi Ali with similar fate, there was no mistaking the Islamist war against the West had arrived in Holland and for her had also become personal.

The mood of people in Holland and beyond in Europe was troubled. The peril of radical Islamism was undeniable as Europe became home for a growing Muslim immigrant population variously estimated to be somewhere between 15 and 20 million. In March 2004 and eight months before the murder of Theo van Gogh, Islamists brought their war to Spain when they bombed a passenger-train in Madrid. A Europe-wide debate began, and continues, on how to contend with Islamist threat and accommodate or assimilate Muslims without risking the Islamist war against the West be turned into the West's war against Islam.

Hirsi Ali found herself at the centre of this political debate in Europe on Islam, Islamism as a political ideology, status of women in Islam and violence against women by Muslims, and the proper European response in engaging with Muslims at home and with the Muslim world. Hirsi Ali's conclusion on these matters was unequivocal; Europe and Islam confronted each other as polar opposites.

"When people say that the values of Islam are compassion, tolerance, and freedom," Hirsi Ali writes in *Infidel*, "I look at reality, at real cultures and governments, and I see that it simply isn't so." In contrast, she opines, life is "better in Europe than it is in the Muslim world because human relations are better, and one reason human relations are better is that in the West, life on earth is valued in the here and now, and individuals enjoy rights and freedom that are recognized and protected by the state."

European opinion is divided, and some of Europe's intellectuals view Hirsi Ali, her courage aside, as Enlightenment "radical" or "fundamentalist" and hence, the flip-side of a Muslim fundamentalist. In this opinion Hirsi Ali having renounced her faith scorns Islam just as Muslim fundamentalists and Islamist warriors view Europe as the land of kufr (unbelief). But any comparison made of Hirsi Ali with Islamists is disgusting. Her struggle to be free of any dogmatically proscribed inhibitions is one waged by words and reason; for the Islamist defenders of the faith she renounced, their weapon is violence and murder.

Many Europeans skeptical of Hirsi Ali's views believe enraging Muslims by disparaging their faith and traditions closes any promise of rapprochement between Europe and Islam. A pluralist Europe where cultures co-exist together in evolving harmony is the promise to strive for, they argue, and this promise despite difficulties reside in the politics of multiculturalism that countries such as Holland and Britain adopted.

Other Europeans view multiculturalism differently. In this perspective multiculturalism in the guise of accommodating other cultures results in the dilution of Enlightenment legacy of individual liberty, separation of religion and politics in the public sphere, secularism and democracy. Multicultural accommodation amounts to one-way concessions to other cultures, in particular to Islam as Muslims generally seek acceptance of their traditional practices without embracing European values.

This debate once simmering below the relatively placid European surface burst furiously into the open following the murder of Theo van Gogh and Hirsi Ali's outspoken views on Islam. It has been carried forward in the pages, for instance, of the webmagazine *signandsight.com*.

Ian Buruma, author of *Murder in Amsterdam* that explores the killing of Theo van Gogh and the politics surrounding it, wrote "I admire Ayaan Hirsi Ali, and agree with most of what she stands for." This was in reply to Pascal Bruckner, a very staunch defender of Hirsi Ali. But then Buruma went on to write that he is "not convinced that public statements, such as Ayaan Hirsi Ali has made, that Islam in general is 'backward' and its prophet 'perverse', are helpful." In other words Hirsi Ali's views and those of her admirers subvert the promise of multiculturalism.

Timothy Garton Ash writing in *signandsight.com* agreed with Buruma. Ash also published a lengthy book review essay in the *New York Review* about "Islam in Europe", and while he expressed like Buruma admiration for Hirsi Ali he wrote, "I do not believe that she is showing the way forward for most Muslims in Europe, at least not for many years to come. A policy based on the expectation that millions of Muslims will so suddenly abandon the faith of their fathers and mothers is simply not realistic. If the message they hear from us is that the necessary condition for being European is to abandon their religion, then they will choose not to be European. For secular Europeans to demand that Muslims adopt their faith – secular humanism – would be almost as intolerant as the Islamist jihadist demand that we should adopt theirs. But, the Enlightenment fundamentalist will protest, our faith is based on reason! Well, they reply, ours is based on truth!"

Pascal Bruckner had in some ways kicked off the debate in his essay reviewing the views of Buruma and Ash on Hirsi Ali. Bruckner was scathingly dismissive of Hirsi Ali's critics in the name of multiculturalism. He wrote of multiculturalism as a "racism of the anti-racists: it chains people to their roots." Bruckner approvingly quoted Hirsi Ali from her memoir. "I moved from the world of faith," writes Hirsi Ali, "to the world of reason – from the world of excision and forced marriage to the world of sexual emancipation. Having made that journey, I know that one of those worlds is simply better than the other. Not because of its flashy gadgets, but fundamentally because of its values."

The worlds of Europe and Islam are not alike, nor equal in terms of values. Muslims bent on proselytizing will, if unchecked, erode Europe of its Enlightenment legacy that makes of it a better place than the world of Islam; or Europe will need to turn Muslims around to accepting its values. In a subsequent response to Buruma and Ash, Bruckner wrote, "It's not enough to condemn terrorism. The religion that engenders it and on which it is based, right or wrong, must also be reformed. Can one understand the Inquisition, the witches burned at the stake, the Crusades and the condemnation of heretics without referring to the dogmas of Roman Catholicism? The time has come to do for Islam what was done for Christianity as of the 15th century: by bending it to modernity and adapting it to contemporary mentalities."

How can Islam be reformed as Bruckner insists, or is it open to reform? There is no simple answer. But any possibility of reform rests with Muslims, and any effort directed at reform must begin by Muslims acknowledging the state of their society. The malaise of the Muslim world indisputably burden and oppress most acutely the female half of its population. And when Muslim women bearing that burden speak out, though not often enough from fear of violence or other forms of punishment, their testimony of the living practice of Islam demolishes all the banal apologetics of Muslims and their non-Muslim friends.

Hirsi Ali's testimony regarding the existing situation within Muslim societies, irrespective of her renunciation of Islam, comes from lived experience and not mere observation of an outsider or through academic study. She writes, "I first encountered the full strength of Islam as a young child in Saudi Arabia… the source of Islam and its quintessence. It is the place where the Muslim religion is practiced in its purest form…In Saudi Arabia, every breath, every step we took, was infused with concepts of purity or sinning, and with fear. Wishful thinking about the peaceful tolerance of Islam cannot interpret this reality: hands are still cut off, women still stoned and enslaved, just as the Prophet Muhammad decided centuries ago."

Muslim reform can only progress by Muslims first taking an honest and unflinching look at their world. And the most urgent of reforms is bringing to an end the religiously sanctioned denial of women as equal in all respect to men that lies at the source of violence directed at women. But the emergence of Islamism has become a formidable obstacle for Muslims to engage without fear in critically examining the state of their society and the role of Islam in inhibiting reform and progress. The situation has worsened since 9/11, and it is only someone with extraordinary courage and total disregard of the inevitable harm might engage publicly in speaking from within about Islam and the ills of the Muslim world.

Hirsi Ali is not alone as a woman in discussing and examining the malaise of the Muslim world. There are other female voices as noble and brave as those of Taslima Nasrin, Wafa Sultan, Nonie Darwish, Azar Nafisi, Necla Kelek, or those of an older generation such as Assia Djebar and Fatema Mernissi. It is the woman's voice within Islam that is most searing in illuminating inequities and injustices of the Muslim society, and will remain the most powerful agent of change. The circumstances of the post-9/11 world provided Hirsi Ali with a deserving prominence in the Western media for her biography is riveting.

Yet all Muslim criticisms of Hirsi Ali cannot be simply dismissed as apologetics, especially when they come from reputable scholars such as Bassam Tibi. Tibi is an Arab of Syrian origin and German citizen teaching at Gottingen. In the debate carried in the pages of *signandsight.com* Tibi observed, "What Hirsi Ali says about Islam is an affront to Muslims and to anyone who knows anything about Islam. When, for instance, she claims that our prophet and our holy book, the Quran, are a fiction, she insults all Muslims and puts a smirk on the faces of all historians of Islam. Of course, Hirsi Ali has every right to turn her back on Islam in the name of religious freedom and this is what she has done. But she should not abuse the religion just to score points cheaply for herself" (emphasis given).

Muslims are upset with Hirsi Ali. In my conversations with Muslim women in three continents, particularly in Europe (France), I have found women irrespective of their social background or professional occupation distancing themselves from Hirsi Ali's views on the Quran and the prophet even as they agree with her on the malaise retarding Muslim societies. Admittedly my sampling is of limited statistical value, and yet it is anecdotally revealing for many of the women with whom I have conversed on the matter are highly educated, emancipated and professional women. For them, as for me, the vulgarity of Muslim fundamentalists and Islamists in display – (Taliban in Afghanistan, Iranian clerics and their medievalism, Wahhabis, Salafists and other variety of Islamists and their obsession with returning Muslim societies to the dictates of seventh century Arabia, and the limitless capacity of Muslim dictators to inflict cruelty on their people) – cannot be the only lens through which to read the Quran, the prophet's life and the history of Islam over fourteen centuries.

The abuse of and violence against women did not originate with Islam, nor are they confined within the Muslim world. Jack Holland in a remarkable study of misogyny – he labeled it "the world's oldest prejudice" – unveiled how ancient and how widespread across cultures and faiths has been the organized prejudice of men against women and the crimes committed as a result. This history should be, however, of little comfort to Muslims or provide them polemical escape from confronting the reality of misogyny in the here and now of Muslim societies. The misogynist history of Christianity and Christians is mostly in the past; the lesson for Muslims in this instance as in the wider case of Islamic reform is to draw upon that history of Christianity, hence Europe, by which Christians promulgated the reform of their faith and culture in adapting to the values of science and democracy as the pillars on which rests the modern world.

Hirsi Ali has much to contribute in the future even as she has done this far in a relatively young life. She has looked deep and hard at the world from which she made her break, and in the process she has done what Voltaire did in his time. Hirsi Ali has challenged Muslims to think equally deep and hard, even if they are upset with some of the language she has used, and if they refuse to engage with her it is more revealing of them in being in denial of their world's broken reality than her so publicly visible stand on issues that can be mortally wounding.

A final thought, Ayaan Hirsi Ali's use of the word "infidel" (meaning simply an unbeliever) as title of her memoir and her identity brim with irony. She wears the word mockingly and boldly. But in Muslim perspective is unbelief unredeemable, and is an unbeliever condemned to an eternity in hell? For Muslim agitators and Islamist warriors from the late Ayatollah Khomeini to the lowly suicide-bomber in the ranks of al Qaeda the matter is settled; the place of unbelievers is indisputably in God's inferno and they need to be dispatched there speedily and mercilessly.

Yet the matter is not simple nor settled as Muslims might think. Islamic history, apart from history in general, records how many an unbeliever has shown superior conduct in goodness than believers and God's infinite compassion and justice give assurance of their redemption. The most instructive example of this in the history of Islam is that of Abu Talib, the paternal uncle of the prophet. Abu Talib raised Muhammad, who was an orphan, then protected him through his adult years and when he started preaching Islam in Mecca without ever abjuring the idol-worshipping faith of his ancestors.

The Quran indicts hypocrite (*munafiq*) as a worse offender of moral laws than an infidel. It devotes chapter 63 titled "The Hypocrites" to the perfidy of those who feign belief in public and behave perversely. In place where justice prevails and where the ruler in heaven as in earth is just, those Muslims learned and ignorant who have abused women or have failed to prevent their abuse, will stand condemned as hypocrites and for them redemption will be justly delayed.

PajamasMedia.com, 24 June 2007

16

Reconciling revelation with reason

The subject of reform, Islam or Muslim, is old, but now has assumed an urgency that is unprecedented.

It is glib to speak about reforming Islam. Islam, as the breath and light of Muhammad, is the spiritual nourishment equally for beggars and princes of the Muslim world.

It is proper to speak about the reform of Muslims. For whatever is Islam in practice – or for that matter Judaism and Christianity – and how it is received, understood and made the template of cultures, it will remain at the human level merely a reflection and refraction of the conduct of Muslims.

Muhammad said, "Islam began as a stranger and will become once more a stranger." He meant Muslims, like other communities preceding them, would become corrupt and the message that elevated them in history would be forgotten.

But he also said, "God will send to this community, at the head of every hundred years, one who will renew for it its religion." He confirmed reform and renewal are inherent aspects of any people's willingness to be receptive to the spirit of their age.

The Prophet's words are reassuring, there is also a prerequisite. A wellknown Quranic verse reads, "Verily God does not change the condition of a people till they change themselves."

The events of 9/11 have a much wider context than simply the deranged, or evil, psychology of Muslim fanatics who perpetrated them. This is the failure of the Muslim world – which is almost entirely situated within the developing countries of Asia and Africa – to meet the multi-layered challenge of modernity and democracy in the 20th century.

For the Muslim world, its centre collapsed a long time ago. So long as the world was predominantly an agrarian economy, the diversity of Muslim countries and the Islamic civilization remained vibrant. Once the Europeans pioneered the basis of a new scientific-industrial civilization, the Muslim world fell behind, its vitality sapped, its centre depleted.

It is not that the Word of God no longer addressed the condition of the Muslim world. On the contrary, the vast majority of Muslims no longer hear God in the dramatically altered conditions of the world in which they appear as a poor specimen of bygone times.

Herein lies the problem and challenge of Muslim reform. The political and cultural realm Muslims inhabit belongs to another age, and is incongruent with the requirements of our times. This system now weighs upon Muslims with deadening effect, and its inertia prevents them from becoming open and receptive to a world that mocks them for their failure they may only deny by compounding the problem.

As the poet William Butler Yeats noted – it now seems a long time ago – when the centre of a culture collapses, "Mere anarchy is loosed upon the world,/The blood-dimmed tide is loosed, and everywhere/ The ceremony of innocence is drowned." In such times there is paucity of hope for reason to prevail, and good may only be expected when once the poison in the bloodstream of that culture has exhausted itself.

Any serious student of Muslim world can provide countless names of Muslim thinkers during the past 200 years tinkering with some aspect of hermeneutics, the science of textual readings, that might contribute to an understanding of the sacred text of Islam, the Quran, in keeping with the spirit of the modern age. The irony is, however, that the cultural system within which Muslims reside, enclose and remove them from hearing ever fresh the Word of God when they read the Quran. Textual interpretations may help individual Muslims reorient themselves to their world, but there is insufficient evidence from Muslim history that it would bring about a Muslim reform.

There was a moment in Muslim history, the 8th-9th century, when a rationalist theology flourished briefly in Baghdad. But the zealotry of the literalminded reactionary men of the mosques and religious schools snuffed this earliest venture of reconciling revelation with reason.

This banishment of Muslim version of Spinoza anticipated what took place in Europe with the Inquisition and religious wars during several centuries of the medieval age. The difference is illuminating. Europe eventually emerged from the close-mindedness of that history into the open-mindedness of the modern world it created for itself and others.

Muslims have much to learn from Christians, for Christianity has the longest, most profound and liberating experience with that entire reform process initiated by Christians of Europe, and spread over more than 300 years through which the world of the Inquisition made its transition to the world of modern science and democracy. Christianity as an institutionalized faith not only survived but came out, as a result of this process, renewed and strengthened, its ideals more brightly restored, more widely spread, more deeply sown in a world not less wanting of spiritual sustenance.

There is no one singular towering personality of Christian reformation who Muslims can take for their guide. They can draw benefit learning from Augustine and Luther as they may from Galileo and Newton. They also need to learn from Cromwell and Washington.

The discovery of America with Tocqueville is no less essential than discovering the inquisitiveness and openness of the mind that brought desert Arabs to embrace Persian and Greek, Indian and Chinese civilizations as Muslims encountered them, and then achieving greatness in the process of assimilating their knowledge.

Muslims of the first generation took to heart what the Prophet advised, "Go unto China seeking knowledge." Muslims of the present generation not only misread the Quran, they have denigrated the Prophet into their self-image of men without love, seething with rage.

The Quran speaks of peoples and cultures in failing to reform their beliefs vanished. It warns, "If God please, He will remove you and bring a new creation [in your place]."

Muslims have been standing indecisively for a long time at the fork of world history. It is their choice to embrace the modern world and prosper, or remaining inconsequentially enclosed within their cultural system vanish into oblivion.

3 October 2003, *National Post* (Toronto)

17

The father of all assassins

There is no example from modern history of a great superpower and its allies launching their flotilla of war machines against an individual for "waging war against civilization." But if we are to understand Osama bin Laden and his fanaticism, we have to reach back a thousand years to when the Arab-Islamic civilization was at its apogee.

In 1092, Nizam al-Mulk, the influential chief minister of the Seljuq ruler, was assassinated. The assassin, dressed as a Sufi or Islamic mystic, dealt his blow in public and serenely accepted his own death.

This assassination sent a shiver down the spine of the Seljuq realm. At its height, under Nizam al-Mulk's direction, the Seljuq kingdom stretched from the Anatolian plateau to the edge of the Hindu Kush mountains in Afghanistan, and from the River Oxus south to the Persian Gulf.

The Seljuq rulers were of Turkish origin; their great rivals were the Cairo-based Fatimid rulers. The Fatimids claimed descent from the Prophet Mohammed through his only surviving daughter, Fatima. Within a few decades of the Prophet's death in 632, political quarrels and fratricide split the Muslims into two groups, the Sunni and the Shi'i. The majority Sunni, horrified by violence, preferred political order over anarchy. They recognized as legitimate any dynasty of rulers adhering to Islamic laws based on the consensus of the majority of religious scholars and jurists.

The Sunni scholars (Sunni derived from the word sunnah, "traditions of the Prophet") viewed the corporate unity of the Muslim world as henceforth resting on adherence to the Islamic laws, the *shari'ah*. The Shi'i minority insisted that the only legitimate ruler could come from the Prophet's family, and their religious scholars developed an alternative political theory of the just ruler.

The Fatimids, who were Shi'i, established their kingdom in North Africa at the beginning of the 10th century. Their power began to disintegrate around the time Nizam al-Mulk was murdered, but generated subsects of Shi'i extremists ready to wage a secret war against Sunni authority. One such subsect was an extremist Ismaili movement led by Hasan Sabbah.

Sabbah, a contemporary of Nizam al-Mulk and Omar Khayyam, the great Persian poet and mathematician, traveled widely, studied philosophy and esoteric sciences; as a Shi'i he was appalled by the growth of Sunni power under Seljuq rulers. He saw himself as the incarnation of the just ruler, and gathered around him loyal followers sworn to secrecy and committed to ignite a revolution by subverting existing authority. His preferred strategy was to strike fear in his enemies' hearts through selected assassinations.

From his castle in a mountain fortress known as Alamut ("Eagle's Lesson"), on the southern shore of the Caspian Sea, Sabbah directed his war against the Muslim world.

To kill authority figures, he set out hand-picked martyrs or assassins, the word according to some authorities derived from the Arabic *hashishi* (plural, *hashishiyyin*), meaning those who smoked hemp, cannabis sativa, for narcotic effects.

This was, in effect, Sabbah's invention of "terrorism" – of a political program of subversion and fear conducted by an organization with limited means, but inspired by a large-scale utopian program.

Hasan Sabbah died in 1124. His Order survived until Alamut was destroyed by Mongol invaders a century later. During this period, his fanatical movement of extreme deviants from mainstream Islam terrorized opponents far and wide. One of their most daring assassinations was that of Conrad of Montferrat, the Crusader king of the Latin kingdom of Jerusalem in 1192. In the end, however, Sabbah and his followers failed in their mission. The Sunni authorities survived and the Arab-Islamic civilization flourished again under the Mongols and the Turks.

Osama bin Laden and his band of fanatical warriors are a contemporary version of Hasan Sabbah and his Order of Assassins. Mr. bin Laden's hideout in the mountains of Afghanistan is a reminder of Sabbah's mountain stronghold. Like Sabbah, Mr. bin Laden has raised his warriors from boyhood to accept death for a political program dressed in religious slogans that set him apart from mainstream Islam.

Mr. bin Laden's beliefs, drawn from Wahhabi teachings, reflect the most narrow, bigoted deviation from the catholicity of Sunni Islam. The puritanical Wahhabi version of Islam is a sectarian movement that emerged from a remote region of Arabia in the 18th century; it resurfaced at the beginning of the 20th century with the foundation of the Saudi kingdom.

According to Ibn Khaldun, the great 14th-century Arab-Muslim historian, a recurring theme in Muslim history is the periodic assault on civilization by primitive nomads of the desert. Wahhabism illustrates this history. Its extreme practitioners – such as Mr. bin Laden – in breaking ranks with their Saudi patrons confirm Ibn Khaldun's theory of the cyclical struggle between inhabitants of the desert and those who have settled into a sedentary culture of cities.

Mr. bin Laden's views are primitivism writ large, and have done immense harm to Islam and to civilization. But in Sabbah's case, the 130 Islam's Predicament failure of his program did not extinguish the fanaticism of his followers for 100 years after his death. Mr. bin Laden and his organization are also doomed – but sadly, civilization may have to remain on guard indefinitely to contain the fanaticism of his hidden warriors.

11 October 2001, *The Globe and Mail* (Toronto)

18

Osama's godfathers

Nine days after the London bombings of July 7, Tony Blair gave a clear-headed speech about the threat to the West. "What we are confronting here is an evil ideology," he said. "This ideology and the violence that is inherent in it did not start a few years ago in response to a particular policy. Over the past 12 years, al-Qaeda and its associates have attacked 26 countries, killed thousands of people, many of them Muslims. Their cause is not founded on an injustice. It is founded on a belief, one whose fanaticism is such it can't be moderated. It can't be remedied. It has to be stood up to."

What Blair did not say, however, is that al-Qaeda's ideology is deeply entrenched in the Muslim tradition and reaches far back, into the earliest years of Islam.

Al-Qaeda's terrorists are a throwback to those Muslims in the first decades of Islam who believed their faith was the purest, while doubting the belief of others around them, and approved of violence as the right way to advance their views of faith and power. They are known as *khwarij* (meaning those who secede) or *Kharijites*.

Muslims in general, fundamentalists in particular, hearken back to the founding years of Islam as the perfect age when the Prophet Muhammad and his companions instituted the divine plan on Earth. In this view, what followed was a regression from belief to unbelief. This picture of Islam's early years is a myth that deprives most Muslims of a critical and rational perspective on history.

The reality, as documented by the earliest Arab-Muslim commentators on Islam's founding decades – from Ibn Ishaq (d. 761) to Al-Tabari (d. 923) – was one of internecine strife, bloodshed and war. Immediately after the Prophet died in 632, wars were fought to compel Arabs of contemporary Saudi Arabia and Yemen to re-submit to Islam as the only permissible religion of the new empire. Three of the Prophet's first four successors as rulers of the expanding realm of Islam – Umar, Uthman and Ali – were murdered as a result of grievances and factional strife. The Prophet's immediate family members were the most conspicuous massacre victims in these seventh-century conflicts. The wars of succession left permanent schisms within Islam.

Ever since those early blood-lettings, Muslims have been the primary victims of Muslim violence.

The *Kharijites* held the view that since a perfect religious and political order had been instituted, anything outside it was impure and corrupting. Any diminution of this pure system of worship and rule, and any compromise with the outside world, reflected a weakening of faith, a commission of sin and a departure into apostasy that had to be fought and annihilated. Consequently, any Muslim who differed from the impossibly rigid *Kharijite* view of faith and politics was to be hunted down.

Politically and militarily, *Kharijites* were systematically eliminated by Muslim rulers within their domain in the first century of Islam. But *Kharijite* ideas persisted, breeding an exclusive, militant and sectarian body of followers outside the mainstream of Muslim belief and practice. The *Kharijite* view would re-surface through the influence of Ibn Hanbal (780-855), a founder of one of the four legal schools in Sunni Islam, and in the work of Ibn Taimiyya (1263-1328), who in turn was influential in shaping the view of Muhammad ibn Abd al-Wahhab (1703-87), the founder of the Wahhabi sect that is the dominant school of Islamic thinking in Saudi Arabia.

The Wahhabis are the contemporary version of the *Kharijites*, and their extreme sectarian views, funded by the oil wealth of Saudi Arabia, have permeated much of the Muslim world. Their atavistic thinking was given a modern facade by Syed Qutb (1906-66), an Egyptian thinker revered by Muslim fundamentalists for formulating Islamism as an ideology of power and jihad. Gamal Abdel Nasser, the populist Egyptian dictator, hanged Qutb for his politics, which were associated with the Muslim Brotherhood (the antecedent group of al-Qaeda and Hamas) in Egypt and the wider Arab world. Later, Qutb's followers were responsible for the killing of Anwar Sadat, Nasser's successor, in October 1981. Osama bin Laden is only the most recent face of the Wahhabi bigotry that has origins going back to the foundational years of Islam.

The arguments in the West that organized Muslim terrorism associated with al-Qaeda and its global network can be ended through concessions are ignorant and naive. Muslim violence is independent of anything Western democracies might do to accommodate grievances that are mostly rooted in their own dismal failures to meet the modern world's political and economic challenges.

In the pre-modern world, Muslim rulers from the Ummayad dynasty in Damascus, the Abbasid dynasty in Baghdad to the Ottoman sultans in Istanbul contained and destroyed *Kharijites* and their ideological progeny. They knew there could be no toleration of these killers who used religion as an ideological shield.

We should do the same: The modern-day *Kharijites* need to be eliminated by force, like their predecessors. Eventually, Muslims themselves must confront the mentality that proselytizes for violence in the name of Islam. It is a disease that mutates over time into a variant of fascism. Only through long-term commitment to reform can this disease be cured.

24 August 2005, *National Post* (Toronto)

19

Two solitudes that aren't

In the weeks since September 11, there has been much effort placed to explain the war against terrorism in civilizational terms. *The Clash of Civilizations*, by Samuel Huntington, a Harvard professor, gets regularly and authoritatively cited in these discussions.

In seeking to make sense of the emerging global politics after the collapse of the Soviet Union and the end of the Cold War, Mr. Huntington seized upon the idea of civilization. He viewed the world moving from bipolar division of the Cold War years to more complex multipolar and multicivilizational divisions with greater potential for instability and conflict. The new lines separating people, he suggested, would not be the boundaries of states and political ideologies, but cultural differences demarcating civilizations. Hence conflicts of the emergent post-Cold War world would be civilizational.

Among all the names of thinkers cited by Mr. Huntington in his densely written book there is one name prominently missing. It is the name of an Arab-Muslim philosopher who made the subject of civilization his life long meditation and the theme of his study of history.

Ibn Khaldun, the most famous of Arab historians, was born in Tunis in North Africa in 1332 and died in Cairo in 1406. He came from a notable family of Yemeni origin, arriving in Spain with the first wave of Arab conquerors in the early 8th century. The family earned prominence as scholars and administrators in the service of Arab rulers of Seville. But by the time of Ibn Khaldun's birth, the slow disintegration of Arab power forced the family to leave for the Maghreb (North Africa).

Ibn Khaldun distinguished himself as statesman, judge and diplomat in the service of several royal houses. His political career was caught in the turmoil of dynastic ambitions, wars and Mongol invasions. These brought him insights and enriched his writings as a man of contemplation and action.

His fame spread and his wisdom was widely sought. The most famous episode of his life was the meeting with Timur or Tamarlane, the great conqueror from Samarkand. Timur had Ibn Khaldun brought to his court in Damascus and kept him as his guest for an extended period. Each was impressed by the other's accomplishments, and their conversations remain one of the most fascinating records of interviews in history.

The abiding fame of Ibn Khaldun rests in his study of history in several volumes. He sought history's inner meaning or, in his words, a "subtle explanation of the causes and origins of existing things, and deep knowledge of the how and why of events." In this effort, he coined the term civilization, or its Arabic equivalent, *umran*, and wrote of how it comes about, evolves, spreads and then declines. It is Ibn Khaldun's insight into this process that sets him apart from all other historians before and after him. Yves Lacoste, a French scholar, noting this observed, "Thucydides invented history but Ibn Khaldun turned it into a science."

In the first volume of Ibn Khaldun's history, the opening sentence reads, "History is information about social organization, which itself is identical with world civilization." In contrast to Mr. Huntington, Ibn Khaldun conceived of civilization in the singular, as a human enterprise global in scope, assimilative in process and cumulative in its unfolding.

Mr. Huntington mapped out seven civilizations. He conceived civilizations as close cultural entities, distinct from one another. These entities may or may not be hostile to one another, but as cultural tectonic plates they are in constant movement, with the proximate ones inevitably colliding. The most volatile boundary, he suggested, is the one separating the West from Islam.

In Ibn Khaldun's view, the history of mankind is a movement from ignorance to knowledge, and knowledge in all its aspects is a common resource of humanity. In civilization, knowledge is of a higher sort – organized, progressively cultivated and shared among people who commonly appreciate arts and sciences.

The critical distinction he made in explaining civilization was between primitive culture (*umran badawi*) and civilized culture (*umran hadari*). Primitive culture belongs to people who live outside of cities where civilized culture is organized and developed. The Arab-Islamic civilization was urban, found in great cities of Baghdad, Damascus, Cairo, Fez, Cordoba, Granada, Delhi, Samarkand, Bukhara, Isfahan. Outside of cities were deserts and mountains where people lived nomadic lives of primitive simplicity.

City life was sedentary. Here leisure and consumption of luxury created demand for arts and sciences, and the progressive expansion of knowledge.

All of this, however, came at a cost. Civilized culture was prey to men of the deserts, the bedouins who periodically emerged to wage war on civilization. The bedouins possessed group solidarity lacking among city dwellers, and this gave them the military edge to contest for power when attracted by the richness of urban centres.

Ibn Khaldun greatly expanded on this theme. Like Aristotle before him, Ibn Khaldun surveyed politics as a science. He made state and religion, the structure of religious law, the basis of industry (crafts) and economy subjects of *ilm al-umran* (the science of civilization).

Ibn Khaldun's work, rich in detail and bold in speculative thought, is unique. Arnold Toynbee, author of the monumental 10-volume *Study of History*, in commenting on Ibn Khaldun wrote, "He has conceived and formulated a philosophy of history which is undoubtedly the greatest work of its kind that has ever yet been produced by any mind in any time or place."

Ibn Khaldun's theme of civilization provides a rich and subtle understanding of September 11 and after. He would have recognized the terrorists, and all those who practice politics of a similar nature anywhere in our highly interdependent world, as people with a mind-set of primitive culture.

And he would have said that the present war against terrorism is not a clash of civilizations, but of civilization seeking to contain, bring to justice and punish those who wage war against it.

19 November 2001, *The Globe and Mail* (Toronto)

20

Perverting Islam for politics

Our normal inclination in understanding and explaining events such as the war in Lebanon is to focus on immediate causes.

Seeking perspective or distance to place events in context is an acquired discipline. The effort needed to view things and events in perspective is a ceaseless struggle against one's own inclinations driven by emotions of familial, nationalist or tribal attachments that undermine universal values.

Since 9/11 – discounting the prior long history of conflicts in the Middle East – debate has raged in the West on the causes of Muslim terrorism. As terrorist atrocities have mounted, this debate has become increasingly acrimonious with respect to fixing blame or responsibility for its spread and its mounting casualties.

Focusing the immediate causes of these political firestorms might be a necessary recourse for diplomacy – to put the fires out momentarily and give some sort of negotiated truce a chance to work. It does not, however, lend itself to understanding why such firestorms keep repeating, and what needs to occur for them to end.

Anyone familiar with the Middle East's history must know the current war triggered by Hezbollah's Hassan Nasrallah against Israel is part of a long scenario reaching back to the founding of the Jewish state in 1947. In fact, it goes even further back to the Balfour Declaration of November 1917, announcing the British government's support for the establishment of a Jewish home in what was then called Palestine.

The defining aspect of this history is Arab-Muslim refusal to recognize Jewish rights in Palestine. Apologists for recent Arab-Muslim history continue to mount endless arguments over the immediate causes of firestorms like this latest one – Nasrallah's war as a proxy of his Iranian paymasters – in a fraudulent effort to fix blame on Jews, Zionism, or some Israeli version of apartheid and the U.S. as Israel's staunch defender.

The wars against Israel – whether mounted from the left by pan-Arab nationalists such as Egypt's Gamal Abdel Nasser and his acolytes, or directed from the right by Islamists such as Iran's Ayatollah Khomeini and his followers – are motivated by a single purpose. We have heard this goal articulated repeatedly in recent times by Mahmoud Ahmedinejad, the Iranian president: Eliminating the Jewish state.

Consequently, Israel has been forced into wars since its founding in 1947 for survival. When we focus only on immediate causes of current conflicts, this context is missing.

But it seems to me there is also an insidious psychology pervasive in the thinking and politics of perhaps a majority of Arabs and Muslims. Their anti-Israeli attitude is saturated with anti-Semitism – partly borrowed from Europe and partly reflecting a strain of anti-Jewish bigotry in their own history. Instead of purging themselves of this bigotry and reconciling with Jews and Israel, they have perverted Islam into an anti-Jewish faith.

In the mixing of politics and faith lies the ruin of both. The history of perverting Islam for political purposes goes back to its earliest years, and it has continued into our times when Islam has been practically emptied by Islamists of its universal values and made into an instrument of their vicious politics.

Muhammad, the prophet and founder of Islam, reputedly said: "Islam began as a stranger and will become once more a stranger." Although I am a Muslim, for me and many others, Islam in the Middle East has for the longest while – certainly during my life time – been a stranger.

Those Arabs and Muslims who have perverted their faith and pursued politics of cultivated hatred towards people of other faiths have made their own lives and history miserable. Moreover, as victims of their own bigotry, they remain blind to their own faults.

In these circumstances, unless there is a change of heart among Arabs and Muslims as the Qur'an instructs, peace in the Middle East will remain elusive – and firestorms will rage every now and then.

12 August 2006, *Toronto Sun*

21

The cost of two denials

There are two denials working in tandem at least since September 11, 2001, that undermine liberal-democracies and their efforts to eliminate the scourge of Islamist brigandage from our world.

One denial is the Muslim majority refusing to denounce without equivocation the Islamist thugs from Osama bin Laden down to the street-corner spokesman for al Qaida, or similar organizations – and their apologists from Sheikh al Qaradawi featured on the Arab television *al Jazeerah* down to the prayer leader in the local mosque – for being "warmongers of darkness" at war with the modern civilization and Islam.

This Muslim denial to confront the now ugly reality of their world emanates in large measure from fear of the "a-word" and what then might follow.

The fear of being labeled an "apostate" by other Muslims, or Muslim authority, cripples the Muslim mind to silence and inaction when confronted with what is undeniably wrong gets espoused in the name of Islam.

While this fear can be explained at length sociologically and historically – it goes back to the first century of Islam when majority of Arab-Muslims, for instance, prayed behind the leadership that sanctioned the murder of members of the Prophet Muhammad's family instead of repudiating such leaders and their apologists in mosques – one of its effects is an erosion of trust between non-Muslims and Muslims.

The other denial is the liberal "white man" refusing to speak clearly about the wrongs of the other – the "non-white" – and, especially, when such wrongs as Islamist terrorism places in peril everyone without any distinction of ethnicity, gender and belief. The "white man's" denial these days is framed as being politically correct, and the aversion of being incorrect comes from the fear to get labelled with the "b" or "r"-words as a "bigot" or "racist."

There could be nothing worse for a liberal "white man" than being called a racist. It stupefies him into incoherence as the deer is frozen into inaction when caught in the headlights of an approaching car.

This fear is bound up with the liberal or "white man's" guilt over the past sins of Europe's colonial-imperial history – the 500 years since Christopher Columbus's voyage represented in this "liberal" version of the "revised" world history as an unrelenting abuse and exploitation by the "white man" of Asians, Africans and the indigenous populations of the Americas, Australia and the farflung islands of the Pacific.

Shelby Steele at the Hoover Institution, Stanford University, has written most incisively about the "white guilt" and what it has meant in terms of race relations in America since the 1960s, or when it becomes necessary to fight in defending freedom.

"Today, the white West," writes the Afro-American Steele, "lives in a kind of secular penitence in which the slightest echo of past sins brings down withering condemnation. There is now a cloud over white skin where there was once unquestioned authority."

America's retreat from Vietnam was somewhat hastened by white guilt, and the foreseen consequences for the Vietnamese mattered little to those who sought America's defeat in south-east Asia.

Similarly, the full-throated cry of "liberal" penitence subverts the West's ability to defeat terrorists and their sponsors in Iraq and elsewhere. Between the two denials at work, Islamist murderers reap their harvest of the innocent dead.

28 July 2007, *Toronto Sun*

22

The Mideast: A cesspool of hate

Since 9/11, the roll call of cities across the world bombed by Muslim terrorists in league with Osama bin Laden, or recruits of his organization, al-Qaida, keeps growing.

One of the latest is Istanbul, Turkey, whose citizens were terrorized in a series of suicide bombings within the span of a week.

In those attacks, Jews, long and peaceful residents of Turkey – with whose history they share an ancient connection – were once again the victims of anti-Semitism. An anti-Semitism which is now turning the Arab-Muslim world into a version of what Europe became during the first half of the previous century – a cesspool of hate where Jews were, and today are, blamed for all things wrong in a culture hurtling toward self-destruction.

When U.S. journalist Daniel Pearl is murdered in Karachi, Pakistan, for being a Jew, and when Neve Shalom, Istanbul's main synagogue, is bombed for being what it is and for its place in Turkey's history, it represents a rising tide of anti-Semitism among Arab Muslims that can no longer be denied by their demagogic representatives.

Can it be explained? Should it be?

Writing as a Muslim, I believe it must. For what is involved here in the spreading slime of anti-Semitism among many Arabs and Muslims – as it once was in Europe – is the wreckage of Islam.

A wreckage in the making by those committing crimes against humanity in humanity's name, while others, professing the faith, acquiesce by remaining silent.

Old World

The Islamic civilization pre-dates the modern world, and the eclipse of that civilization began with the making and the triumph of the modern, secular, democratic and liberal world we now live in.

To understand the Islamic civilization of the past, it needs to be judged according to the prevalent standards of the time. In the pre-modern world, Islamic civilization, when compared to Europe, was relatively more advanced, wealthier, more liberal, more tolerant and more assimilative. For all those reasons, it was poised to become a far more innovative force in the modern world than it ever did.

Jewish relations with Arabs and Muslims are as old as Islam, and as intimate as were their relations with Christians in the foundational years of Christianity.

Jewish presence and contributions in the making of Islamic civilization were of no lesser significance than in the making of the modern world. Jews in pre-modern times were relatively more secure, as a people, within the domain of Islam than they were in Europe.

Bernard Lewis and S.D. Goitein, just two of many Jewish scholars, have explored this complex history with great care.

Lewis writes in *The Jews of Islam*, "For most of the Middle Ages the Jews of Islam comprised the greater and more active part of the Jewish people…With few exceptions, whatever was creative and significant in Jewish life, happened in Islamic lands."

Similarly, Goitein, in *Jews and Arabs*, admirably catalogues the intensive contacts of the two Semitic peoples through the centuries in both good and bad times.

So what happened? How can the present situation be explained?

In the circumstances of the 20th century history, a relationship of rivalry emerged between the two peoples, layered with past history in which the Arab self-perception was one of being superior to Jews, both politically and culturally.

That perception dramatically reversed over time.

Goitein writes, "The resurgence of the two peoples was effected after a prolonged period of suffering and humiliation, a period during which neither formed a nation in the ordinary sense of the word."

Longest exile

But then, following World War II, Jews returned to Palestine after their longest period of exile to found a state for themselves, and successfully defended it against tremendous odds.

By contrast, noted Ibn Khaldun, the remarkable Arab philosopher from the 14th century, Arabs were displaced in history from the position of prominence they once occupied.

As he wrote in 1377, "The realm of the Arabs has been wiped out completely; the power now rests in the hand of non-Arabs, such as the Turks in the East ... and the Franks (Europeans) in the North."

In the modern post-colonial resurgence – the creation of Israel and the emergence of independent Arab states – the success of the one contrasts with the failures of the others.

From the point of view of many Arabs, Jews are today an even more unbearable power than those who displaced them several centuries ago, as was pointed out at the time by Ibn Khaldun.

Jews, as a people, despite the terrible injustices inflicted on them which finally culminated in the Holocaust, survived and succeeded. Arabs, as a people, despite the resources gifted them by nature and the support received from others in modern times, on the whole displayed incapacity to assimilate into the modern world.

The widening gap between success and failure of the two peoples in meeting their respective goals requires explaining.

One explanation would be that offered by Cassius to Brutus in another circumstance, that the fault "is not in our stars, but in ourselves."

The contrary explanation is to blame the stars, or others, while avoiding at all costs looking within "ourselves" and in "our" culture and history for the reasons for failing to meet desired goals.

Tribalism persists as a characteristic of Arab politics and culture. Tribal politics is a closed circle, and in such a system, insiders and outsiders are clearly marked.

Jews are the perennial outsiders, instinctively held responsible for the problems of the insiders. Within the closed circle of tribal politics, Jewish success grates upon Arab thinking, sometimes in venomous forms.

Breeding ground

To be sure, anti-Semitism is bound up with European history as well. But even purged from its European locale, the plague of anti-Semitism found a breeding ground in Arab resentment against Europe, and then America, for supporting Jewish nationalism – Zionism – in the creation of Israel.

Anti-Semitic bile became a crutch to explain Arab failure as a vast machination of Jewish conspiracy, abetted by the West, constant in its purpose to divide and control the Arab world since the time of the Crusades.

This view of history has become the ur-text, or the holy grail, of Arab nationalism, and morphed into religious fundamentalism. It explains away any responsibility Arabs owe to themselves for their failures.

While Arabs are a minority in the wider Muslim world, they have claimed a position greater than others in interpreting Islam because of being native to the language and culture into which Muhammad, the prophet, was born, and the Quran was revealed.

In modern times, this has meant the experience of Arab politics in general, and of the Palestinians in particular, has been ground into the lens by which Islam as a faith and tradition is viewed within the wider Muslim world.

Consequently, while Arabs have sought to legitimize their politics with an appeal to Islam, non-Arab Muslims have generally accepted Arab views and interpretations as legitimately Islamic. That is the conduit through which Arab anti-Semitism has spread into the wider Muslim world.

The situation in which the Arab-Muslim world now finds itself can only be reversed with external assistance.

Here it is worth reminding ourselves that fascism and anti-Semitism in Europe, which precipitated a world war and Holocaust, were only purged by greater force intervening from the outside.

1 January 2004, *Toronto Sun*

23

Exposed in Gaza

Forty years is somewhat more than a generation, and a large enough span of time to assess the fruits from seeds sowed by one generation and reaped by the next. The Palestinian civil war and the trashing of Gaza in the days following the 40th anniversary of the June 1967 Arab-Israeli war signify the death knell of a politics by which a people continue to innovate new ways for self-abuse. The seeds Yasser Arafat and his generation sowed just as they had inherited – and are leaving for their children to harvest as they have gone full throttle in murdering each other – were rotten.

Palestinian unity was mostly a charade. But with the Hamas faction of the Palestinian Authority seizing control of Gaza through civil war, effectively removing it politically and by arms from the West Bank, an unforeseen reality has emerged in the long bitter Arab-Israeli conflict. This Palestinian fratricide poses for the western powers, particularly the U.S. and European Union, a big question: how long will these nurturers of Palestinian corruption and intransigence persist in their own delusion that more appeasement and bribes for Palestinians can furnish the final settlement of two states, one Arab and one Jew, as envisaged by the November 1947 UN plan for the partition of what remained of the Palestine Mandate?

The history lesson from the last century is irrefutable. Beginning with the announcement of the Balfour Declaration in November 1917, in which Britain promised to establish a Jewish homeland in Palestine, the sole objective of Arab politics has been to nullify Jewish rights by any and all means available. Between the two world wars, Haj Amin al-Husseini – a Palestinian-Arab and Muslim leader, appointed Mufti of Jerusalem by Herbert Samuel, a Jew and Britain's High Commissioner in the Palestine Mandate – led the fight against Jews by making common cause with Hitler and the German Nazis.

The West's response following the June 1967 Six-Day War (in which Israel pre-empted what they had reason to fear was an imminent attack by Gamal Abdel Nasser's Egypt) came in the form of UN Security Council Resolution 242. It set the principle of exchanging land for peace on the premise that Arabs would eventually accept the UN partition of Palestine and the right of Israel to a secure peace.

But while Palestinian Arabs led by Arafat went through the motion of accepting Resolution 242 in 1988, 10 years after Egypt signed its peace treaty with Israel, the Mufti's policy of annihilating the Jewish state was never repudiated. Instead, the Mufti's Jew-hatred was passed on to his successors as the lodestar of Palestinian-Arab politics.

Arafat and the Palestine Liberation Organization learned that terrorism can be rewarding. Instead of being shunned after Palestinian gunmen killed Israeli athletes at the 1972 Munich Olympics, Arafat was invited two years later to address the UN General Assembly. When Arafat's politics of extortion, terror and airline hijacking almost destroyed Lebanon, the EU went ahead with its 1980 Venice Declaration to recognize the PLO as a legitimate negotiating partner. And after his embrace of Saddam Hussein, Arafat went on to sign the Oslo Accords, receive a Nobel peace prize and enjoy regular invitations to the White House – all the while assuring his people and supporters in the Arab-Muslim world that his diplomacy was merely a pause, a temporary truce with the enemy, in the struggle to "liberate" all of Palestine. The Mufti as the archetypal Arab Jew-hater could not have hoped for a more effective successor than the mendacious Arafat.

The West has persisted in its self-deception by adhering to Resolution 242 for mediating the final settlement between Israelis and Palestinians. This policy, however, could only work so long as all Palestinian factions went along with the diplomatic charade.

The civil war has wrecked the charade and should disabuse the West of pursuing any further its failed policy of appeasing and bribing

Palestinians to be partners in a negotiated final settlement. Instead, the West should recognize Jerusalem as the undivided capital of the Jewish state, and work out with the Israelis the shape of a non-negotiable final settlement to be imposed on the Palestinian Authority. The progeny of the Mufti, Arafat's terrorist-trained children, can then be left on their own to work their way back into respectability and civil order, or continue descending into the hell of their making.

30 July 2007, *Western Standard* (Calgary)

24

A choice awaits Arab states

History does not progress in a straight line for people from whichever point they set forth to their desired end.

This illusion is served by retrospective view, and then deviations explained as results of people's ignorance or the caprice or duplicity of leaders as those today on the liberal-left – those on the right in their time displayed the same tendency – mindlessly repeat the silly phrase "Bush lies and people die."

The politics of the Arab Mideast show how improbable is the idea of history's linear progress in the region.

More than 500 years of Turkish rule of this region ended not as a result of the indigenous peoples' capacity to gain their own independence. It was won for the Arabs by Britain with soldiers from its empire, men bearing arms from India, Australia and New Zealand, in the war of 1914-18.

The story of the Arab Revolt as told by the Englishman T.E. Lawrence in his book *Seven Pillars of Wisdom* is a magnificent record of the effort invested on behalf of a people, the desert Arabs (Bedouins), so they may have a claim on their history that was being shaped by forces from outside of their lives.

This effort continues with all its various meanderings as witnessed this week at Annapolis, Md., to make the Arab states grapple with their shortcomings, to turn the page on the politics of resentment and grievances against each other and outsiders, to take responsibility for their failings as an essential requirement to become alert in defending their own interests.

The practicality of politics lies in the capacity to distinguish between all that is desired and what is possible, and make it happen.

This is also the lesson of the Jews to the Arabs in making Israel happen from what was the least desirable held out to them. U.S. President George W. Bush, unlike any of his predecessors, has gone the furthest in committing the United States to support the establishment of the Palestinian state. Like Lawrence with the desert Arabs, Bush has leaned forward to save the Palestinians from themselves and their past folly of repeatedly snatching defeat from the jaws of sanity.

But the desert Arabs – Palestinians among them – are, as Lawrence described them, "a people of starts, for whom the abstract was the strongest motive, the process of infinite courage and variety, and the end nothing."

It was men like Lawrence, and General Sir Edmund Allenby in command of the British forces in the Mideast most of all, who were responsible for returning history and independence to the Arabs after 500 years of their slumbering in the shadows of Turkish rule.

Then, 90 years later, it is Bush investing the resources of the United States to turn the Arab states around against their self-defeating instinct and squander another century in recrimination.

There is urgency for the Arab states to recognize how their interests are being undermined by Iran and its clients, Hamas and Hezbollah. This was the subtext of the Annapolis meeting.

The Arab states led by Saudi Arabia have a choice to make.

They can either settle with Israel and join the United States in preventing Iran from acquiring nuclear weapon capability, or let their disunity work in favour of Tehran's ambition to become the dominant power in the Mideast as once were the Turks.

1 December 2007, *Toronto Sun*

25

The intellectual defence of tyranny

In an essay titled "Dignity and solidarity" published recently in Egypt's leading English journal *Al-Ahram Weekly*, Edward Said writes: "Whatever one thinks of Saddam Hussein, and he was a vicious tyrant, he provided the people of Iraq with the best infrastructure of services like water, electricity, health, and education of any Arab country. None of this is any longer in place."

Said is professor of comparative literature in New York's Columbia University.

His well known book *Orientalism* (1978) has had a wide influence within and outside the Middle East.

As one of the sophisticated voices of Arab intellectuals – nationalist and secular – Said's latest reflection on Saddam Hussein does not come as a surprise.

He belongs to that modern school of Arab thinking, shaped by the traumatic defeat of the 1967 Arab-Israeli war, that readily faults the West for most of the ills in the Arab-Muslim world.

On this matter, Kanan Makiya, the Iraqi-Arab writer who has toiled to expose the tyranny of Saddam Hussein, observed pointedly that Said's major work "is premised on the morally wrong idea that the West is to be blamed in the here-and-now for its long nefarious history of association with the Middle East."

The surprise is in the phrasing of Said's apologetic for Saddam, in that it echoes those offered by other apologists for tyrants and dictators in the past.

It is a reminder of the sort of excuses made for Hitler and Mussolini, the leaders of German and Italian fascism – that, whatever their faults, they ran the trains on time.

But of greater interest in Said's remarks about the Iraqi despot, is to witness again the performance of those intellectuals who see themselves as defenders of common people, as anti-imperialists, as swimming with the currents of history to liberate the down-trodden and the oppressed and at the end becoming, at least in part, apologists for mass murderers.

Said is only the most recent example. The most prominent is that of the French philosopher, Jean-Paul Sartre.

Said has written about the influence of Sartre in his thinking, of Sartre as the public philosopher who "opposed France in Algeria and Vietnam."

But what is most remembered about Sartre is not what Said writes, not about his declining the 1964 Nobel Prize in literature, nor his Marxism and the intricacies of his existentialist philosophy, but his defence of Stalin even after the details of his crimes were denounced from the altars of Bolshevism by his successor, Nikita Khrushchev, in 1956.

Apart from eccentricity, there are complex reasons why an intellectual defends Stalin in the case of Sartre, or Hitler and the Nazis in the case of Martin Heidegger.

Sartre offered a clue – self-loathing – in an essay titled "Situations" (1961). He wrote: "In the name of the principles my class had inculcated in me, in the name of its humanism and humanities, in the name of liberty, equality and fraternity, I dedicated to the bourgeoisie a hatred which will end only with myself."

Sartre, like Heidegger, was not a solitary intellectual, nor his views inconsequential for the public to which he wrote and spoke. He remained loyal to the Soviet Union, he was an establishment figure of the left, and his views buttressed the position of the French Communists in the period when Soviet communism appeared to be invulnerable.

Similarly, Said is no mere academic, or a lonely writer with his views confined within a narrow circle of students specializing in contemporary literature and literary criticism.

He is a celebrated public figure in the Middle East, a widely published author in America, a former member of the Palestinian National Council, and the most eloquent representative of Arab nationalists in the West.

Yet Said's faulting of the West, and America in particular, for the Palestinian condition, led him to become an apparent apologist for Saddam Hussein.

Consequently, again, like Sartre, Said has provided false comfort to a great many Arabs and Muslims in their morbid self-deception to escape responsibility from a history that is partly of their own making.

10 July 2003, *Toronto Sun*

26

Reasonableness and rage

This week 59 years ago May 14, 1948, David Ben-Gurion read out the declaration proclaiming Israel's independence.

Some six months earlier in November 1947 the UN voted for the partition of Palestine under British Mandate into two states, one Arab and one Jewish.

Jewish leaders accepted the UN resolution, while the Arab League representing Arab opinion repudiated the UN plan and refused to accept the making of modern Israel.

The history of this period, and of the decades preceding and following Israel's re-birth, is layered with controversy, yet one dominant motif of this history stands out. Arab misery is in part a self-inflicted consequence of Arab vindictiveness toward Jews, making the Arab-Israeli dispute the most intractable of conflicts over the past 100 years and counting.

Arab refusal to accept Jewish rights to statehood has been accompanied by wars with the intent to annihilate Israel. Bigotry and hate toward Jews on the Arab side has masqueraded as religious edict, and then morphed into the sheer evil of indiscriminate suicide bombings.

Arabs have not been alone in their malice towards Jews and Israel. Big powers have also connived and colluded with Arab states to keep alive Arab-Muslim animus towards Israel.

Britain's promise made to Jews in the Balfour Declaration of November 1917 laid the grounds for a Jewish home in the lands where God – so does the Quran (5:20-21) of the Muslims record – instructed Moses to take his people. It was from these lands and the temples Jews built to God that the Romans evicted them 2,000 years ago.

But when Jews, threatened in the 1930s with Hitler's Final Solution for European Jewry needed most urgently support to find refuge, Britain imposed stringent restrictions on Jewish emigration into Palestine. If with British help – instead of London's opposition to Jews and appeasement of Arabs – Israel had been founded 10 years earlier then many of those Jews who perished in the Holocaust would have survived.

An acceptance of Israel, at any time during the past six decades, would have made for permanent peace between two people claiming rights over the same lands. Israel's peace treaties with Egypt (1979) and Jordan (1994) are instructive that neither nationalism nor religion are insurmountable obstacles to reaching an Arab-Israeli settlement on Palestine as proposed in the UN plan of 1947.

What is missing on the Arab side, in particular with Palestinians, is reasonableness, a quality amply demonstrated by Jews despite the anguish of their tragedy and the rightness of their claims to statehood. Unlike Arabs, Jews accepted what was offered by the UN in 1947 as the least good, and then worked hard to make the best of the circumstances provided.

Elias Khoury, a Palestinian-Christian writer, reflecting on the twists and turns of his native land comments, "Palestine isn't a country for it to have a flag. Palestine is a condition. Every Arab is a Palestinian... Palestine is the condition of us all." In other words, Palestine for Arabs is pathology or a rage and tribal call for rallying in an endless conflict with tribal enemies.

Israel's success in building a modern economy within a democratic setting holds a mirror to the Arab-Muslim world's abject failure to meet demands of the modern world with reasonableness.

Arab politics instead burns self-destructively with rage whether it is in the savagery of violence at display in Iraq, in the ethnic genocide unleashed in Darfur, or Palestinians shooting each other as the world watches in disbelief or wrong-headed sympathy.

19 May 2007, *Toronto Sun*

27

Muslim contradiction

The world, perhaps, is exhausted with trying to understand what malady torments some Muslims to behave insanely. And with their propensity to violence as in the latest saga over the Danish cartoons of the Prophet Muhammad.

How does one explain how cartoons – however objectionable to religious sensibility – can spark violence in the name of Islam, which means peace?

Or, for that matter, why the late Iranian clerical leader Ayatollah Khomeini, in February 1989, pronounced a death sentence on Salman Rushdie for his novel, *The Satanic Verses*, that alluded allegorically to the Prophet Muhammad.

Experts have engaged for some time in explaining contemporary Muslim politics, as the historian Bernard Lewis does in his book, *What Went Wrong?* Such efforts continue in the hope of making sense of this behaviour that bewilders non-Muslims.

But even as Muslims insist their faith-tradition is one of peace, the conduct of at least a considerable segment of the Muslim population contradicts their public faith.

Some writers such as Ibn Warraq, a pseudonym, suggest the problem with Muslim conduct is inherent in Islam.

They contend Muslim violence is symptomatic of an intolerant religion.

But the Quran, Islam's sacred text, calls upon its readers to engage in introspection. Muslims who engage in what the Quran invites them to do would eschew violence as a requisite of their faith.

Why, then, is there such disconnect between what Muslims insist their faith represents and the conduct of some Muslims, as we witness in recent times?

For a plausible figurative explanation consider the following: Chronologically speaking Islam is in its 15th century, Christianity in its 21st and Judaism in its 58th.

We might express the ages of these three faith-traditions in terms of human life span, with Islam being in its adolescent years, Christianity having entered into its adult years and Judaism being well past its middle age.

Several centuries ago when Christianity was about the same age as Islam is today, it too often showed characteristics of adolescents lacking in introspection, readily prone to committing violence and in taking offence, behaving uncharitably toward others and being self-righteous.

The remarkable achievement of Judaism, from the perspective of its relatively long life, is survival against terrible odds.

This has provided Judaism with the wisdom of respectful coexistence with other faith traditions.

What we view in the behaviour of radical Muslims as bewildering – people who have, for instance, dynamited the Buddha statues of Bamiyan in Afghanistan, gutted churches, repeatedly insulted people of other faiths – is consistent with the conduct of an adolescent, yet to grow up and understand that actions have consequences.

Not all Muslims are adolescents, or engage in violence and reprehensible behaviour. But it is undeniable that Muslims who indulge in violence, irrespective of the reasons they offer, have not been effectively repudiated and checked by the Muslim majority.

The majority then, troubled and saddened as it is with watching its faith-tradition wrecked by its religious compatriots, is not entirely blameless.

This explanation of mentality in terms of age would suggest that many Muslims are yet to mature and grasps the precepts of their own faith traditions.

Those who did – for example the little-known Sufis who seek the hidden treasure of Islam within their hearts and minds – were often abused by fanatics, reflecting the mindlessness of adolescents.

This also suggests the world must find the means to adequately deal with those Muslims who behave as destructive adolescents, until they grow up and become responsible.

11 February 2006, *Toronto Sun*

28

Achieving freedom a fragile fight

Four years after the fall of Baghdad to American forces, current pictures from Iraq show us a culture seething with tribal rivalries and violence that was once kept in check by the even greater violence of a regime headed by Saddam Hussein.

The sectarian violence between Sunnis and Shi'ites has created a river of blood that reaches back to the first century of Islam. The tribal violence never ceased as it transformed into conflicts among the successor states of the Ottoman Empire created by the British-French agreement following World War I.

It is the West's loss of confidence in itself and its contribution to the making of the modern world – its ideals enshrined in the United Nations Charter – that raise blinders to seeing things for what they are in the Middle East, and speaking about them plainly without insulting the memory or experience of victims of that region's political culture.

In observing the Middle East now for some time, I am reminded of what Umar ibn al-Khattab, the prophet's companion and second caliph, said about his people. Umar remarked, as it is recorded, "The Arabians are truly an unruly camel and, by God, I am he who can keep them on the right path."

Saddam Hussein and his like, who ruled the Arab-Muslim world with undisguised cruelty, imagined they had the warrant of Umar to tear apart limbs of men, make women widows and children orphans in order to perpetuate their rule indefinitely through their clans.

As I write, Darfur burns and the Arab-Muslim rulers shrug their shoulders dismissively for this is the way of their world.

Terrorists are the cruel progeny of the Arab-Muslim rulers, and their excesses in savagery recorded daily in Baghdad and elsewhere are lessons they learned in societies run by these rulers.

But people in Egypt, Darfur, Syria, Iran and much of the Arab-Muslim world want to escape from their rulers. They dream of the possibilities inherent in freedom.

Four years ago, Americans and their coalition-partners brought freedom for Iraqis. Historians in the future, not contemporaries with their blinkered views and partisan politics, will assess how much of that freedom was sold short by mistakes made by the liberators of Iraq.

Four years later much of Iraq, except for Baghdad and its neighbourhood, has been slowly progressing to acquire the culture of freedom where it never existed.

Kurds were denied by the British to have a state of their own while being mercilessly abused by Saddam Hussein, yet they have turned the page on their past to build a society with much promise of civility and basic decency.

Similarly, Iraqi Shi'ites – haltingly and without any precedent of selfrule to guide them into the future – have been making gains even as terrorists without any reprise batter them daily.

In these four years we have also seen a people, deeply troubled and abused, defiantly defend their newly won freedom.

Violence failed to intimidate Iraqis as they ratified their constitution and elected their government, nor did the recent bombing of the parliament stop the elected members reconvening to discharge their responsibilities.

These four years have shown, lest we forget, how fragile and difficult is the birth of freedom anywhere. These years have also shown how irresolute and unmindful of history are an increasing number of people in the West taking their own freedom for granted.

21 April 2007, *Toronto Sun*

29

The Malady of Islam

Since 9/11, the West, and the United States in particular, has been wrestling with the problem of how to deal with the pathology, or what Abdelwahab Meddeb, the Paris-based Tunisian writer, calls the "malady of Islam." There seems to be no relevant past experience that the West might draw upon in confronting this malady.

The pathologies of German-Italian fascism and Japanese militarism were eventually severely dealt with by the Allied powers, and their defeat followed by reform of those societies made the world more secure and prosperous. Similarly, a combination of diplomacy and military force by the West contained the pathology of the former Soviet Union until the communist system collapsed. But presently, there is great reluctance in the West — especially from the new Obama administration in Washington — to learn from the past and to tackle the challenges the Arab-Muslim world will continue to pose in the years ahead if the malady remains uncured.

Much has been written in recent years about Islam. I will comment here on an aspect of the problem of Islam and our modern world as a Muslim drawing upon my own lived experience.

First, the Arabs constitute less than a fifth of the world's Muslim population. Yet despite their minority position Arabs are the center of gravity in the Islamic world. Non-Arab Muslims, for a host of reasons, look to Arabs for their understanding and practice of Islam. Hence, the malady of the Arab-Muslim world is intimately bound with the cultural norms of Arabs. Regionwise, the most affected areas extend from the Atlantic to the River Indus.

Secondly, the malady has been exacerbated by the Arab response to modernity. Modernity has multiple meanings: industrialization, urbanization, adoption of liberal values, women's rights, elected governments, etc. I want to emphasize here the concept of citizenship as a core component of modernity. The idea of citizenship is linked to the idea of individuals in society possessing unalienable rights. The evolution of this idea has meant that even though society is a collection of individuals, individual rights override collective rights and distinguish modern society from mob rule. On this idea rests the modern democratic society, wherein political leaders are elected by citizens to whom they are accountable. They hold office with citizen approval; they make laws, but none might be passed that override the unalienable rights of citizens written into the constitution. They govern with support of the citizens and are replaced when they fail to meet the goals that saw them elected.

Let us now consider the malady of Islam given the above description of the problem as I see it. Modernity, and its concept of individual rights, is Western in origin. It evolved through centuries of philosophical and political debates, and then equally long periods of war to defeat those who opposed the principle of individual liberty. Eventually modernity and its off-shoot, citizenship, prevailed over the opposition and were more or less firmly established in the West and places beyond by the end of the last century.

Arabs were in close proximity to these ideas and the struggle that accompanied them. What, it might be asked of the Arabs, was their response to modernity? Even with all the apologia and obfuscation, the answer that cannot be evaded is that the collective Arab response has shown a preference for totalitarian ideology. In the period following the end of the World War II and European colonialism, there were three ideological responses that marked out the Arabs into three groups: secular Muslims, and orthodox Muslims divided into the majority Sunni and minority Shi'i sects.

Secular Muslims were mobilized by Arab nationalism embodied in the Ba'ath party. Sunni Muslims chose Wahhabism/Salafism embodied in the politics of the Muslim Brotherhood and the Taliban. Shi'i Muslims followed Khomeinism embodied in the politics of the clerical regime in Iran, Hezbollah in Lebanon, and the Sadrists in Iraq.

All three ideologies and movements they spawned are totalitarian. For all their professed belief in Islam's sacred scripture, Arabs — given their bloodsoaked history of suppressing dissent and despite their close proximity to the evolution of liberal movements in Europe — have been engaged in suppressing or eradicating any form of individual liberty while making no allowance for their opponents. Arabs have shown by their conduct that tyranny is their preferred response to modernity.

Liberalism in the Arab-Muslim world is peripheral. Muslim liberals are scorned, or treated worse. They look for support in the West or flee to the West. Those who have fled are viewed as stooges of the West in their native countries. Then many among them torn by remorse and guilt turn against their Western hosts and become caricatures of their past lives, railing against the West even as they prosper personally and professionally in the freedom West provides.

America's response to 9/11 under President George W. Bush has been hugely consequential for the advance of freedom over tyranny in the Arab-Muslim world. Two of the three tyrannies (Iraq under the Ba'ath and Afghanistan under the Taliban) have been destroyed.

The remaining tyranny (Iran under Khomeinism) is in a unique situation. It is trapped between emerging democracies, even as it is seen as a bastion of reactionary hope among besieged tyrannies and their defenders. This circumstance has opened a second front in the war against Islamist terrorism, and one may observe the rise of proxy armies far and wide as a result.

Among supporters of the defeated tyrannies are the urban elite. Members of the urban elite, particularly among non-Arab Muslims, are Westernized, share little in common with the populace, live in privileged enclaves, and send their offspring to schools in the West. Their rule has brought much ruin to their people, as in Egypt and Pakistan. But they have avoided taking any responsibility by railing against the West and blaming it for their failure. This blame game will not end soon, especially as the West continues to contort itself in making apologies for the colonialism that ended some time ago.

Muslims need to ask themselves what they have against modernity. Does it go against their scripture? Does it undermine their political interests? Does it impede their progress from poverty to a life of dignity and improved well-being? Except for the obstacle posed by the urban elite and the influence of Arab culture, Muslims in general have no reason not to embrace modernity.

Freedom and democracy have been planted by American arms in the heart of the Arab-Muslim world. Violent reactions were predictable given the history of the people and the region. But the defeat of two tyrannies and their accompanying ideologies is a beginning. It opens a new chapter for Muslims to prove to themselves they can be free people respecting of individual liberty and making progress with a better and reformed understanding of Islam. Conversely, if the malady of Islam is not cured it will increasingly infect the West; hence, apart from any other reason, prudence itself demands the West steadfastly remain committed to the curing of Islam's malady.

8 March 2009, *Pajamas Media*

30

Barbarians kill as West drifts

There comes a point at which diminishing returns on most issues begin to go negative.

Such a point in denouncing Islamist terrorism and equally the Muslim majority's silence against this menace was reached sometime ago.

As Islamist terrorism, however despicable, became mundane occurrence in the daily news cycle, the deafening silence of Muslims – except for lonely voices of feeble opposition – has given credence to growing numbers of non-Muslims that Islam is as much a religion of peace as the Klanmen's politics is an expression of multiculturalism.

But there is another side to this abject reality. The Muslim majority's silence is greatly compounded by the appeasement mentality in the West of the mainstream liberal-left media, politicians trolling for ethnic votes and bureaucrats running public institutions.

An evidence of this comes from Scotland. Theodore Dalrymple, a retired physician and prolific writer, in New York's *City Journal* reports:

"In an effort to ensure that no Muslim doctors ever again try to bomb Glasgow Airport, bureaucrats at Glasgow's public hospitals have decreed that henceforth no staff may eat lunch at their desks or in their offices during the holy month of Ramadan, so that fasting Muslims shall not be offended by the sight or smell of their food. Vending machines will also disappear from the premises during that period."

It is as if more diversity training for public officials, more accommodation of demands made by fundamentalist Muslims, greater willingness to selfflagellate for sins long past of western colonialism, more policing of what might be politically incorrect speech and writing about Islamists or Saudi Arabia's official cult (Wahhabism) of bigotry masquerading as a world religion, will somehow mysteriously translate into taming suicide-bombers and their masters to reciprocate kindly to the liberal-left sensibilities of people in the West.

Dalrymple observes stories such as the one from Scotland tell us something about how civilizations commit suicide – they "collapse not because the barbarians are so strong, but because they themselves are so morally enfeebled."

What do barbarians do? Kill indiscriminately as in the recent August 14 massacre in northern Iraq reported by the New York Post with the headline "Savages Kill 175 in Iraq Bombings."

Four trucks were exploded west of Mosul – Iraq's third largest city in the Kurdish north – in an area predominantly inhabited by Yazidis, a people practising pre-Islamic faith. The toll of dead and wounded among this poor dwindling minority living at the edge of the Iraqi society far exceeds the numbers first reported.

This savagery is the work of al-Qaida associates preparing more predictable bombings ahead of the mid-September report in Washington to be given by Gen. David Petraeus, the top U.S. commander in Iraq.

There is now a pattern in al-Qaida bombings arranged to influence American public opinion during key moments in public policy debates and general elections.

But the liberal-left media, such as the *New York Times*, remains fixated with faulting the Bush administration for the savagery of Islamists while providing oxygen to apologists of terror spinning their endless refrain of "root cause" being oil and Israel for violence originating in the Middle East.

How morally enfeebled, as Dalrymple opines, is the West? Imagine the uproar denouncing any suggestion that the mainstream liberal-left media, in appearance at least, is treasonously on side with the newest enemies of freedom and democracy.

25 August 2007, *Toronto Sun*

31

How the West was duped

When Ayatollah Ruhollah Khomeini announced on Valentine's Day 1989 the death sentence on Salman Rushdie for writing *The Satanic Verses*, and others associated with its publication and translation, it was his last major pronouncement as the radical religious leader and founder of the Islamic Republic of Iran.

Khomeini died in June 1989. His notorious edict as the opening salvo of the Islamist war against the West, however, still remains lethal in censoring free speech and driving fear into the hearts of anyone daring to submit Islam and Muslim history to critical scrutiny.

It would be fair to say the West did not know what to make of Khomeini's incitement to murder 20 years ago. Or of Rushdie who was forced to hide under British protection from those who might kill him for the $5.2 million bounty on offer.

The edict against Rushdie was lifted officially by Khomeini's successors in 1998. But to the ever-lasting shame of many around the world, the edict sparked a debate over the propriety of any expression, such as Rushdie's book, that could be viewed as insulting Islam.

This debate is far from over and it continues to cast a chilling spell over freedom of expression that could well be characterized as the essential value of the secular West. Khomeini's success in confounding the West came from a simple, yet ingenious tactic of dressing his politics in the garment of religion.

Instead of repudiating Khomeini's politics, and that of the Islamists, the West contorted itself, with its policy of official multiculturalism, to accommodate the vulgar and neo-barbaric politics aggressively promoted as religion.

Twenty years on and it would be fair to say the West has become somewhat complicit in the politics unleashed by Khomeini, and pushed relentlessly by Islamists ever since, to silence and punish critics of Islam and Muslim history.

The profound irony here is that Muslims can only be politically liberated by subjecting Islam to unfettered critical inquiry as was done with Christianity. Only then they may recover their faith as a matter of personal conscience, instead of being suffocated by an Islam perverted into a tool of totalitarian politics ever since the early years of Arab-Muslim history.

Within the Muslim world any effort to engage in such a task, that Salim Mansur 163 eventually demolishes the totalitarian control of the power holders over Islam, carries with it mortal risks. Khomeini's edict against Rushdie was to set a forbidding example.

Only in a relatively free and secure environment could anyone, especially Muslims, engage in the task of salvaging Islam's pristine message of monotheism and God's mercy in a world of unending struggle between good and evil. It is also through such efforts, and by not appeasing Islamists, that a mutually respectful and genuine coexistence of non-Muslims and Muslims might be constructed.

But when the West concedes to Islamists in the mistaken belief that subjecting Islam and Muslim history to intensive criticism amounts to "hate speech" and must not be allowed, then freedom is undermined and totalitarianism in the Arab-Muslim world gets further entrenched.

Muslims need to become free of totalitarian Islam and the least the West can do in support is not concede an inch of its own hard-won freedom in quest of false peace with Islamists.

14 February 2009, *Toronto Sun*

32

Europe placates foes of freedom

Europe, or a significant segment of Europe, unfailingly discloses its frequent willingness to appease totalitarian foes of freedom.

In modern times Europe gladly has served as a cradle of fascism on the right, communism on the left and in between all sorts of variations of the two, joined at the hip with a common blood-soaked bigotry directed at Jews.

Since 9/11, and despite Muslim terrorists striking on European soil, that segment of Europe ready to appease any totalitarian assault on freedom has contorted itself to accommodate the Islamist agenda. The latest evidence of this is the Amsterdam Court of Appeal's decision to prosecute Geert Wilders, an elected member of the Dutch Parliament, for hate speech offending Islam and Muslims.

Wilders is the most daring critic of the Islamist assault on Holland, and Europe, since the murder of Theo van Gogh in November 2004 by a self-confessed Muslim fanatic of Moroccan origin, and the marginalization in Dutch politics of Ayaan Hirsi Ali, the Somali-born critic of Islam.

What brings Wilders into legal trouble with Dutch jurists is the 15- minute video he produced last year on Islam titled *Fitna*. In this short film Wilders juxtaposed verses from the Quran with passages from Hitler's rant, *Mein Kampf*, and urged Muslims to push for reform by removing "hate-filled" verses from their sacred text.

I do not share Wilders' views on the Quran, or on Islam, and I would be quite prepared to engage him if an opportunity presented itself. But I categorically disagree with the Amsterdam Court of Appeal's decision to prosecute him on the grounds of hate speech, thereby abridging the principle of free speech, for expressing his views on the Quran.

It is ironic that the announcement to prosecute Wilders comes on the eve of the 20th anniversary of Ayatollah Ruhollah Khomeini's notorious incitement (fatwa) to murder Salman Rushdie, the Indian-born writer, for his satirical novel *The Satanic Verses*.

Khomeini's incitement was an opening salvo in the Islamist agenda to silence any critic, Muslim or non-Muslim, of Islam and Arab-Muslim history.

Following Khomeini's directive to murder, Farag Foda – a courageous and brilliant Egyptian critic of fundamentalist Muslims and Islam – was gunned down in Cairo in April 1992. However Foda's compatriot and winner of the 1988 Nobel Prize in literature, Naguib Mahfouz, survived a knife assault by Islamists in 1994.

Islamist effort to silence critics is part of a larger agenda for the full and unreformed imposition of *shari'ah* – laws derived from the Quran and codified in the first millennium of the Christian era – within the Arab-Muslim world, and its acceptance by governments in Europe and North America to enable Muslims residing in the West to live by a pre-modern legal code.

This push is backed by the 57-member Organization of Islamic Countries (OIC) at the UN to combat "defamation of religions" under the international human rights code for the purpose of judicially silencing critics of Islam and Muslims.

The prosecution of Wilders, as the Dutch judges contort themselves to do the bidding of the OIC, will warm the hearts of Islamists everywhere. But Europe and the West could not be more warned of what embracing the Islamist agenda means than taking full measure of the Arab-Muslim world turned into a cultural wasteland by the unremitting Islamist assault on civilization.

31 January 2009, *Toronto Sun*

33

Muslim world not a monolith

It's time to leave aside the controversy over the Danish cartoons of Prophet Muhammad that has dominated the news in the past few weeks – and examine instead what is at the heart of the violent reaction of some Muslim protesters.

The virulent protests themselves are not new – we saw something similar decades ago with the Iranian fatwa against novelist Salman Rushdie for his book *The Satanic Verses*.

But debate is necessary on this subject. Without the freedom to question, affirm, deny, revise or dismiss deeply held beliefs and values, there is only dogma that invariably becomes stale, lifeless and suffocating.

The kind of rage we have seen from some extremists is indicative in part of their incapacity to provide a persuasive argument in defence of their position.

Whatever reasonable arguments they might have for limiting freedom of expression on grounds of religious propriety, these have been shredded by the recourse to violence.

There is no such argument, however, in liberal-democratic society. To pretend that freedom of expression as a principle is not subverted when restrictions are imposed out of fear of causing offence, is to trade in hypocrisy – just as commissars of totalitarian societies do.

A segment of the Muslim population has, by indulging in violence, demanded that free societies restrict freedom of expression. If free societies, including Canada, concede to this demand, then one of their foundational principles is irreparably compromised.

What has been lost in the sound and fury of the present controversy is the rather simple question: Is the Muslim world a monolith? If it is not, then surely there exists a diversity of opinions among Muslims on matters sacred and profane.

To consider the Muslim world a monolith – and Muslims in general beholden to the opinion of some religious authority or power-holder – is a greater insult to Islam than any perverse imaginings of cartoonists or the even more perverse reaction of that segment of Muslims so readily driven to rage, be it contrived or genuinely felt.

"There is no compulsion in religion," declares the Quran, Islam's sacred text. A faith born of compulsion would be akin to demanding love following rape.

Since God in his infinite majesty neither compels, nor takes offence, it is reasonable to believe his prophets, including Muhammad, instructed their followers accordingly.

Hence, the recent rage really has little to do with Islam, and much to do with the sociology of parts of the Muslim world, where freedom remains an alien idea and dissent a crime.

Yet Muslims, such as Omar Khayyam (d. 1131) – dissident poet and astronomer-mathematician – defied authoritarian rulers, tyrants, and establishment gatekeepers of Islam to worship God and honour the Prophet in freedom of their conscience.

Khayyam's spirit persists even though the Western media has become greatly devoted to portraying only Muslim rage, and not the quiet courage of Muslims who are more offended by the perversity of violence within their societies.

As a few Muslims readily rage over some perceived injury or another, and demagogues in their midst spin excuses, it is worth recalling Khayyam's admonishment:

> Oh Canon Jurist, we work better than you
>
> With all this drunkenness, we're more sober:
>
> You drink men's blood, we, the vine's,
>
> Be honest – which of us is the more bloodthirsty?

18 February 2006, *Toronto Sun*

34

Getting a read on the Quran

I will not rehearse here, since space forbids, the arguments on how ludicrous is the display of Gordon Brown's Labour government in banning Geert Wilders from entering Britain.

What needs noting, however, is the irony that Brown, Wilders, the liberal elite in the West with their insistence on limiting free speech, and the Muslim thugs – from the potentates who rule in the Arab-Muslim world to those who riot in the streets – are all in agreement that Muslims generally are programmed by Islam and its sacred text, the Quran, to engage in violence.

The difference between Wilders and Muslim fanatics is in how they assess the rightness or wrongness of violence to be found in the Quran. Wilders sees the Quran as a Muslim version of Adolf Hitler's *Mein Kampf*, and Muslim fanatics see the Quran as heavenly license to trample over those in disagreement with their views of the world.

But the Quran does not speak. The verses of the Quran – if we go by Muslim belief – were heavenly words spoken to Muhammad or impressed into his heart by the angel Gabriel.

It was Muhammad who spoke the heavenly words and acted upon them. After him there is silence, and the words of the Quran as we have them are scratches on parchments collected into a text by those who heard Muhammad utter them.

After Muhammad it is the tongue of man, of Muslims, that speaks and gives meaning to the words originally addressed to him. The tongue of man can be straight or forked, pure or vile, and what such tongues utter reveal the state of men's minds and hearts.

The wonderful poet-philosopher from the 13th century, Jalal ad-Din Rumi – many revere him as the greatest mystical poet of Islam – likened the Quran to the mysteriousness of women. His exact words cannot be quoted here due to the political correctness code of our time.

What Rumi alluded to was how a woman chose to disclose her mystery depended on the circumstances, with whom and under what condition she engaged with that person. Similarly, the Quran's mystery remains locked or gets gradually unfolded in relation to the man, given his abilities, who engages with it.

Rumi cautioned Muslims rape is not love even though the motions might appear to be similar.

My mentor and friend the late Wilfred Cantwell Smith – he was perhaps Canada's greatest scholar of Islam – would remind his audience the Quran is to Muslims what Jesus is to Christians. Hence, in terms of belief the Quran, not Muhammad, is divine to Muslims as is Jesus for Christians.

The Quran categorically instructs there is no compulsion in religion. Muslim thugs read the text even as the Quran's instruction fails to register in their hearts and minds while its mysteriousness completely eludes them.

The Quran is violated by Muslim thugs. The result is to be found in the misery of the Arab-Muslim world as a broken civilization.

One of the profound mysteries surrounding the divine in its descent into our corrupt world is the response it generates, and the extent to which it is mutilated.

Jesus was crucified. The Qur'an is daily mutilated by Muslim fanatics, and they insist their reading of it is an act of devotion.

21 February 2009, *Toronto Sun*

35

Let's not monkey with the Quran

There is not a day passes when the world does not hear cursing of Jews pouring out of the Arab-Muslim world.

The verses from the Quran cited in these hate fests masquerading as prayers, are ones in which Muhammad was reminded how Jews in transgression of sacred laws were admonished.

In Yusuf Ali's translation the verses – Quran chapter 2: 65-66 – read, "Those among you who transgressed in the matter of Sabbath We said unto them: 'Be ye apes, despised and rejected.' So We made it an example to their own time and to their posterity, and a lesson to those who fear God."

In Yusuf Ali's commentary the verses are to be understood allegorically. Ali's commentary also recalls the Quran's cautionary note to readers that the text contains verses at minimum of two kinds (3:7), those of clearly understood meaning and those being allegorical that require careful reading to avoid discord.

The context for these verses was Muhammad's encounter with Jews of Medina. Any relevance of these verses, or verses of similar kind, after Muhammad, lies in understanding the allegory as a warning to all people – not Jews alone – that transgressors of sacred laws and universal moral codes will resemble apes by their conduct.

As I wrote in an earlier column, the Quran does not speak. It is the tongue of men, pure or vile, that gives meaning to words of the Quran.

The most important distinguishing characteristic between man endowed with God's gift of free will and lesser creation such as apes, lies in the human capacity to reason, to choose between good and evil – in other words assume responsibility for one's deeds – and to be introspective.

The Quran was revealed to an Arab of noble lineage born among idol worshippers so that they may learn of Abraham's God. Muhammad's mission was to bring to pagan Arabs what God revealed to Jews through prophets raised among them.

The unambiguous words of the Quran instructing Muhammad on how to contend with evil are of universal import. It would be right to suggest, for instance, when the Allied leaders insisted by force of arms on the unconditional surrender of the German Nazis and Japanese militarists they acted in accordance with the Quran's precept.

We do not need to fast forward to our times to know who greatly violated the Quran. Among the immediate followers of Muhammad were those who would have shamed Macbeth as they committed murder and mayhem, including killing members of the prophet's immediate family.

Iran's ayatollahs, imams and potentates of the Arab-Muslim world, and some Muslims – wherever alone or collectively spewing anti-Jew bigotry overflowing from their blackened hearts – are the progeny of those from Islam's earliest days of post-prophetic history who gave tongue to the Quran to varnish their evil deeds.

The Quran is regularly mutilated by some Muslims, and in keeping with its warning no other people in our time may be more likened to apes than those Muslims who engage in or condone terrorism, honour killing and oppressing minorities.

History is a cautionary tale of civilizations ruined when wicked people go unchecked and unpunished. Hence, those who fight those Muslim perpetrators of evil to protect civilization are the just warriors of good faith acting in accordance with the teachings of Islam's sacred text.

28 February 2009, *Toronto Sun*

36

Democracy breeds bravery

Last weekend's protests in cities across North America and Europe against the war and American presence in Iraq were once again a vivid confirmation of democracy's vitality and moral superiority over all other political systems.

In Canadian cities the protest was also against Canada's military role in Afghanistan. Protesters chanted for peace, opposed violence, denounced George Bush, Tony Blair and Stephen Harper – no doubt feeling good about themselves and their politics, the sort that can only be practiced in a democracy such as ours.

The core constituency of these crowds in Paris, London, Rome, New York and Toronto, has remained the same over the years. Their protests against war and for peace have always tilted alarmingly in favour of such monstrous regimes as those of Stalin and Mao, Ho Chi Minh and Fidel Castro, in support of gnome-headed members of the politburo in Beijing or Havana or their cruel caricatures in Damascus, Baghdad and Tehran.

And predictably for this constituency, the enemy invariably remains the same: The democratically elected leaders of free and open societies in Washington, London or Ottawa.

In my years of folly – when youthful ignorance, I recall now with embarrassment, made me think Noam Chomsky to be wiser than Winston Churchill, Franklin Roosevelt and Ronald Reagan – I, too, on occasion walked with the crowd to protest the seeming perfidy of the United States and its allies.

It does not take knowledge, reflection or, most importantly, courage to join such crowds in democratic societies where the right to protest, to insult, and throw insidious labels at elected leaders is constitutionally protected.

Courage is the conviction to stand alone and, knowing the peril, to speak against evil and evildoers.

I found such courage recently in Paris among some remarkable Muslim women who came together to expose the cruelties of radical Islamism that maim, kill and silence individuals in the societies from which they fled to freedom.

Samia Labidi is of Tunisian origin and resides in Paris. She is a writer devoted to exposing al-Qaida as a cult of criminals and killers. She published an account of how her younger brother was recruited by al-Qaida and taken to Afghanistan – and eventually escaped the entrapment of those who make of Islam an ideology of suicide bombings.

I was humbled by Samia Labidi's quiet demonstration of courage, intelligence and unyielding spirit to defend freedom in a culture where women pay the price for men's honour. She reminded me of another immensely brave woman who was recently profiled by John M. Broder in *The New York Times*.

Many by now have heard of Dr. Wafa Sultan, the Syrian-born psychiatrist residing outside of Los Angeles. Her recent appearance on the Arab TV network *al-Jazeera*, speaking forcefully the sort of truth that few dare voice in her culture, raised a storm across the Arab world.

Wafa Sultan is now deemed an apostate by those Muslim religious leaders who contort themselves in apologetics for al-Qaida criminals.

This, because she declared, among other things: "Knowledge has released me from this backward thinking ... Only the Muslims defend their beliefs by burning down churches, killing people and destroying embassies... Muslims must ask themselves what they can do for humankind before they demand that humankind respect them."

There are for sure many more women, and men, such as Samia Labidi and Wafa Sultan.

They will not be found in demonstrating crowds, but their hearts pump with courage and their eyes recognize the difference between the evil of closed societies and the fallibility of democracies.

25 March 2006, *Toronto Sun*

37

Democracy can heal

Democracy never arrived anywhere impeccable and fully dressed. Not in ancient Greece, nor in modern Europe and North America.

Democracy is a tedious process, often flawed, requiring patient work for improvement and a lot of luck. Democracy is a journey, rarely a destination to step down and call it over.

It is a messy journey, frequently accompanied with disquiet, often beginning in quarrels amidst smoke and blood, and no one is ever content with the nature of the journey, the direction taken or the distance travelled.

But whatever the discontent, there is a near global consensus, today painfully reached, that despite democracy's flaws there is no better alternative.

The simple definition offered by Abraham Lincoln, the 16th U.S. president – in the midst of a civil war that was the bloodiest conflict of the 19th century – that democracy is government "of the people, by the people, for the people" perhaps cannot be improved upon.

Yet democracy as an idea and as a form of government remains contested.

One of Canada's highly respected political philosophers, the late C.B. Macpherson of the University of Toronto, devoted his 1964 CBC Massey Lectures to the subject of democracy. He began by observing, "There is a good deal of muddle about democracy... At bottom, the muddle about democracy is due to a genuine confusion as to what democracy is supposed to be about."

If the West, despite its long and rich experience with democracy as politics and culture, still remains "muddled" about it, then the situation elsewhere – particularly in the Arab-Muslim world – is terribly bleak, given the absence of or scant experience with democracy when it comes to putting together the bare minimum of a representative government.

The democratic journey is hazardous, and yet it is the only proven path for any people striving to live in a decent society. Despite endless arguments about democracy's flaws, its opponents and enemies have failed to do better in measurable terms than the achievements anywhere of an imperfect democracy at work.

In Iraq, the anguish of a people wrestling with the promises of democracy is unmistakably visible in the daily toll of death and destruction wrought by its enemies. Iraq is the evidence for those who forget how high is the costs of democracy, and how implacable is the enemy of freedom.

But on what basis can anyone make the argument that the costs of building a democratic society in Iraq have become too steep and should be abandoned? Will anyone credibly argue that the costs for keeping the United States together through the civil war and in ending slavery were too high?

On the contrary, it can be shown that the costs of tyranny in Iraq were unbearably high – as is being demonstrated in the ongoing trials of Saddam Hussein, which the mainstream media in the West are barely reporting.

The Iraqi dictator was recently found guilty for the killings of 148 Shiites in Dujail during the 1980s. His sentence, very likely the death penalty, will be announced in October.

A second trial has opened. Saddam is charged in the 1987-88 campaign against the Kurds of Iraq. It was an Iraqi version of the Final Solution to eliminate Kurds, named "Anfal" – a Quranic reference meaning "spoils of war."

Human Rights Watch estimated between 50,000 and 100,000 Kurds (men, women and children) were killed by the orders of Saddam. The evidence at the trial is massive, indisputable and mostly recovered from the archives of his regime.

The list of Saddam's crimes is immensely long. The shame of the Arab-Muslim world has been its silence over the years of what took place in Saddam's Iraq, just as it presently remains silent over the rape and murder taking place in Darfur.

Iraqis know too well on which side of the ledger – tyranny or democracy – the costs are higher, and it is unlikely they will abandon their freedom journey after the distance they have traveled since Saddam Hussein was toppled.

2 September 2006, *Toronto Sun*

38

I'm sorry...

In a recent column, Michael Coren, my colleague here at the *Sun*, demanded Muslims apologize for wrongs too numerous to list.

Coren is right. I, as a Muslim, apologize without equivocation or reservation for the terrible crimes – small and big – committed by Muslims against non-Muslims and against Muslims, as in Darfur, who are weak and easy prey to those who hold power in the name of Islam.

I imagine, however, Coren is not seeking an apology from a person of Muslim faith such as I, who maintains no rank and cannot speak on behalf of the institutionalized world of Islam.

Like many others who share his frustration and legitimate anger, Coren is asking to hear a contrite voice from within institutionalized Islam – to repent for Muslim misconduct, past and present, that is indefensible by any standard of civility and decency, and seek forgiveness.

But Coren and others might well wait indefinitely for such an apology from those representatives of institutionalized Islam convinced of their own righteousness, even as they are engineers of a civilization's wreckage and prosper in it by the art of bullying.

Muslims and non-Muslims often point to the fact there is no Vatican in contemporary Islam – no figure like the Pope or the Archbishop of Canterbury who authoritatively represents the Muslim world.

This is only partly true, for the lack of a Pope-like figure among Muslims does not mean an absence of an institutionalized setting operative in the Muslim world.

From the earliest years of post-Prophetic Islam, Muslims holding the power of the sword and what constitutes the authoritative meaning of the Quran and the Prophet's traditions have rigged the boundaries of institutionalized Islam. The wielders of the sword and interpreters of faith have worked in tandem to impose their consensus on all Muslims, and those who have questioned their authority have paid a steep price.

This institutionalized reality of Islam and its resulting complexity are not well understood by non-Muslims. Institutionalized Islam is represented by Muslim majority states and their political and religious leaders who share a consensus on matters of politics and faith.

Below institutionalized Islam's scrutiny exist a vast unaccounted number of Muslims who seek anonymity to escape the coercive notice of authorities in mosques and in presidential or monarchical palaces. Their voices, were they heard, would be rudely dismissed as heretical.

From its beginnings, institutionalized Islam's representatives hollowed out the spiritual content of Islam in the service of political expediency. The inevitable followed – politics dressed in the robes of religion.

The faces of institutionalized Islam – political leaders such as Egypt's Hosni Mubarak or religious leaders such as Lebanon's Hasan Nasrallah – are revealing of what politics have done to faith.

Within the Arab Sunni world the Egyptian-born Sheikh Qaradawi, 80, of Qatar, is the face of institutionalized Islam. He is the closest to what might pass for a titular head of Muslims akin to the Pope. Qaradawi's words, now broadcast by television network al-Jazeerah, are taken as authoritative pronouncements of Islam. He is the "spiritual" leader of the Muslim Brotherhood, a movement formed to repudiate freedom and democracy, and a defender of Islam's war against the West by any means, including suicide bombings.

For such representatives of institutionalized Islam, all things are political. They are the authoritative guardians of the ideology that in Islam religion and politics are inseparable, and jihad – holy war – is its defining aspect.

Hence, since this institutionalized Islam is at war with the West, for Coren or anyone else to expect an apology from its generals is rather naïve.

30 September 2006, *Toronto Sun*

39

In gratitude...

As Canada marks its 140th birthday it will be my 34th Canada Day celebration since I landed a generation ago at what is now Pearson International Airport.

My experience is common with most immigrants in Canada. We have been part of Canada's growth, and also its vibrancy as the ethnic profile of Canadians in major urban centres changed during this period.

Each of us came with stories as immigrants from previous generations did and each of our stories became part of the Canadian narrative.

As a young adult I witnessed civil war, mass killings and refugee exodus. I fled the disaster wrought by humans, made my way to Canada sponsored by a relative and found here what one might imagine can be made real by commitment to work and study.

I worked in stores, restaurants and drove a cab while attending night school and then university. I discovered Canadian generosity was not a fable, and I know I would not be where I am without the support and kindness extended to me.

In the years since I landed penniless, my relatives and family have grown and taken root in Canada. My son was born in Toronto and survived his ailment at birth only because of the care he received at the Hospital for Sick Children in Toronto.

I am often asked about my country, meaning from where I came. And I mostly answer my country is where my son was born, and where I laid my mother to rest.

It has been a long time since I stopped seeing myself as a hyphenated Canadian and did what others have done before me in making my unequivocal emotional investment in the country that took me in without any reservation, and gave me a home to be proud of.

During these past three decades there have been great changes within and outside Canada. Quebec separatists pushed Canada, for instance, to its edge, and newcomers from developing countries have made demands on the country for causes which should have been left behind whence they came.

The Cold War ended without a catastrophic bang, but conflicts have not abated and Canada is drawn by its commitment to protect freedom and democracy to support those struggling for the same.

Yet there are never-ending complaints. I take the Biblical story of Cain and Abel as an apt metaphor of the human condition, and no amount of social engineering will make a utopia where Cains embrace Abels and make their lands flow with milk and honey.

But the West through much bitter experience of its own did eventually discover the means of making a society least vulnerable to the caprices of Cains allowing Abels to prosper in relative security.

Canada is an example of such a society, and yet over the years I have heard too often voices disparage this country which remains generous without demanding much of any sort in return.

Since 9/11 a dark, ominous shadow has fallen across the land.

There are those among us who do not share Canadian values, some publicly rejects them, and others plot to harm us.

It would be best if they left our shores on their own, or the rest of us made certain we do not want them in our midst.

For most of us, I believe, as it is with me on this Canada Day and every day of the year, our hearts brim with gratitude for the land that gave us its shelter.

30 June 2007, *Toronto Sun*

40

We Muslims have work to do

Muslim Canadians, as Muslims elsewhere in Western societies, have felt increasingly besieged for some time now, both from outside their community and from within.

This sense of isolation, of being misrepresented and misunderstood, will inevitably deepen as the full story unfolds of the arrests of 17 Toronto-area Muslims on terrorism charges.

But whose fault is this? Let us, Muslims, be brutally honest.

We have inherited a culture of denial, of too often refusing to acknowledge our own responsibility for the widespread malaise that has left most of the Arab-Muslim countries in economic, political and social disrepair.

Statistics and intergovernmental reports over the past several decades have documented a gap, perhaps now unbridgeable, between Muslim countries and the advanced industrial democracies in the West.

In a recent "failed states index" published in the journal *Foreign Policy* (May/June 2006), Pakistan, for instance, is ranked among the top 10 failed states in the world – ahead of Afghanistan. Pakistan is a Muslim country, a nuclear military power, but it can barely feed, clothe, educate and shelter its population.

The reports on the Arab countries are a dismal catalogue of entrenched tyrannies, failing economies, squandered wealth, gender oppression, persecution of minorities and endemic violence.

The cleric-led regime in Iran seeks nuclear weapons and threatens to obliterate Israel, repress domestic opposition, and seek confrontation with the West.

Instead of acknowledging the reality of the Arab-Muslim world as a broken civilization, we Muslims tend to indulge instead in blaming others for our ills; deflecting our responsibilities for failures that have become breeding grounds of violence and terrorism.

Many of our intellectuals in public life and our religious leaders in mosques remain adept in double-speak, saying contrary things in English or French and then in Arabic or Farsi or Urdu.

We have made hypocrisy an art, and have spun for ourselves a web of lies that blinds us to the real world around us.

We seethe with grievances and resentment against the West, even as we have prospered in the freedom and security of Western democracies.

We have inculcated into our children false pride, and given them a sense of history that crumbles under critical scrutiny. We have burdened them with conflicting loyalties – and now some of them have become our nightmare.

We preach tolerance yet we are intolerant. We demand inclusion, yet we practice exclusion of gender, of minorities, of those with whom we disagree.

We repeat endlessly that Islam is a religion of peace, yet too many of us display conduct contrary to what we profess.

We keep assuring ourselves and others that Muslims who violate Islam are a minuscule minority, yet we fail to hold this minority accountable in public.

A bowl of milk turns into curd with a single drop of lemon. The minuscule minority we blame is this drop of lemon that has curdled and made a shambles of our Islam, yet too many of us insist against all evidence our belief somehow sets us apart as better from others.

In Islam, we insist, religion and politics are inseparable. As a result, politics dominates our religion – and our religion has become a cover for tribalism and nationalism.

We regularly quote from the Quran, but do not make repentance for our failings as the Quran instructs, by seeking forgiveness of those who we have harmed. We Muslims are the source of our own misery, and we are not misunderstood by others who see in our conduct a threat to their peace.

10 June 2006, *Toronto Sun*

References

1. Wahid, Abdurrahman. “Right Islam vs. Wrong Islam,” *The Wall Street Journal* (New York), 30 December 2005.
2. For the life of the Prophet based on the earliest sources see M. Lings, *Muhammad* (London: George Allen & Unwin Ltd., 1983).
3. This early history of Muslims is described at length by the great Muslim scholar al-Tabari (d. 923) in his voluminous writings about Islam. See *The History of al-Tabari. Volume IX. The Last years of the Prophet.* Translated and annotated by I. K. Poonawala (Albany, NY: State University of New York Press, 1990. Also see W. Madelung, *The succession to Muhammad: A study of the early Caliphate* (Cambridge, UK: Cambridge University Press, 1997).
4. See *The History of al-Tabari. Volume X. The Conquest of Arabia.* Translated and annotated by F. M. Donner (Albany, NY: State University of New York Press, 1993).
5. For a recent historical survey of the Arab-Muslim conquests see H. Kennedy, *The Great Arab Conquests: How the Spread of Islam Changed the World We Live In* (London: Weidenfeld and Nicolson, 2007).
6. Charfi, M. *Islam and Liberty: The Historical Misunderstanding* (London and New York: Zed Books, 2005), p. 78.
7. On the Mutazilites, see F. Rahman, *Islam. Second Edition* (Chicago and London: University Press of Chicago, 1979) chapter 5. Also see R.C. Martin and M.R. Woodward with D.S Atmaja, *Defenders of Reason in Islam: Mu'tazilism from Medieval School to Modern Symbol* (Oxford: Oneworld Publications, 1997).
8. Cited in Charfi, p. 86.
9. Schwartz, S. *The Other Islam: Sufism and the Road to Global Harmony* (New York: Doubleday, 2008).
10. Quoted by J. Barzun in *From Dawn To Decadence* (New York: HarperCollins Publishers, 2000), p. 441.
11. Arkoun, M. “Is Islam Threatened by Christianity?” in H. Kung and J. Moltmann (eds), *Islam: A Challenge For Christianity* (London: SCM Press Ltd., 1994), p. 54.

12. Stark, R. *The Victory of Reason* (New York: Random House, 2005), p. 233.
13. Jaki, S.L. *The Road of Science And the Ways To God* (Chicago: The University of Chicago Press, 1978), p. 243.
14. Hassan, Z. & C.H. Lai (eds), *Ideals and Realities: Selected Essays of Abdus Salam* (Singapore: World Scientific Publishing Co. Ltd., 1984), pp. 48-49.
15. Smith, W.C. *Islam in Modern History* (Princeton, NJ: Princeton University Press, 1957), p. 298.
16. Gibb, H.A.R. *Whither Islam: A Survey of Modern Movements in the Moslem World* (London: Victor Gollancz Ltd., 1932), p. 319.
17. Kennedy, P. *Preparing for the Twenty-First Century* (Toronto: Harper Perennial, 1994) p. 208.
18. Quran, 13:11.
19. London: Oxford University Press, 1934.
20. Gibb, H.A.R. *Modern Trends in Islam* (New York: Octagon Books, 1978), p. 81.
21. Adonis is the penname of Ali Ahmad Said.
22. See A. Ahmad, *Islamic Modernism in India and Pakistan 1857-1964* (London: Oxford University Press, 1967) pp. 224-36.
23. Chicago: The University of Chicago Press, 1982.
24. New York: Addison-Wesley Publishing Company, 1992.
25. Gibb, H.A.R. *Whither Islam: A Survey of Modern Movements in the Moslem World* (London: Victor Gollancz Ltd., 1932), p. 319.
26. Kennedy, P. *Preparing for the Twenty-First Century* (Toronto: HarperPerennial, 1994), p. 208.
27. Ibid.
28. Hodgson, M. *The Venture of Islam*, vol. 3 (Chicago: University of Chicago Press, 1974), p. 176.
29. Giddens, A. *The Consequences of Modernity* (Stanford: Stanford University Press, 1990), p. 1.
30. "Introduction," in W. I. Jennings, ed, *Constitutional Problems in Pakistan* (London: Cambridge University Press, 1957), also reference to Pakistan's supreme court judgment, pp. 298-9, 307.
31. Arblaster, A. *Democracy* (Minneapolis: University of Minnesota Press, 1987), p. 8.
32. See the collection of his essays in G. Kateb, *The Inner Ocean: Individualism and Democratic Culture* (Ithaca: Cornell University Press, 1992).
33. Kateb, G. "Moral Distinctiveness of Representative Democracy," in *Inner Ocean*, p. 43.
34. Zakaria, F. "The Rise of Illiberal Democracy," *Foreign Affairs*, Nov./Dec. 1997, pp. 22-43.

35. Finer, S.E. *Comparative Government* (London: Allen Lane The Penguin Press, 1970), chap. 9.
36. Said, E. *Peace and Its Discontents: Essays on Palestine in the Middle East Process* (New York: Vintage Books, 1996), p. 89.
37. Lipset, S.L. *American Exceptionalism: A Double-Edged Sword* (New York: W.W. Norton & Co., 1996), p. 14.
38. Kateb, G. "Whitman and the Culture of Democracy," in *Inner Ocean*, p. 240.
39. Quran, 35:15-16.
40. Lewis, B. *What Went Wrong? Western Impact and Middle Eastern Response* (New York: Oxford University Press, 2002).
41. *Arab Human Development Report 2002* (New York: United Nations Development Program, July 2, 2002); see "How the Arabs Compare: Arab Human Development Report 2002," *Middle East Quarterly*, Fall 2002, pp. 59-67.
42. Heggy, T. *Culture, Civilization and Humanity* (London and Portland: Frank Cass, 2003), pp. 54-5.
43. London and New York: Oxford University Press, 1962.
44. Heggy, *Culture, Civilization and Humanity*, p. 59.
45. Ibid.
46. Ibid., p. 64.
47. *Time*, Dec. 11, 2000.
48. Pipes, D. "Why Revoke Tariq Ramadan's U.S. Visa?" *The New York Sun*, Aug. 27, 2004; *The Washington Post*, Aug., 28, 2004; T. Ramadan, "Scholar under Siege Defends his Record," *The Chicago Tribune*, Aug. 31, 2004; T. Ramadan, "Too Scary for the Classroom?" *The New York Times*, Sept. 1, 2004.
49. Ajami, F. "Tariq Ramadan," *The Wall Street Journal*, Sept. 7, 2004.
50. Ibid.
51. Ramadan, T. "What You Fear Is Not Who I Am," *The Globe and Mail* (Toronto), Aug. 30, 2004.
52. Leicester, U.K.: The Islamic Foundation, 1998.
53. Ramadan, T. *Western Muslims and the Future of Islam* (New York: Oxford University Press, 2004).
54. Ibid., p. 71.
55. Papanek, G.F. *Pakistan's Development: Social Goals and Private Incentives* (Cambridge: Harvard University Press, 1967), pp. 1-26.
56. Ibn Khaldun, *The Muqaddimah: An Introduction to History*, N.J. Dawood, ed., F. Rosenthal, trans. (Princeton: Princeton University Press, 1969), pp. 98-115.

57. Ahmed, A.S. *Islam under Siege* (Cambridge, U.K.: Polity Press, 2003), p. 77.
58. Ibid., p. 57.
59. Ibid.
60. Safran, N. *Egypt in search of Political Community* (Cambridge, MA: Harvard University Press, 1981), p. 231.
61. Sadat, A. *In Search of Identity* (New York: Harper & Row, 1978), p. 13.
62. Ibid., p. 21.
63. Ibid., p. 303.
64. Dimont, M.I. *Jews, God and History* (New York: New American Library, 2004), p. 191.
65. Carlyle, T. *On Heroes and Hero-Worship* (London: Ward, Lock & Co. Ltd., 1911), p. 101-2.
66. Kung, H. *Global Responsibility* (New York: Crossroad, 1991), p. xv.
67. Mansur, S. "Ramadan is time for Muslims to face facts," in the *Toronto Sun*, 22 October 2004.
68. Dimont, M.I. *Jews, God and History* (New York: New American Library, 2004), p. 6.
69. Paris, E. *The End of Days* (Toronto: Lester Publishing Ltd., 1995), p. 39.
70. Lewis, B. *The Jews of Islam* (Princeton, NJ: Princeton University Press, 1984), p. 8.
71. Cited by B. Lewis, *Islam in History* (Chicago and La Salle, IL: Open Court, 1993), pp. 139-40.
72. Patai, R. *The Arab Mind* (New York: Charles Scribner's Sons, 1973), p. 1.
73. Lewis, B. "Introduction," p. ix in I. Goldziher, *Introduction to Islamic Theology and Law* (Princeton, NJ: Princeton University Press, 1981).
74. Patai, R. *Ignaz Goldziher and His Oriental Diary* (Detroit: Wayne State University, 1987), p. 28.
75. Ormsby, E. "Remembering the Schulmeister," in *The New Criterion*, September 2003, vol. 22, no.1, p. 35.
76. Lewis, B. *The Crisis of Islam Holy War and Unholy Terror* (New York: Random House, 2004), p. 3.
77. Ramadan, T. "Cartoon conflicts," in *The Guardian* (UK), Monday 6 February 2006.
78. Guillaume, A. *The Life of Muhammad*. A translation of Ishaq's *Sirat Rasul Allah* (Karachi: Oxford University Press, 1955), p. 552.
79. Rose, F. "Why I published the cartoons," reprinted in *National Post* (Toronto), Thursday, 23 February 2006.
80. Mill, J.S. *On Liberty* (Harmondsworth: Penguin Books Ltd, 1978; reprint), p. 81.

81. Ibn Warraq, "Democracy in a cartoon," in *Speigel Online* 3 February 2006.
82. Ibn Khaldun, *The Muqaddimah: An Introduction to History*. Translated from the Arabic by Franz Rosenthal. Abridged and edited by N.J. Dawood (Princeton, NJ: Princeton University Press, 1969), p. 118.
83. Ibid., p. 119.
84. Bennabi, M. *Islam in History and Society* (Kuala Lumpur, Malaysia: Berita Publishing, 1991), p. 10.
85. Said, E. *Orientalism* (New York: Vintage Books, 1979), p. 49.
86. Ibid., p. 3.
87. Ibid., p. 5.
88. Ibid., p. 204.
89. Cited in Z. Sardar, *Desperately Seeking Paradise: Journeys of a Sceptical Muslim* (London: Granta Books, 2004), p. 202.
90. Sartre, J.P. "Preface" in Frantz Fanon, *The Wretched of the Earth* (New York: Grove Press, Inc., 1968), p. 10.
91. Taheri, A. "Bonfire of the Pieties," in *The Wall Street Journal*, 8 February 2006.
92. Lewis, B. "The Roots of Muslim Rage," in *The Atlantic Monthly* (September 1990), p. 60.
93. Revel quoted from his essay in *National Review* (2000) in the obituary notice for J.F. Revel in *The Wall Street Journal*, "online edition", 3 May 2006.
94. Steele, S. "White Guilt and the Western Past," in the *Wall Street Journal*, 2 May 2006.
95. Faiz, F.A. "Freedom's Dawn," in *The Penguin Book of Modern Urdu Poetry* (1986). Selected and translated by M. Jamal.
96. Cited by G. Salahuddin, "A 'sad and wonderful' visit," *The Daily Jang* (Pakistan), Sunday, March 28, 2004.
97. See S. Wolpert, *Jinnah of Pakistan* (New York: Oxford University Press, 1984), p. 340.
98. See *Foreign Policy*, May/June 2006, pp. 50-58.
99. Ibid., p. 52.
100. For a recent overview of Pakistan's history and politics, see O. B. Jones, *Pakistan: The Eye of the Storm* (New Haven & London: Yale University Press, 2002).
101. On the making of Pakistan, see K. B. Sayeed, *Pakistan: The Formative Phase 1857-1948* (London: Oxford University Press, 1968). Also see H. Malik, *Moslem Nationalism in India and Pakistan* (Washington, DC: Public Affairs Press, 1963).

102. See M. Hasan, *Legacy of a Divided Nation: India's Muslims since Independence* (Boulder, CO: Westview Press, 1997), chapters 1-4.
103. Cited in S. Wolpert, *Jinnah of Pakistan* (New York: Oxford University Press, 1984), p. 340.
104. On the history of the Mughals see A. Eraly, *The Last Spring: The Lives and Times of the Great Mughals* (New Delhi: Penguin Books, 1997).
105. On Muslims in Bengal, see R.M. Eaton, *The Rise of Islam and the Bengal Frontier1204-1760* (Berkeley: University of California Press, 1996).
106. On 1971 see G.W. Choudhury, *The Last Days of United Pakistan* (Karachi: Oxford University Press, 1993). Also see A. Mascarenhas, *The Rape of Bangla Desh* (New Delhi: Vikas Publications, n.d.).
107. W. Madelung, *The succession to Muhammad: A study of the early Caliphate* (Cambridge:Cambridge university Press, 1997).
108. Al-Azmeh, A. *Ibn Khaldun* (London: Routledge, 1990), p. 32.
109. Ibn Khaldun, *The Muqaddimah: An Introduction to History*, p. 166. Translated from the Arabic by F. Rosenthal. Edited and abridged by N.J. Dawood. (Princeton, NJ: Princeton University Press, Bollingen Series, 1967).
110. See A. Schimmel, *Islam in the Indian Subcontinent* (Leiden: E.J. Brill, 1980).
111. Pipes, D., *Militant Islam Reaches America* (New York: W.W. Norton & Co., 2002), pp. 3-4.
112. Such seekers of truth and God are known as Sufis. On Sufis and Sufism there is a vast corpus of writing. Three of my favourite books on the subject are those by T. Burckhardt, *Introduction to Sufism* (London and San Francisco: HarperCollins, Thorsons edition, 1995), A.J. Arberry, *Sufism: An Account of the Mystics of Islam* (London: Unwin, 1950, 1979), and M. Lings, *What is Sufism?* (London: George Allen & Unwin, 1975).
113. Quran, chapter 2, verse 256.
114. Quran, chapter 4, verse 59.
115. On Shi'i Islam see al-Tabataba'i, *Shi'ite Islam* (Albany: SUNY Press, 1977); on Sunni Islam see F. Rahman *Islam*, second edition (Chicago: The University of Chicago Press, 1979).
116. Goldziher, I., *Introduction to Islamic Theology and Law* (Princeton, New Jersey: Princeton University Press, 1981), pp. 3-4.
117. Esposito, J.L. *The Islamic Threat: Myth or Reality* (New York: Oxford University Press, 1992).
118. Pryce-Jones, D., *At War With Modernity: Islam's Challenge to the West* (London: Institute for European Defence and Strategic Studies, 1992).
119. Pryce-Jones, p. 10.

120. See M. Ruthven, *A Fury For God: The Islamist Attack on America* (London: Granta Books, 2002); and L. Wright, *The Looming Tower: Al-Qaeda and the Road to 9/11* (New York: Random House, 2006).
121. Imam Khomeini, *Islam and Revolution*. Translated and Annotated by H. Algar (Berkeley: Mizan Press, 1981), p. 305.
122. Philadelphia, PA: Fellowship Press, 2003.
123. See the main text of Bawa Muhaiyaddeen's discourses on Islam as a Sufi master, *Islam and World Peace: Explanations of a Sufi*, second edition (Philadelphia, PA: Fellowship Press, 1987; reprint 2007).
124. Quran, chapter 5, verse 48.
125. See *The Truth and Unity of Man: Letters in Response To a Crisis by His Holiness M.R. Bawa Muhaiyaddeen* (Philadelphia, PA: Fellowship Press, 1980).
126. Ibid.
127. Havel, V., *The Art of the Impossible* (New York: Alfred A. Knopf, 1997), p. 20.
128. Freud, S., *Civilization and its Discontents* (New York: W.W. Norton & Co., 1961), p. 43.
129. Kung, H., *Global Responsibility* (New York: Crossroad, 1991), p. xv.
130. Smith, H., *Why Religion Matters* (New York: Harper Collins Publishers, 2001), p. 12.
131. Freud, p. 43.
132. Weber, M., *The Protestant Ethic and the Spirit of Capitalism* (New York: Scribner's 1958), p. 182.
133. Smith, p. 16.
134. Coolidge, C. "Speech on the Occasion of the One Hundred and Fiftieth Anniversary of the Declaration of Independence, July 5, 1926, Philadelphia, Pennsylvania" in *TeachingAmericanHistory.org*.
135. Havel, p. 9.
136. *The Upanishads* translated by J. Mascaro. (Penguin Classics, 1965), p. 110.
137. Ibid., p.111.
138. *Bhagavad Gita* translated by S. Mitchell (New York: Harmony Books, 2000), p. 55.
139. Radhakrishnan, *An Idealist View of Life* (London: Unwin Hyman Ltd, 1932, 1988), p. 34.